THE LOST WORD OF GOD

Dear Mathew,

Enjoy the book!

— [signature]

THE LOST WORD OF GOD

HOWARD SCHATZ

TONE CIRCLE PUBLISHING • NEW YORK

Published by Tone Circle Publishing, LLC
Copyright © 2007 by Howard Schatz

www.tonecircle.com

ISBN-13: 978-0-9787264-0-9
ISBN-10: 0-9787264-0-5

Printed in the United States of America

Cover art by Anita Weiss

Notice of Rights

To Ernest McClain
musician, philosopher, friend

From a word of Torah is formed a sound... that sound ascends and breaks through the heavens.

- Zohar, part III, 31b, 121b

Contents

Acknowledgements

A heartfelt thanks to my friend and mentor, Dr. Ernest McClain, for teaching me that musical "string theory" is the basis of religion, philosophy and metaphysics in the ancient world. His breakthrough thesis grew out of an effort to expound the musical/mathematical allegories in Plato that had eluded scholars for centuries — an effort that began in the late 1860's with Albert Von Thimus' insights into Pythagoreanism. Von Thimus' ideas were expounded by Hans Kayser, Ernst Levy and Siegmund Levarie. Both Levy and Levarie had been colleagues of McCLain. My book develops the theological and scientific implications of Dr. McClain's methods and applies them to the oldest and most mysterious theological work within monotheisim, the *Sefer Yetzirah* (Book of Creation). I would also like to express my gratitude to Dr. Marty Kerner and Dr. Robert Ehrlich for helping me clarify many of the manuscript's mathematical and scientific ideas and historical references.

Grateful acknowledgement is made to the following for permission to reprint previously published material:

Excerpted from *Sefer Yetzirah: The Book of Creation* by Aryeh Kaplan, Used by permission of Red Wheel/Weiser, Newburyport, MA and San Francisco, CA. To order please call 1-800-423-7087.

Excerpted from *Islam: A Short History,* copyright 2000 by Karen Armstrong. Used by permission of Modern Library, a division of Random House, Inc.

Excerpted from *Kabbalah* by Gershom Scholem, copyright © 1974 by Keter Publishing House Jerusalem Ltd. Used by permission of Quadrangle Books, a division of Random House, Inc.

Excerpted from *The Arabs in History*, copyright 2002 by Bernard Lewis. Used by permission of Oxford University Press.

Excerpted from *Superstrings and the Search for the Theory of Everything,* copyright 1989 by F.David Peat. Used by permission of McGraw-Hill Companies.

Foreword

Here is the dawn of a new age in Bible scholarship. With the breath-taking vision of Judaism, Christianity, and Islam as three inter-related faces of the same monotheism, Howard Schatz dares to return to the mystical roots of orthodox religion, and to read the Bible with the assumptions of its original authors. In prose that is always clear, often beautiful, and eminently quotable, and with a numerology carefully explained to uncover the science behind traditional Kabbalism, Schatz employs his own comfortable grasp of modern science to do justice to our common ancestors by employing the principles eventually abstracted from the Pentateuch by the Jews themselves and stripped bare of verbal excess in *Sefer Yezirah*, the Book of Creation — that few people of any faith, or no faith, ever read. To say anything more about this seminal study that treats the Tanakh, the New Testament, and the Quran as a priceless unity — perceived through its author's own musical experience — would delay a delight for which his readers need no further preparation. His intent is to expose the "mind-set" that created the Bible. Be ready, then, for what the great English philosopher Alfred North Whitehead describes in one of his own titles as, "Adventures of Ideas."

Dr. Ernest G. McClain, Emeritus Professor of Music,
Brooklyn College of the City University of New York.

Preface

When we use everyday language to communicate our reflections about God, we enter into the most subjective and emotionally charged of all arenas — one that has, sadly, given birth to countless wars. Throughout history, there have been a few who believed that the road to peace requires the reconciliation of rationalism and science with revelation and religion. To quote the noted religious scholar Karen Armstrong, "They wanted to find the kernel of truth that lay at the heart of all the various historical religions, which, since the dawn of history, had been trying to define the reality of the same God."[1] Many of us share Ms. Armstrong's longings for an "objective, generalized truth" about God to which all can subscribe. Her despair is evident when she speaks of the "death of God" in the minds of many: "All our old conceptions of divinity had to die before theology could be reborn. We are waiting for a language and a style in which God could once more become a possibility."[2]

Perhaps the rationalistic, objective truth about God that Ms. Armstrong is looking for requires a universal language that bypasses the need for spoken language with all its linguistic and cultural overtones. Both mathematics and music are said to be universal languages that speak directly to our innermost being. Imagine a world in which the murkiness and violent emotions of language and religious culture are all washed away by the clarity and precision of mathematics, or a world in which the human soul is bathed in the colors of the rainbow and soothed by the celestial harmonies of David's ten-string lyre. This is exactly how most of us think of heaven, but is this just fantasy, biblical allegory, or perhaps Greek myth? Could there possibly be any truth to it?

Thirty years ago, as an undergraduate student at Brooklyn College, I had the good fortune of studying with Dr. Ernest McClain, who taught me how to solve the mathematical riddles embedded within Plato's dialogues, riddles that have troubled classical scholars for centuries. At the same time,

---

1 Karen Armstrong, *A History of God* (New York: Random House, 1993), 173.
2 Karen Armstrong, *A History of God*, 380.

I was spending evenings studying in a Chasidic rabbinical seminary. To my surprise and delight I discovered that mathematical riddles, very much like the ones Dr. McClain taught me to recognize and solve in Plato's dialogues, also appeared in important Jewish writings. My findings were published in Dr. McClain's first book, *The Myth of Invariance*.[3]

After more than 30 years of research and analysis I have applied Dr. McClain's methods to what I believe is mankind's most precious book – a "little scroll"[4] called the *Sefer Yetzirah* (Book of Creation). Within the Jewish tradition it is the only work attributed to Abraham, the great patriarch of Judaism, Christianity and Islam.[5] Many believe it to be the oldest and most mysterious of all Jewish texts, and the one text that holds the most authoritative answers to God's great mysteries. Thirty years of research and analysis corroborates that it is both the chronological starting point and theological foundation for the Hebrew, Christian and Islamic Scriptures. More important, it points us toward an objective and completely empirical definition of God and Creation.

Abraham's Book of Creation may be the first monotheistic work to be conceived and the last to be understood. It is virtually unknown outside orthodox Jewish circles, and it has remained an impenetrable mystery until now. What sets this effort apart from the work of those highly respected religious and secular scholars through the ages who have tried but failed to unlock the mysteries of this ancient text? There is a saying that the correct approach is half the solution. In this case, the correct approach is to realize that Abraham speaks to us in terms that are both mathematical and musical, in what can only be described as the language of God: ancient string theory.

Abraham saw the hand of God in his scientific exploration of sound using ancient string theory, the forerunner of acoustics, a branch of modern physics. The Book of Creation chronicles Abraham's scientific exploration of this inner, unseen world of God. He defines God, the soul, time, and the cosmos using the terminology of musical string theory, which is one of four ancient mathematical disciplines: arithmetic, music, geometry, and astronomy. During the Middle

3 Ernest G. McClain, *The Myth of Invariance: The Origin of the Gods, Mathematics and Music from the RG Veda to Plato* (New York: Nicolas Hays, 1976), 124-128.
4 It will be demonstrated that the complex symbolism within the Book of Revelations and the Book of Ezekiel both derive from Abraham's text. Since the *Sefer Yetzirah* is less than 2000 words, it appears to qualify as the "little scroll" mentioned in Revelations 10:1-4.
5 The *Sefer Yetzirah* is not to be confused with Mormon founder Joseph Smith's "Book of Abraham."

Ages they were collectively referred to as the Quadrivium. According to Jewish tradition the "Pillars of Seth" preserved these mathematical secrets when "God destroyed the world by flood and flame."

We can intuitively grasp Abraham's approach if we look into the way sunlight refracts through a prism into a rainbow of colors. Just as with the prism, a complex sound can be put through a prismlike harmonic analyzer to become a rainbow of sine waves. Today we are discovering that this "rainbow principle" exists not only within white light and complex sound but also within the most elemental building blocks of matter. Each type of atom on the periodic table of elements can be considered a rainbow of subatomic wave-particles. All matter and energy in the universe, including the multitude of living beings, share this organizing rainbow principle called the harmonic series. It is the common thread that runs through all of Creation, bringing scientific rigor to the much debated topic of intelligent design. Abraham defines God as the vibrational essence of Creation described by a harmonic series – while the Blueprint of Creation describes a mathematical extension of this harmonic series into matter!

In 1984, almost four millennia after Abraham, modern theoretical physicists discovered, and became intent on empirically proving, that superstring theory describes a "theory of everything" for understanding the deep structure of all matter and energy in the cosmos. Superstring theory is a direct descendant of Abraham's string theory, and proving superstring theory would corroborate Abraham's cosmology as real and scientific. The ancient origins of superstring theory, usually associated with Pythagoras, will now be seen as having been introduced much earlier than Pythagoras. Abraham, the great patriarch, should properly be considered the father of string theory.[6]

Given the dire conflict between Judeo-Christian traditions and the Islamic "culture of martyrdom" within the "post-9/11 world," only the words of Abraham, patriarch of the three faiths, have the cultural authority to reach across political and religious boundaries with the potency to heal these ancient rifts. The Jewish people have been the traditional caretakers for Abraham's Book of Creation. Years of comparative religious studies have led me to conclude that this seminal treatise on theology rightfully belongs to *all* of Abraham's descendants. And all must learn its theological lessons if there is ever to be peace. I am convinced that it is the only theological work describing the religion of Abraham as it existed before Judaism, Christianity,

6 Although the Book of Creation appears to be the earliest extant text on the subject, string theory can be traced back to Babylon and Sumer as early as the fourth millennium BCE.

and Islam. Although each of the three faiths has traveled a different path from these origins, a proper understanding of the Book of Creation presents an opportunity for each of the three faiths to embrace a profound common theological ground – a prerequisite for real and lasting peace.

Understanding God and Creation in the mathematical terms of ancient string theory is not a simple task. I am hopeful that my efforts constitute something of a breakthrough for all people of faith, as well for people of little or no faith. My thesis attempts to establish that the key to unlocking the deepest meaning of Scripture is contained in monotheism's most ancient teachings, as expressed in the Book of Creation. My approach was to focus on the Book of Creation's content and meaning, rather than the usual philological analysis of the extant text. The Book of Creation appears to be the culmination of an ancient oral tradition of biblical sexigesimal harmonics, with roots in ancient Sumer, circa 4000-3200 BCE. The Book of Creation is effectively the seminal treatise on Kabbalah, and as such:

- It serves as a guide to the deepest meaning of Scripture.
- It is the foundation document and cradle of religion and science.
- It teaches us the method of prayer used by the great prophets.
- It provides a new framework for interfaith reconciliation.

Parts 1 and 2 of this book offers a broad and accessible theological perspective, and I would consider myself successful if these sections found a wide readership. Parts 3-5 describe "a science of theology" that is intended to reach an academic audience, serious students of Kabbalah, and scientifically minded atheists. Part 2 also explores the root cause of tensions among the three faiths from Abraham's perspective and attempts to apply that same perspective to tensions that have developed within each faith. It allows us to see how monotheism's most authoritative source provides a new framework for interfaith discussion, and fertile ground for theological reconciliation.

This book contends that Abraham's writings are capable of reuniting the three faiths, reuniting science and religion, and reuniting mankind with God. In answer to Ms. Armstrong's prayers, the Book of Creation provides "a language and a style in which God could once more become a possibility." It would be most fitting if the words of Abraham himself, patriarch of the three faiths, were capable of bringing the world together in peace to fulfill the great promise of Scripture.

Introduction

The Bible is generally considered the most influential book in Western history. It has greatly influenced civilization by its effort to define morality within the monotheistic world. It is also important to recognize that the Bible has not accomplished its most cherished goal – peace! Of course, that may be too much to ask of a book — even if it is "the Book." Before we can achieve peace, however, we must seek a more objective perspective when we speak about God. Explaining God and Creation in the universal terms of music and mathematics provides the kernel of truth that lies at the heart of Judaism, Christianity, and Islam. The Book of Creation reveals the scientific foundation of religion. Once Abraham's writings reveal God's great mysteries, we will have the missing piece of the puzzle that empowers the Bible to fulfill its promise of peace by reconciling the Tanakh,[1] the New Testament, and the Koran.

Jews, Christians and Muslims who each believe their way is the right way, or the only way, take great pride in proclaiming that their holy book, being the "Word of God," can never be disputed by mere mortals. However, the original meaning of that phrase came from a much older holy book, Abraham's Book of Creation. For Abraham, there was only one "Word of God," the Holy Tetragrammaton (יהוה = *YHVH*), known to the English-speaking world as *Jehovah* or *Yahweh*. It is the holiest, unspeakable Name of God, and it will be demonstrated that this "Word of God" was set forth in the Book of Creation long before the earliest pages of the Bible were written. Joseph Gikatilla in his *Sha'arei Orah* states, "The entire Torah is like an explication of, and a commentary on, the Ineffable Name of God."[2] Since the time of Solomon's Temple, the Jewish High Priests and the general Jewish population must say *Adonai*

---

1 The Tanakh is the Hebrew Scriptures, whereas the term "Old Testament" is a Christian term given to the Church's reordering of the Tanakh. The Tanakh consists of three sections: the Torah, Prophets, and Writings.
2 Scholem, Gershom, <u>Kabbalah</u> (New York- Jerusalem: Keter Publishing House, 1974), 171.

(אדני) instead of the unspeakable Name.[3] This is supposed to continue until the true vocalization and transcendental meaning of the Ineffable Name is revealed in the "world to come."

The secret society of Freemasons believe that even Christianity's Sacred Mystery of the Holy Trinity is dependent on the "Holy Trinity" of Hebrew letters (יהו = *YHV)* contained within the Word *Yahweh* (יהוה = *YHVH).*[4] The last High Priest of Solomon's Temple died protecting the great mysteries of this "Lost Word." The only true Bible code is Abraham's mathematical encryption of the transcendental meaning and pronunciation of this Lost Word. An understanding of Abraham's mathematics reveals the definitive explanation of the Father, Son and Holy Spirit, as well as the lost details of all covenants between man and God.

Once the Word of God is properly understood, it will teach us how to bind our mind, body and soul to God in order to purify our mind and body and liberate our soul. A transfigured soul has access to God's wellspring of prophecy, healing and magic. This lost practice is mathematically encoded within Abraham's writings as "seven circuits around the sacred cube." It is a technique of prayerful meditation that "binds" or "marries" our soul to God.

Every Jewish wedding is performed under a Chuppah (a sacred cube) while the bride's family marches, in a circle, seven times around the groom. Abraham's practice also manifests itself within Judaism every weekday morning, when Jewish adult males "bind" or "marry" their soul to God by putting on phylacteries (Hebrew: *tefillin*). A leather strap is wrapped seven times around ones arm, while two small sacred cubes are worn on the arm and head. "Seven circuits around the sacred cube" also became one of the five pillars of Islam, called the hajj. The hajj is the annual pilgrimage to Mecca to pay homage to Abraham and circumambulate the Ka'bah (literally: square building) seven times.[5]

Unlike Jews and Muslims, Christians have no sacred practice of performing seven circuits around a sacred cube, however, within <u>Christianity's </u>Book of Revelation, seven trumpet tones correspond to

3 It must be said that even God's name Adonai (אדני) is not to be uttered in vain. The point to be made here is that when praying and reading יהוה one pronounces Adonai.
4 Robert Macoy, *General History, Cyclopedia and Dictionary of Freemasonry* (New York: Masonic Publishing Company, 1869), 554.
5 According to Arab tradition, the Ka'bah was originally Adam and Eve's dwelling place after their exile from Eden. It had fallen into disrepair and was rebuilt by Abraham and Ishmael upon God's command.

seven "tone circles" that herald the descent from heaven of the New Jerusalem in the form of a sacred cube. This demonstrates that Abraham's core teaching plays a central role within all three faiths. Why then do we consider Abraham's ancient practice lost?

Although the great symbols of Abraham's practice have always held a place of prominence within the three faiths, the Book of Creation's definition of those symbols and their transcendental meaning have been lost for thousands of years. Christians wait for the "End of Days" when, according to Christian prophecy within the Book of Revelation, the great mysteries of God that enshroud the seven trumpet tones and the sacred cube of the New Jerusalem will be revealed by a "little scroll."

A proper understanding of the Book of Creation will reveal that the ancient symbols of the three faiths comprise Abraham's secret method of prayerful meditation used by the High Priests of Solomon's Temple on the Day of Atonement[6] to pass through the veil that separates life and death to what Christians call the "eternal priesthood." Abraham mathematically encrypted this lost sacred practice and the Blueprint of Creation within the Lost Word of God, *Yahweh.* The Tefillin, the Ka'bah , and the New Jerusalem are "the symbolic point of origin of all creation"[7] because "seven circuits around the sacred cube" is Abraham's depiction of the Lost Word of God responsible for Creation.

We will come to understand *Yahweh* as the embodiment of a global rainbow principle revealing 32 paths of Wisdom that will lead man back to God and Paradise with the correct pronunciation of God's Great Name, a pronunciation that will put man into a deep state of meditation and empower him to liberate his soul. These great mysteries, revealed in elaborate detail within the Book of Creation, link the three monotheistic faiths to each other, and to what might be called a fourth faith – superstring theory!

Perhaps the main reasons the Book of Creation has not been studied outside of orthodox Jewish circles are its status as a cherished Jewish text, plus the impenetrability and complexity of the text itself. Once this true "Bible code" is deciphered, it becomes clear that Abraham defines God as the vibrational essence of Creation described by the harmonic

---

6 Rabbi Schneer Zalman of Liadi, *Likutei Amarim-Tanya*, trans. by Rabbi N. Mindel, Rabbi N. Mangel, Rabbi Z.I. Posner, Rabbi J.I. Schochet (first published 1796; New York-London: Kehot Publication Society, 1973), 279.

7 John Renard, *Understanding the Islamic Experience* (New York/Mahwah, NJ: Paulist Press, 1992), 89.

series,[8] while the mathematical Blueprint of Creation that is embedded in the Lost Word derives from that harmonic series. In other words, God's divine light — the harmonic series – "descends into matter" to become the vibrational essence of Creation.

With regard to the Book of Creation's age and authenticity many biblical scholars, including the preeminent tenth-century scholar and rabbi, Saadia Gaon,[9] writes that, "The ancients say that Abraham wrote it."[10] Aryeh Kaplan writes:

> The *Sefer Yetzirah* is without question the oldest and most mysterious of all Kabbalistic texts... so ancient is this book that its origins are no longer accessible to historians. We are totally dependent on traditions with regard to its authorship.[11] A number of very old manuscripts of *Sefer Yetzirah* begin with a colophon calling it "the Letters of Abraham our Father, which is called *Sefer Yetzirah*."[12]

One of the leading modern authorities on Kabbalah, Gershom Scholem, states that the Book of Creation might need to be understood "in the spirit of the Pythagorean School."[13] Philo of Alexandria (20 BCE-50 CE) was perhaps the first scholar to try to harmonize the Hebrew Scriptures with Platonic accounts of Creation by interpreting the Torah's Genesis allegory using Greek scientific categories and concepts. Saadia Gaon was among the earliest Jewish scholars to attempt to reconcile Judaism with the philosophical tradition of Pythagoras and Plato.[14] The twelfth-century Jewish sage Maimonides (the Rambam) also spoke of

8 The harmonic series was not discovered as a naturally occurring phenomenon until the eighteenth-century.

9 Saadia Gaon, *Commentary on Sefer Yetzirah*, translated into Hebrew by Yosef Kapach, (Jerusalem, 1972), 34. Saadia lived in Babylonia during the time that the Muslims ruled Asia Minor. He wrote the first Arabic translation of the Tanakh. The Rambam (Maimonides) has stated, "If not for our master Saadia Gaon, Torah would have been forgotten in Israel."

10 Aryeh Kaplan, *Sefer Yetzirah* (York Beach, ME: Samuel Weiser, 1990), xii. For a list of early commentators who support this position see Kaplan's footnote #15.

11 Kaplan, ix.

12 Kaplan, xii.

13 Scholem, *Kabbalah*, 27.

14 Saadia Gaon, *The Book of Beliefs and Opinions,* trans. S. Rosenblatt (New Haven: Yale, 2002), xxxi.

the "wise men of Athens" in his *Guide to the Perplexed*. Yet none of the great scholars knew enough "Pythagorean" mathematical detail to offer the appropriate acoustical interpretation, and thus the Book of Creation remained a deep mystery.

Until now, modern scholars have been limited mostly to a philological interpretation of *Yetzirah*, and until now, the *Zohar* may have been the first work to approach Kabbalah within the context of a theory of light emanations. I am quite sure that Scholem is correct regarding the need to understand *Yetzirah* within a Pythagorean context, and *The Lost Word of God* explains the ancient string theory necessary to realize that it is the content of *Yetzirah* that predates Scripture (and Pythagoreas), if not the text itself. It provides the lost details of Ezekiel's Chariot-Throne as depicted on the cover.

Rediscovering the meaning of both the "Old" and "New" Covenants in the discerning light of the Book of Creation reveals nothing less than the Messianic message: a specific method of prayerful meditation that enables all of Abraham's descendants to become "anointed ones." An "anointed one" is capable of transfiguring his soul at will according to Abraham's instructions. The Koran states that Abraham's book will "lead mankind from darkness to light,"[15] in steps all men must take to enjoy Scripture's promise of peace.

The three greatest prophets of monotheism, Moses, Jesus and Mohammed, were descendants of Abraham who somehow learned Abraham's sacred practice. All Abraham's descendants should feel obliged to understand the Book of Creation and measure the distance their thinking has traveled from Abraham's theology. This understanding will enable us to see that Scripture may be divinely inspired, but it is not the "Word of God." Scripture is based on, and derives from *Yahweh*, the only true Word of God. With this revelation we will finally understand "the power of the Word."

Abraham's tiny treatise is mankind's greatest treasure, the cradle of both science and religion, and the oldest extant foundation document of civilization. If we are willing to make the effort required to understand Abraham's teaching, we can begin to contemplate God in the manner of the prophets, and we will have real tools to follow in their footsteps. We will also come to appreciate what is now within reach: modern science's empirical proof of God's existence.

---

15 Koran 14:1.

PART I. THE TORAH AND ITS SONG

Figure 1 – The Encrypted Building Secret
(Robert Fludd: Temple of Music)

The Legacy of Abraham

God's Covenants with Man

Within the Hebrew Scriptures, the Book of Genesis tells us that God waited ten generations from Adam until Noah to make a covenant with man, and then waited another ten generations, until Abraham, to find another righteous man worthy of His covenant. God's Covenant with Abraham would be Abraham's legacy, a cherished birthright, passed down to his son Isaac and then to his son Jacob. God renamed Jacob, Israel. God blessed Israel with the promise that a new nation *shall issue from your loins. The land that I assigned to Abraham and Issac, I assign to you.*[16] As promised by God, Israel's twelve sons led the twelve tribes that would form the nation of Israel. Abraham, Isaac and Jacob were considered its founding fathers.

Before the tribes grew into a nation, Israel's youngest son Joseph was sold into slavery by his brothers for 20 pieces of silver, and brought to Egypt. This set off a chain of events that would culminate in the Jewish exile in Egypt. After the death of Jacob and Joseph, during the Jewish exile, the Covenant with God — Abraham's legacy — was lost and had to be renewed. Seven generations after God's Covenant with Abraham, "the Word of God" was once again revealed to the Jews through Abraham's direct descendent Moses, on Mount Sinai, following the exodus from Egypt. Moses received the tablets of the Ten Commandments and the revelations that would become the Written Law: the Torah.

Today, Abraham is considered the founding father of Judaism, but it is Moses who is considered its greatest prophet. Judaism's most important text, the Torah, was revealed to Moses in five books: Genesis, Exodus, Leviticus, Numbers and Deuteronomy. The "Five Books of Moses" (Torah), "Prophets" (Nevium) and "Writings" (Kituvim) comprise the acrostic called the Tanakh (Hebrew Scriptures). The familiar title, "Old Testament" is really a Christian term that indicates a slight, but significant, reordering

16 Genesis 35:12.

of the Tanakh. Mosaic Law derives from the Torah's codification into 613 commandments that provide guidelines for every aspect of Jewish life; they are understood to derive from the Ten Commandments.[17]

Tradition tells us that in addition to the Written Law, Moses received the Oral Law on Mount Sinai, which reveals the Word of God, and is believed to explain the inner meaning of the Written Law. Tradition tells us that Rabbi Juda wrote down the Oral Law for the first time around the year 200 CE. His 63 tractates, called the *Mishnah,* explain details of how each of the Torah's 613 commandments should be carried out. Over the next 300 years, rabbinic discussions about the Mishnah were also written down and called the *Gemara.* The Talmud, comprising the Mishnah and Gemara, is usually published along with later commentaries, and is considered the most authoritative work after the Torah. The Torah and the Talmud are considered the foundation documents of Judaism

Kabbalah is considered the esoteric part of the Jewish Oral Law that covers the entire range of Jewish mysticism. It is generally understood to embody the deepest meaning of the Written Law. Most scholars believe the most authoritative written kabbalistic work is the thirteenth-century Aramaic text called the *Zohar.* As we read the Zohar, however, it speaks of *"deep and hidden things which issue from God's thought and are taken up by the Voice which are not disclosed till the Word reveals them."*[18] Elsewhere the Zohar speaks of *"secret paths which cannot be discovered."*[19] We will demonstrate that only Abraham's Book of Creation reveals *the Voice,* and *the Word,* as the key to understanding *deep and hidden things,* and *secret paths which cannot be discovered.* We will also demonstrate that the seminal and definitive work of Kabbalah is the Book of Creation, and, further, that it is older than the oldest pages of Scripture.

Given the long-standing Jewish model of Torah exposition and elaboration just outlined (the Torah, the Mishnah, the Gemara, and later commentaries) it is not unreasonable to believe that Abraham's tiny treatise of less than 2000 words might actually require the entire Hebrew Scriptures to explain. We will argue that the allegories of the Torah, and all subsequent writings of the Oral Law, were revealed to mankind in order to make the intricacies of Abraham's Book of Creation more accessible to

---

17 Zalman, *Tanya,* 83.
18 Zohar, 32a.
19 Zohar, 30b.

the common man. In other words, only the Book of Creation contains the *Pnimiyut*[20] of the 613 commandments revealing their hidden reasons.

Once the transcendental meaning and pronunciation of the Word of God was lost it had to be revealed to Moses on Mount Sinai, who passed it on to the secret order of High Priests. The order of High Priests who possessed knowledge of the Word, *Yahweh*, continued until Solomon's temple was destroyed, and the last High Priest died protecting its transcendental meaning and pronunciation.

The Lost Word of God

A secret fraternity of sacred builders known as Freemasons, understands that God used the "Blueprint of Creation," hidden in His Great Name, *Yahweh*, to construct the known universe. As we can see in the passage below, they believe that mankind once had direct knowledge of this Lost Word and used it to build sacred edifices, such as the Great Pyramids of Egypt and Solomon's Temple. We should note that they believe this secret knowledge is buried somewhere in Jewish kabbalistic writings:

> The existence of a building secret, represented as a Master-Word, is like a pivot upon which rests the Legend of the Third Degree. The Master-Builder died to preserve the secret of this Word…the Grade of Knowledge represented by that Word, of which every Master Mason is still upon the quest… The root matter of much, which is shadowed forth in the Legend, as regards the meaning of the Temple and the search for the Lost Word, is to be found in certain great texts known to scholars under the generic name of Kabbalah.[21]

As the many details of this book unfolds, we will begin to see that the Freemasons are correct to perpetuate these core beliefs, but like most people who study Kabbalah, they point to the Zohar as the authoritative

---

20 Zalman, *Tanya*, 563, fn.117: "Pnimiyut of Torah is the esoteric part composed of the deeper and sublime reasons of Torah and the commandments (as they are in their root, prior to becoming vested in directives that require specific physical objects and actions)."
21 Waite, 416-17.

kabbalistic work. As already mentioned, the Zohar speaks of unknowable mysteries but lacks the mathematical detail of the "Blueprint" itself. According to an important Talmudic teaching, Betzalel, who accompanied Moses in the desert after the Exodus from Egypt, "knew how to permute the letters with which heaven and earth were created."[22] He was therefore able to build all elements of the Tabernacle in such a manner that it would act as a channel for the spiritual energies of creation. The lost "building secret" is both mathematical and musical, and has been depicted throughout the writings and artwork of Robert Fludd (1574 - 1637), as seen here and the beginning of this chapter.

Figure 2 – Mandalas or Tone Circles as part of the Building Secret
(Robert Fludd: Temple of Music)

---

22 Kaplan, *Sefer Yetzirah*, 26.

From a Christian perspective, Abraham's book also reveals the great mysteries of Christianity by defining the theological basis of the Transfiguration, the Incarnation, the Holy Trinity, the Resurrection, the New Covenant, the New Jerusalem, and even for the relatively modern Protestant concept of the Rapture.

From the Muslim perspective, the Lost Word provides the theological origins for the ancient practice of seven circumambulations around Islam's holiest shrine, the Ka'bah in Mecca. Abraham provides the authoritative explanation of the "inner struggle" that defines the deepest meaning of *jihad.* The Book of Creation's detailed explanation of the ancient Arab cult of the Ka'bah may also allow us to tie the approximate date of the book's origins to the approximate date of the Ka'bah's construction.[23] We will see that the mathematics of the Book of Creation provides the metaphysical and theological framework of the Torah — providing proof that it precedes the Torah's oldest passages — also proving that it must be considerably older than the ancient Greek origins the Book of Creation is suspected of having by today's scholars.

Abraham's legacy teaches mankind how to pray! He provides specific and detailed instructions that describe sophisticated techniques of prayerful meditation and then mathematically encrypts them within the Lost Word of God. Without in-depth knowledge of this legacy, Abraham's theological "compass" was lost to the three faiths. One can speculate that had this knowledge not been lost, Jesus and Mohammed may well have been accepted by the rabbis as great prophets, and Christianity and Islam would never have had reason to split from Judaism.

Once properly understood, Abraham's teaching replaces all subjective notions of God with an objective reality, accompanied by specific techniques of prayerful meditation that enable each of us to realize that objective reality. These techniques empower us to peacefully raise our consciousness above both love and hate in order to bind our soul to God. Whenever man is not engaged in prayerful meditation, his body, thoughts, and emotions will tend to distract him from God. Abraham teaches us that God is not a bearded old man in the sky, but rather that man must "tune in" to the image of God that lives within each of us.

23 Presuming, of course, that Muslims would ever allow the Ka'bah to be scientifically dated. Considerable room for error must also be allowed for determining when an oral transmission is finally written down, as with other ancient kabbalistic texts, such as the Bahir and the Zohar.

Abraham's core practice will liberate a man's soul from the prison of his body, thoughts, and emotions and provide the means to reenter Paradise while still very much alive – the ultimate "gift" of Scripture.

The Book of Creation is associated with magic; its contents, viewed through the lens of history, have become the basis for countless novels, legends, secret societies, conspiracy theories, and miracles. Within Jewish tradition, the general population has never been considered ready or even able to understand and use this knowledge wisely. The fragments of Abraham's text that have been understood have been zealously guarded and obscured since ancient times.

Studying the Book of Creation or other kabbalistic works, such as the Zohar or the Bahir, is traditionally considered dangerous and is recommended only for adult males over 40 years of age who are learned, pious, and already wise in the ways of the Torah. "The whole science of the Kabbalah was hidden in their days and concealed from all the scholars of Torah, except for a select few, and even then in a mode of 'walking hiddenly' and not publicly."[24] Unfortunately, by limiting the transmission of these teachings to a select few, the risk of corrupting or misinterpreting critical information grows. It is therefore not difficult to understand how Abraham's legacy was lost.

The Deep Structure of Creation

In ancient Greece, Plato believed that music was the most potent force in the universe. For Pythagoras, Aristotle, Plato, and Abraham, music spoke directly to man's soul, while music's mathematical basis linked his soul to the "deep structure" of Creation. In the following passage Plato explains that music is the foundation of knowledge:

Moreover as I have now stated several times, he who has not contemplated the mind of nature which is said to exist in the stars, and gone through the previous training, and seen the connection of music with these things, and harmonized them all with laws and institutions, is not able to give a reason of such things as have a reason.[25]

24 Zalman, Tanya, 551.
25 Plato, "The Laws," in Collected Dialogues, trans. by A.E. Taylor (Princeton, NJ: Princeton University Press, 1999), 967e.

From Plato's words we can begin to see why music was so important in the educational system of ancient Greece. The Greek doctrine of *ethos* describes how music affects the human soul.[26] Pythagoras, Plato, and Aristotle were in agreement that laws should regulate what was musically permissible.[27]

Ethos of character:

> If one listens to the wrong kind of music he will become the wrong kind of person; but, conversely, if he listens to the right kind of music he will tend to become the right kind of person. Aristotle, Politics, 8, 1340a,b

For the soul:

> Music training is a more potent instrument than any other, because rhythm and harmony find their way into the inward places of the soul, on which they mightily fasten, imparting grace, and making the soul of him who is rightly educated graceful... Plato, Republic III

> (The just man) will always be seen adjusting the body's harmony for the sake of the accord in the soul. Plato, Republic 591d

For the city:

> The city's guardians must "build their guardhouse" in music and permit "no innovations, for never are the ways of music moved without the greatest political laws being moved." Plato, Republic 424c, d

For society:

> ...The foundations of music, once established must not be changed, for lawlessness in art and education inevitably leads to license in manners and anarchy in society. – Plato, Republic, IV, 424; also Laws, III, 700C

The ancient Greeks believed that music could tap into a man's emotions and physiology, and either corrupt or enhance the stillness of

26 Donald Grout, *A History of Western Music* (New York: New York, 1973), 7-9.
27 Grout, 8.

his inner being. This ancient belief appears to have some corroboration in the recent work of Daniel Schneck and Dorita Berger:

> Our treatise discusses what this "essence" — the "me" embedded within the human being — entails, using a paradigm that, for the first time, establishes a theoretical framework that can be quantified, subjected to rigorous research protocols, and thereafter be applied clinically[28]...Music communicates with the body by speaking the language of physiology.[29]

The Roman Catholic Church adopted the Greek notions of ethos for well over 1000 years. It was the writings of the great scholar Amicus Manlius Severinus Boethius (ca. 480-524) that taught the Church these principles. It tried to control music according to the Platonic model from the time of Boethius in the early Middle Ages, until the Renaissance. "Boethius was the most influential authority on music in the Early Middle Ages... Like the Pythagoreans and Plato, he regards music as a corollary of arithmetic, thus as exemplifying in sounds the fundamental principles of order and harmony that prevail throughout the universe."[30]

The Language of God

The use of music to explain the universe was clearly not intended to describe audible everyday sounds. It was meant to describe the inaudible vibrations of spirit, more subtle forms of energy and matter that happens to follow the same mathematical principles as audible sound. There is a beautiful passage by John Keats, in his poem "Ode on a Grecian Urn," that eloquently communicates this idea:

> *Heard melodies are sweet, but those unheard*
> *Are sweeter; therefore, ye soft pipes, play on;*
> *Not to the sensual ear, but, more endear'd,*
> *Pipe to the spirit ditties of no tone.*

---

28 Daniel J. Schneck and Dorita S. Berger, *The Music Effect: Music Physiology and Clinical Applications* (London: Jessica Kinglsey Publishers, 2006), 26.
29 Schneck and Berger, 24.
30 Grout, 23-24.

Today's liberal arts education derives from the "seven liberal arts" that were the basis of education in the Middle Ages. They comprised four mathematical disciplines known as the Quadrivium – arithmetic, music, geometry and astronomy – and three language disciplines known as the Trivium – grammar, rhetoric, and logic. According to the *Antiquities of the Jews* by Jewish historian Flavius Josephus (37 CE - ca. 100 CE), the Quadrivium goes back much further than the Middle Ages. Inscriptions on the "Pillars of Seth"[31] are said to have preserved this knowledge when "God destroyed the world by flood and flame."

Here is an explanation of the Quadrivium in very general terms: Arithmetic includes the study of numbers and numerical operations, such as addition, subtraction, multiplication, and division, which we are all familiar with. Music is considered a mathematical discipline because musical tones formed by vibrating strings are the foundation of music theory, and they can be described in terms of integer ratios. For example, if a musical instrument has two vibrating strings, and the second string is vibrating at twice the rate as the first object, the frequency of the string's vibrations would be in a ratio of 1:2. The distance between these two vibrating strings would be a musical octave, i.e., eight notes apart. Similarly, a ratio of 2:3 yields the musical interval of a perfect fifth; 3:4 yields a perfect fourth, etc. Whether we're talking about the length of a vibrating string or the volume of air in an organ pipe, these numerical ratios determine the musical tones produced. This is not music in the sense that it is composed and played for enjoyment. The music of the Quadrivium should be understood as the ancient science of sound, a precursor to modern acoustics.

Within the context of the Quadrivium, geometry would then take these numbers and have them define geometric shapes. For example, 6 is a composite number, measured by the prime factors 2 and 3. The composite numbers that are the product of two prime numbers are described as planar; they are considered to have two dimensions, length and width. Those composite numbers that are the product of three prime numbers, such as $27 = 3^3$, are described as solids, since they possess the third

---

31 It is said that Adam's son Seth acquired this secret knowledge from his father, who acquired it from the angel Raziel. Seth then engraved it on two columns, one of brick and the other of stone. Josephus says, these were still to be seen, in his day, in the Siriadic land. In the works of Manetho, some 300 years before Josephus, Manetho declares that he had seen them, but that they were engraved by the first Thoth (Hermes), and, after the deluge, the Son of the Second Thoth translated the inscription into the language of the Priests.

dimension. Each composite number fell within its own particular class of geometric forms – triangles, squares, etc., or pyramids, cubes, etc.

Arithmetic, music, and geometry each contribute an additional layer of complexity to the universe's mathematics. It is as if God were first sketching the geometric shapes that lay underneath Creation's finished canvas. When we add astronomy to the mix, God sets these numerical, musical, and geometric shapes in motion, creating what many of today's scholars call the "Music of the Spheres." The ancient Greeks would describe Creation as an abstract world of integers and geometric forms in motion -- rotating, vibrating, undulating and interacting in a way that might describe the hustle and bustle of daily life in a city or village. This mathematical mélange was used to describe the dynamics of the heavenly bodies, as well as the complexities and inner workings of man's body and soul. In this manner, the Music of the Spheres mathematically encodes a detailed scientific description of a unified cosmology and cosmogony that links the microcosm of the soul to the macrocosm of the universe.[32]

Figure 3 – Standing Wave

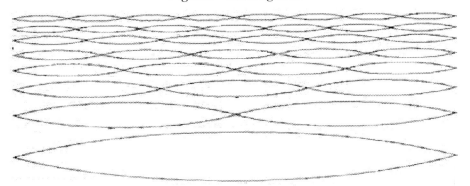

In the diagram above we can see how the number of oscillations or "cycles" (frequency) are determined by the ratio of integers that define counting, 1, 2, 3, 4, 5, 6, etc., while measuring the length of each cycle (wavelength) decreases by a reciprocal ratio 1/1, 1/2, 1/3, 1/4, etc. Frequency is a measure of time (measured today in terms of cycles per second), and its mathematical reciprocal, wavelength, is a measure of length (meters, nanometers, etc.). Also in the diagram, we can see a string vibrating to create

32 S.K. Heninger Jr., *Touches of Sweet Harmony: Pythagorean Cosmology and Renaissance Poetics* (San Marino, CA: Huntington Library, 1974), 84.

what is called a "standing wave," in which the endpoints are fastened down (as on a violin) and the "rainbow" of different sine waves are all happening at the same time, blending into a single complex tone:

The harmonic series manifests itself not only in the analysis of sound and light – it manifests everywhere. The reason many of today's modern theoretical physicists say that superstring theory is the most viable theory of everything, is because the heart of superstring theory is the harmonic series — an ancient scientific truth that modern science tells us is the organizing principle of Creation.

The harmonic series wasn't discovered as a natural phenomenon until the eighteenth-century. Nevertheless, Abraham's Book of Creation accurately describes the mathematics of the harmonic series and fully elucidates the first "theory of everything" almost 4000 years ago by describing the vibrational essence of God and the "Blueprint of Creation." The acoustical ratios of string theory were "recognized by both Mesopotamia and Egypt at least two millennia before the dawn of Greek civilization."[33] In other words, Plato (ca. 427-347 BCE) had a string theory of divine emanation that was established almost 1500 years earlier by Abraham, while the string theory of Abraham's Book of Creation and the Hebrew Scriptures, can be traced to Babylon and Sumer as early as the fourth millennium BCE. McClain writes:

> What is certain is that by the beginning of the second millennium B.C. Semitic mathematicians were virtuosi in computation ... the Hebrew Bible is thus the product of a Semitic culture which had masterminded the fundamentals of music and mathematics a thousand years before its oldest pages were written."[34]

The Hebrew Scriptures state that Abraham was born in the land of Ur of the Chaldeans (Mesopotamia ca. 2000 BCE), and he later spent time in Egypt. Considering Dr. McClain's comments, he would have been well situated, both chronologically and geographically, to write the seminal work on string theory and Kabbalah.

---

33 McClain, *The Myth of Invariance*, 130; Henry George Farmer, "The Music of Ancient Egypt," in *The New Oxford History of Music* (London: Oxford University Press, 1957), Vol.1, 275.
34 McClain, *The Myth of Invariance*, 130.

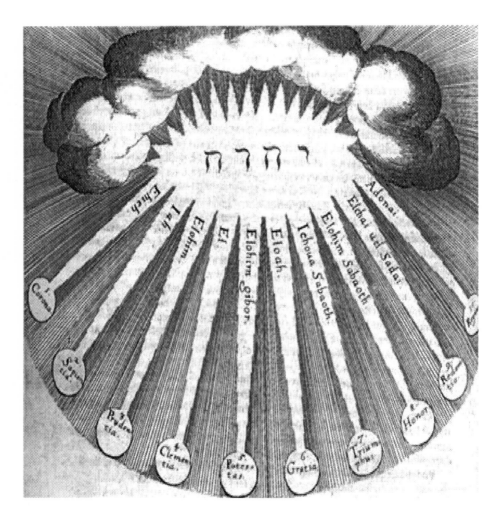

Figure 4 – The Ten Utterances of God
(Robert Fludd: Philosophia Sacra)

The Book of Creation

Thirty-Two Mystical Paths of Wisdom

The Book of Creation tells us that God engraved His universe with "*32 mystical paths of Wisdom*" and "*with three books, with text, with number and with communication* [i.e., sound]."

1.1 With *32 mystical paths of Wisdom*
  engraved Yah
    the Lord of Hosts
    the God of Israel
  the Living God
    King of the universe
  El Shaddai
    Merciful and Gracious
    High and Exalted
    Dwelling in eternity
  Whose name is Holy –
    He is lofty and holy ---
And create His universe
  with three books (Sepharim),
    with text (Sepher)
    with number (Sephar)
    and with communication (Sippur).

In his 1990 translation of the Book of Creation, Aryeh Kaplan states that the 32 mystical paths described in the passage above, consists of the 10 digits and 22 letters contained in the Hebrew alphabet.[35] Equating the 32 mystical paths with the 22 letters of the Hebrew alphabet and 10 Hebrew numerals points us in the right direction but it does not tell us exactly how God engraved Creation from these numbers and letters.

35 Kaplan, *Sefer Yetzirah*, 5.

Historically, most interpretations of these 32 paths have graphically represented the human soul as some variation of the following diagram, depicting 10 Sefirot joined by 3 horizontal lines, 7 vertical lines, and 12 diagonal lines.

Figure 5 – The 32 Paths of Wisdom[36]

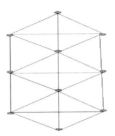

    To explain the true meaning of these 32 paths we must first understand the significance of the three books mentioned in passage 1.1, describing Abraham's three different levels of interpretation: number (*Sephar*), text (*Sepher* – literally: book), and communication (*Sippur* – literally: telling). Kaplan explains that the Hebrew word for text (*Sepher*) is the same word that is used for number (*Sephar*), with only a difference in gender.[37] It is therefore not surprising to learn that Hebrew letters can also be understood as Hebrew numerals.

    Today's understanding of kabbalistic gematria[38] depends on this close relationship between Hebrew letters and numbers, and kabbalistic interpretations typically make some attempt to tie some deeper meaning to the numerical version of the corresponding letters. This is not the correct approach to gematria. Dealing with only two layers of meaning is not enough. Without fully grasping Abraham's three levels of interpretation (text, number and sound), one lacks the skill set necessary to render accurate kabbalistic interpretations of the Bible. Knowledge about the Quadrivium informs us that the Hebrew letters and numerals need to be understood from

---

36 Kaplan, *Sefer Yetzirah*, 26.
37 Kaplan, *Sefer Yetzirah*, 19.
38 The art of gematria, the permutations and combinations of Hebrew letters/numerals, has often been arbitrarily applied within Kabbalah. Abraham's treatise demonstrates that gematria must be understood as the numerical ratios of musical string theory.

the perspective of its four mathematical disciplines, describing Abraham's use of number, sound, shape and motion.

As already stated, in the Hebrew language, two of Abraham's "books" have a built in relationship. Hebrew letters can also be understood as numerals:

Table 1 – The Hebrew Alphabet

Letter		Numeral	Letter		Numeral
Alef	א	1	Lamed	ל	30
Bet	ב	2	Mem	מ	40
Gimel	ג	3	Nun	נ	50
Dalet	ד	4	Samekh	ס	60
Heh	ה	5	Ayin	ע	70
Vav	ו	6	Peh	פ	80
Zayin	ז	7	Tzadi	צ	90
Chet	ח	8	Kof	ק	100
Tet	ט	9	Resh	ר	200
Yud	י	10	Shin	ש	300
Kaf	כ	20	Tav	ת	400

The numerical value of Hebrew letters can be added together. The numerical value of the name Abraham, for example, is אברהם (248). However, the larger mathematical context of the Quadrivium needs to be taken into consideration to thoroughly understand this process. Abraham's conception of number, sound, shape and motion provides the metaphysical basis of theology and, as Plato states, "the mind of nature which is said to exist in the stars."

The importance of sound as the key to unlock the ancient writings was recognized by at least one other historically important Jewish figure, Abraham Abulafia (1240-1292). The extent of Abulafia's knowledge of the Quadrivium's mathematics is not known, but Gershom Scholem writes: "He [Abulafia] drew a clear parallel between 'the science of combination' [gematria] and music."[39]

---

39 Scholem, *Kabbalah*, 180.

The Secret of the Torah

1.2 *Ten Sefirot of Nothingness*
    And 22 Foundation Letters:
      Three Mothers,
      Seven Doubles
      And twelve Elementals.

The "Secret of the Twenty-Two Letters" is known as *Razah D'Oraytah* (the "Secret of the Torah" or the "Secret of Knowledge").[40] It explains how the primal light of God's Ten Sefirot of Nothingness descends across 22 Foundation Letters, extending His light into the essence of man and all living creatures, the essence of time, and the essence of the cosmos. The first hint Abraham gives us to solve this riddle can be found in the word *Sefirot,* which literally means "counting." One might normally expect the use of the word *Mispar* (number) in this passage.[41] For Abraham, counting appears to be the basis of Creation. The obvious question is "What does counting have to do with either music or Creation?

The answer to that question is the key to understanding Abraham's writings. The simple act of counting defines a naturally occurring phenomenon known as the *harmonic series* – a scientific phenomenon not discovered until the eighteenth-century. A Frenchman named Joseph Saveur appears to have been the first "modern" scientist to realize that each sound contained more than just a single note. The basic principle states that each sound of nature is a complex combination of sounds, stacked up, one upon the other. The mathematical relationship between these stacked sounds can be defined by "integer multiples of some fundamental tone." In other words, it is the simple act of counting that describes the mathematical structure of sound.

The act of counting integers gives us an intuitive understanding of the structure of sound. Just as white light refracts through a prism into a rainbow of different colors, a complex sound can be processed by a prism-like device known as a harmonic analyzer and be broken up into a "rainbow" of different sounds, called sine waves. After the time of Saveur, it was discovered that the relationship between sound and light was more <u>than just analogy</u>. The simple mathematics of counting that defines the

40 Zalman, 301.
41 Kaplan, *Sefer Yetzirah*, 23.

structure of sound, also defines the structure of light. Abraham appears to have understood the harmonic series and its cosmological significance thousands of years before its discovery by "modern" science.

The Book of Creation provides the mathematical framework for Scripture. The most important biblical allegory that derives from Abraham's mathematics is the Creation allegory of Genesis:

> *In the beginning of God's creating the heaven and the earth -- when the earth astonishingly empty, with darkness upon the surface of the deep, and the Divine Presence hovered upon the surface of the waters -- God said, "Let there be light," and there was light. God saw that the light was good, and God separated between the light and the darkness. God called to the light "Day," and to the darkness He called "Night." And there was evening and there was morning, one day.*[42]

While Kabbalah stresses the importance of number, without understanding that Abraham's numbers need to be understood from a musical perspective, rabbis and scholars do their best to reconcile Abraham's first two books text (*Sepher*) with number (*Sephar*) — but without addressing sound — Abraham's third book (*Sippur*). For example, a translator's footnote within another Jewish holy book, the *Likutei Amarim-Tanya*, comments on this biblical passage:

The Tanya attempts to reconcile God's Ten Utterances with God's nine utterances of the phrase, "And God said, Let..." by arguing that the first Utterance of God somehow occurs "In the beginning..." or at least prior to the words "Let there be Light."[43] However, this would imply that the second Utterance of God is responsible for creating divine light, which is a somewhat awkward assumption requiring additional explanation. Similarly, Rabbi Kaplan suggests that the Hebrew digits 0 through 9 correspond to the Ten Sefirot, but the concept of zero does not exist within Hebrew numerals; once again an awkward assumption requiring additional explanation. The musical mathematics of Abraham's third book permits an elegant and comprehensive explanation of all biblical allegory.

---

42 *Chumash: Artscroll Series*, ed. Rabbi Nosson Scherman and Rabbi Meir Zlotowitz (Brooklyn, NY: Mesorah Publications, 1998), Genesis 1:1 – 1:5.
43 Zalman, 740 fn. 15.

We begin counting the Sefirot sequentially, in a line (Hebrew: *Kav*), beginning with the numeral 1, which stands alone as "the One," i.e., the unity of God as the Monad. God begins to extend his divine light into Creation with His Utterance of the numeral 2. God's Utterances continue sequentially. Abraham calls them the Ten Sefirot of Nothingness, but later tradition refers to them as either the Kav, or the Ten Utterances of God. On God's last Utterance we would discover that the Arabic number 11 doesn't exist as a Hebrew numeral (see Table 2). The next sequential Hebrew numeral after 10 would translate into Arabic numerals as the number 20. However, the numeral 20 does fall within the harmonic series, and it has a unique function. It serves to define an upper limit to contain God's infinite light.[44] The containers of divine light will be discussed later in considerably more detail. We can summarize what has been said thus far in the following table:

Table 2 – God's Ten Utterances

God		Ten Utterances	
Letter	Numeral	Letter	Numeral
Alef א	1	Bet ב	2
		Gimel ג	3
		Dalet ד	4
		Heh ה	5
		Vav ו	6
		Zayin ז	7
		Chet ח	8
		Tet ט	9
		Yud י	10
		Kaf כ	20

God's Ten Sefirot of Nothingness forms a harmonic series that "echoes" into matter to become the vibrational essence and sustenance of Creation. The Ten Sefirot of Nothingness then descends into matter and appears to radiate across the 22 Foundation Letters, which are assumed to be the 22 letters of the Hebrew alphabet. Once again, however, it is not a straight forward one-to-one correspondence, because Abraham's third book has been omitted from the explanation. All we really know so

44 The paradox of containing God's infinite light is not lost on Abraham. We will see how he incorporates that concept into his mathematical system.

far is that the *22 Foundation Letters* were comprised of: *Three Mothers, Seven Doubles, and Twelve Elementals.*

The Kav's harmonic series enables us to intuitively understood God as the unifying "rainbow principle." Just as rainbows coalesce into the unity of white light, the Ten Sefirot of Nothingness coalesce into a complex unity of God's light. Divine light is the foundation of nature and must be understood from the perspective of God's unity as well as Creation's diversity. It is the unifying principle of rainbows that intuitively defines God for mankind. That is why the Torah associates God's covenant with His "bow."

Since the 1980's, scientists have been finding that the harmonic series is the most basic and pervasive mathematical relationship in nature. A red-letter day for counting occurred in 1984, when Michael Green and John Schwarz discovered that tiny vibrating strings appear to be the key to defining the "deep structure" of all matter and energy in the universe. The mathematical model they developed became the most viable candidate for a theory of everything (TOE): superstring theory.

Superstring theory was discovered only 22 years ago, and the harmonic series was discovered as a single complex entity and natural phenomenon approximately 300 years ago, yet Abraham developed his own "theory of everything," using ancient string theory to define a harmonic series almost 4000 years ago? Like the rainbow that is contained by white light, the diversity of Creation's design was united within a single holistic entity who was the *Living God* — the *King*. Of course, Abraham called the foundation of religion and science GOD and not TOE! Abraham anthropomorphically fashioned "intelligent design" into the Designer called God, but Abraham's *Living God* could be found in the unity of nature, and his monotheism thus encompassed theism, deism, and pantheism.

The Doctrine of Opposites

Now that we know the numbers of the Kav, it is important to remember that Abraham thought of the Kav's numbers as more than just numbers. They represent the integer ratios of all the different vibrations within the complex sound that we call the harmonic series. We have learned that these ratios can be determined by simply counting. For example, if we start with some arbitrary fundamental tone that vibrates at a frequency of 100 cycles per second, then, according to our theory of counting, the next harmonic ratio would be 2 x 100 = 200 cps; the third harmonic would be 3 x 100 cps; then 4 x 100 cps, etc. The rainbow of sound and light can be described by simple integer multiples of any fundamental tone.

The term *frequency* can be characterized by the human ear's perceptions of sound either going up or down in pitch. Tones formed by a higher frequency are perceived by the human ear to be higher in pitch, while tones formed by a lower frequency are perceived as lower in pitch. Frequency is described in terms of the number of vibrations, or cycles per second, a unit of measurement named after Heinrich Hertz, a pioneer in radio wave theory. The human ear can hear a range of about 16 hertz (Hz) up to approximately 20,000 Hz.

From a scientific perspective, wherever there is a frequency, there is a corresponding wavelength. *Wavelength* is a measure of the tiny distance between each of these vibrational cycles; it is the distance separating consecutive peaks or troughs of a wave's complete cycle. Wavelength is a measure of distance and frequency is a measure of time. Frequency and wavelength are in a reciprocal mathematical relationship. Whenever a string's length, which is a function of wavelength, is divided in half, its frequency doubles. Similarly, whenever a string is divided into thirds, its frequency triples. Conversely, doubling the length halves the frequency, while tripling the length corresponds to one-third the frequency. It was Galileo who scientifically proved that ratios between the frequencies of vibration are the inverse of the ratios of string lengths – another scientific phenomenon anticipated by Abraham.

From Abraham's explorations of the structure of sound he saw the hand of God at work. He came to understand the reciprocity of frequency and wavelength, not in the modern terms of cycles per second, but in the ancient terms of integer ratios. In order to decipher the way Abraham's mathematical system is encoded in Scripture, it will be demonstrated that the principle of opposites, embedded throughout Abraham's writings and Scripture, is based on the reciprocity of frequency and wavelength.

Belief in this principle of reciprocity pervaded the ancient world. Everything in the universe was believed to be part of a dualistic framework of reality. A religious culture like Judaism described it as the spiritual world versus the material world, while the humanistic Greek culture preferred to describe this duality in terms of abstract form versus matter.[45] The abstract world and the material world are reflections of one another. Even within the abstract world and within the material world, everything is believed to have a corresponding opposite: heaven and earth, day and night, male and female, right and wrong, etc.

> *God separated between the light and the darkness. God called to the light "Day," and to the darkness He called "Night." And there was evening and there was morning, one day.*[46]

In this passage from Genesis, it is logical to think of "Night" as the absence of divine light, however, commentary to Genesis states that "darkness is not merely the absence of light, but a specific creation."[47] It is only within the context of the reciprocity of frequency and wavelength that we can finally understand the substantiality of darkness as a specific creation. In this same manner, we can understand the substantiality of good and evil, and heaven and hell.

In the Hebrew Scriptures, reciprocity is expressed as an all-encompassing principle.[48] In a passage from Ecclesiastes 7:14, we read: "the Almighty has made one thing opposite the other ... as water mirrors the reflection of a face." In the Tanya, Rabbi Zalman states, "For in each hour there is a different flow from the higher worlds to animate those who dwell here below, while the flow of vitality of the previous hour returns to its source (in accordance with the esoteric principle of 'Advance and Retreat' in the Sefer Yetzirah)."[49] In ancient philosophical and religious works, reciprocity is alternately referred to as: "advance and retreat," "running and returning," "waxing and waning," "ascending and descending," and "the dyad of the great and small."

---

45 For example, the idea of a table corresponds to its abstract form whereas a specific instance of a table would correspond to matter.
46 Genesis 1:1 – 1:5.
47 *Chumash*, Genesis 1:2 fn. 2.
48 Zalman, 21, 241-2, 257, 285; Proverbs 27:19.
49 Zalman, 215; Rabbi Zalman's reference to the *Sefer Yetzirah* underscores the relevance of Abraham's work as authoritative in these matters.

Rediscovering the Lost Tables of Divine Light

2.5 *How?*
He permuted them, weighed them, and transformed them,
    Alef with them all
        and all of them with Alef
Bet with them all
        and all of them with Bet
They repeat in a cycle
    and exist in 231 Gates.
It comes out that all that is formed
        and all that is spoken
    emanates from one Name.

2.6 *He formed substance out of chaos*
        and made nonexistence into existence
He carved great pillars from the air
        that cannot be grasped.
This is a sign
    [Alef with them all, and all of them with Alef]
He forsees, transforms and makes
    all that is formed and all that is spoken:
        one Name.
A sign for this thing:
    Twenty-two objects in a single body.

Abraham first gives us very specific instructions on how to build two mathematical/musical tables, which serve as a sort of Rosetta Stone[50] to help us decipher the rest of his book. We will now begin to reveal and explain these tables in detail. Without knowledge of how ancient string theory was used to describe metaphysical concepts, these tables have been misinterpreted by religious scholars since ancient times, and at some point the oral tradition could no longer explain Abraham's legacy. As a result the transcendental meaning and pronunciation of the Word of God, *Yahweh* was lost to future generations.

The misinterpretation of these two mathematical tables is one of the great tragedies in the history of Western civilization. Without them

---

50 The Rosetta Stone enabled archeologists to decipher hieroglyphics.

there have been few clues that suggest how to decipher Abraham's text. Rediscovering these tables will lead us toward an explanation of the Lost Word of God. The Word, *Yahweh* encodes the Blueprint of Creation that teaches us the specific paths to God, as well as exactly how to "walk" those paths. Abraham's mathematical tables are akin to a "treasure map" that will enable us to explore the great mysteries of God as revealed in the Book of Creation.

"In the beginning…" the Ten Sefirot of Nothingness were represented in the biblical text by the spirit of God *hovering* over the face of the waters. When God said "Let there by light…" the Kav's 11 numerals were extended across a field of 21 out of 22 Hebrew letters to create a mathematical matrix consisting of "231 Gates" of divine light (11 x 21 = 231; see Stanza 2.5). The "Secret of the Torah"[51] describes how the Ten Sefirot of Nothingness descend from God's upper realm, into matter, to construct the vibrational essence of the Soul, Time and the Universe

The Book of Creation's "Rosetta Stone" is a pair of mathematical tables whose essential connection with music must be reestablished for the three faiths to find the paths to God. Abraham's riddles have eluded scholars for thousands of years, cleverly embedding an ancient musical table within a multiplication table. The two traditional methods for interpreting these tables, "the kabbalistic method" and "the logical method," are described in detail by Kaplan.[52] Without the fundamental connection to musical string theory, neither of these two methods allows for a proper understanding of gematria and Kabbalah.

One of the two tables in question was rediscovered by Albert von Thimus in the late nineteenth-century, in the context of explaining the mathematical allegories in Plato's Timaeus.[53] The existence of these tables within the Book of Creation is presented here for the first time. Although the ancient Greeks and Hebrews share this table, we will demonstrate that the mathematical constructions within the Book of Creation were precursors to the mathematical constructions encrypted within the oldest pages of the Bible. This implies that they predate Pythagoras and Plato as well; and it corroborates the position of Philo of Alexandria, who believed that both Pythagoras and Plato learned their theology from the Torah.

---

51 Zalman, 301.
52 Kaplan, *Sefer Yetzirah*, 113-122.
53 McClain, *The Pythagorean Plato* (York Beach, ME: Nicolas-Hays, 1978), 147-148.

Once we understand how these two tables form the basis of Abraham's theory of numbers and sound, we should be able to see how the Creation allegory of Genesis builds upon our knowledge of acoustics in a step-by-step manner, with each passing day of Creation, until a panorama of the complete soundscape is revealed and referenced as the foundation of the book of Scripture.

The need to translate between a mathematical table and a musical table is hinted at in the Hebrew word for "paths," taken from the phrase *32 mystical paths*. Aryeh Kaplan points out that the word is numerically equivalent to the number 462. This suggests that the 231 letters need to be doubled up somehow. The Zohar tells us *"when letters are joined, letters ascend and descend."*[54] Musical tones "ascend" and "descend" in this manner because they are musical pitches, which characteristically "ascend" and "descend." But without a direct application of music theory, the wrong letters have gotten doubled up throughout history, resulting in a long history of misinterpretation.

The first step is to recognize that the ratios of musical string theory hold the key to unlock Abraham's mathematical riddles. Armed with this basic assumption we can begin to examine Abraham's writings. Stanza 2.5, above, suggests a starting point for our detective work by asking the question: *How?* Abraham then proceeds to answer his own question.

We read that *"He permuted them, weighed them, and transformed them,"* but what exactly was it that God permuted, weighed and transformed? The acts of "permuting and weighing" sound like numeric operations of some sort, but these number values were then somehow *"transformed."* If for the moment we assume these numbers were transformed to sound, we should be able to see how far that approach takes us. Abraham's riddle tells us to combine *"Alef with them all,"* which I interpret as combining the Hebrew letter *Alef* with all the Hebrew numerals of the Kav. Alef (= 1), is representative of God Himself, Alef is "the One" who utters the Ten Sefirot of Nothingness. The resulting fractions can then be understood as the integer divisions of a string that defines a harmonic series, in the manner of "Egyptian unit fractions," known in ancient times.[55] We should keep in mind that these are Arabic numeral translations of Hebrew numerals.

---

54 Zohar, 30a-30b.
55 McClain, "A New Look at Plato's Timaeus," *Music and Man* (1, no. 4 (1975)), 351.

Table 3a - God's Ten Utterances as a Harmonic Series

1/1	1/2	1/3	1/4	1/5	1/6	1/7	1/8	1/9	1/10	1/20

Once we have taken *"Alef with them all,"* we are then instructed to take *"all of them with Alef."* Taking our cue from the text, as well as our knowledge that musical ratios can be taken "either in direct or reverse order,"[56] we will now invert these numerals in a manner consistent with the "doctrine of opposites" and the reciprocity of frequency and wavelength. The beginning of a matrix is formed when the "hovering" horizontal x axis, containing the harmonic series defined by the Kav, descends vertically into matter along a y axis. If we are to create a matrix of 231 gates, then we must extend our y axis through 21 of the 22 letters of the Hebrew alphabet (11 x 21 = 231).

Table 3b - God's Ten Utterances "Descending" as an Arithmetic Series

1/1
2/1
3/1
4/1
5/1
6/1
7/1
8/1
9/1
10/1
20/1
30/1
40/1
50/1
60/1
70/1
80/1
90/1
100/1
200/1
300/1

---

56 Zalman, 287.

We then add the next layer to this construction by combining *"Bet with them all and all of them with Bet"* as follows:

Table 3c - The Beginnings of the Divine Light Matrix

1/1	1/2	1/3	1/4	1/5	1/6	1/7	1/8	1/9 ⟹
2/1	2/2	2/3	2/4	2/5	2/6	2/7	2/8	2/9 ⟹
3/1	3/2							
4/1	4/2							
5/1	5/2							
6/1	6/2							
7/1	7/2							
8/1	8/2							
9/1	9/2							
⇓	⇓							

Since *"they repeat in a cycle and exist in 231 Gates,"* our mathematical/musical matrix of divine light begins to take shape as the musical ratios of string theory. It is no coincidence that this table defines the three most significant types of mathematical progression – harmonic, arithmetic and geometric (see Appendix: The Arithmetic of the Quadrivium).

The neo-Platonist Iamblichus called this musical table the 'lambdoma' because if one is accurate in drawing ratios and tones equidistant from one another, then lines resembling the Greek letter lambda (Λ) can be drawn connecting each instance of a musical ratio."[57] "It is with a touch of genius that Albert Von Thimus reconstructed the Pythagorean multiplication table in a way which renders the old tonal implications immediately visible to us."[58]

The *x* axis of the table consists of a harmonic progression, while the *y* axis consists of an arithmetic progression, and any two adjacent numeric rows or columns maintain the same geometric progression. There is a 2:3 ratio maintained across the second and third rows, while there is a reciprocal 3:2 ratio going down the second and third columns.

---

57 Siegmund Levarie and Ernst Levy, *Tone: A Study in Musical Acoustics* (Kent, Ohio: Kent State University Press, 1968), 35-39.
58 McClain, *The Myth of Invariance*, 147.

Table 4 - The Pythagorean Table of Von Thimus[59]

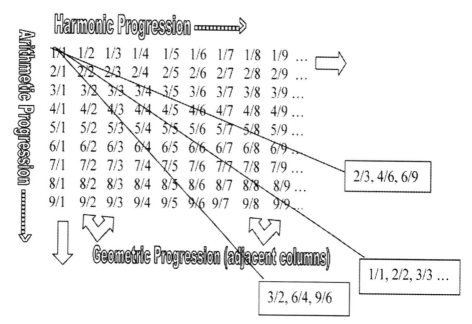

This reciprocal relationship between rows and columns is easier to see if we convert everything to a common denominator. For example, it is easier to assess the value of the fractions in the second and third columns if we use a common denominator of 12 (see Table 5). The converted columns on the right demonstrate a 3:2 ratio in the numerators, all the way down the two columns. Any two adjacent numerators in the converted columns will show the same geometric ratio of 3:2, i.e., 6:4, 12:8, 18:12 and 24:16:

Table 5 – Converting to Like Terms

1/2	1/3		6/12	4/12
2/2	2/3		12/12	8/12
3/2	3/3		18/12	12/12
4/2	4/3		24/12	16/12

In Table 6, each musical tone is labeled with its corresponding musical ratio. In moving from left to right across the *x* axis, each

59 Levarie and Levy, 40; McClain, *The Myth of Invariance*, 148.

fraction describes progressively smaller lengths of the fundamental string (wavelength), which sound increasingly higher frequencies. If one descends along the y axis, then the string lengths get progressively larger, while their frequencies get lower.

Reading the desired musical ratios directly from this table enables us to follow Abraham's acoustical constructions as he relates numbers to the inner workings of our Soul, of Time, and of the Universe. When nineteenth-century music theorist Albert von Thimus rediscovered this table in the works of Plato, he named it "the Pythagorean table" and used it to explain the World Soul in Plato's Timaeus. However, the Book of Creation is likely to be the oldest extant manuscript that makes use of this table.

Abraham has us first construct the table of 462 musical "Paths." But, to enter those "paths" mankind must first discover the location of the 231 "Gates" that lead to these paths. We must understand where to find the gates because Abraham's text often references only the gates. As with any good riddle the answer is right in front of our nose. We close the "gate" to the musical "path" of ratio 3/5 by simply multiplying the two numbers together to get 15 (compare tables 6 and 7). Similarly the musical path 2/3 closes its gate to yield the number 6 – and so on. Once all the gates have been closed we are left with a multiplication table in which Stanza 2.6 tells us *"He carved great pillars from the air that cannot be grasped."* One of the two multipliers would be listed in the top row (along the x axis), while the other would be listed in the leftmost column (along the y axis). The product of these two multipliers would be located at the point of intersection of the respective row and column, thus forming the body of the table. One can toggle between the multiplication table and the musical table at will, metaphorically opening up the gate to enter the path, or closing the gate to return from the path.

We can see that Abraham builds a column of numbers under the number 20 that defines an upper limit of 6000. In the Talmud and Tanya we read, "Six thousand years shall the world exist."[60] One might also wonder why the tone-generating y axis of the 231 Gates table is only 21 letters, rather than 22 letters of the Hebrew alphabet. The subtle variation in the number of Hebrew letters and digits is an important part of the encryption process; a process in which the obvious is successful, but only in a very general way. The parameters of the table are clearly $11 \times 21 = 231$ and

60 Zalman, 441; Sanhedrin 97a.

not 10 x 22 = 220. Without knowledge of how string theory "transforms" those 22 letters one cannot penetrate the "Secret of the Torah": the divine light matrix that God used to "engrave" Creation.

We will soon see that omitting the twenty-second letter, the letter Tav (ת), from the 231 Gates table preempts it from creating a new musical tone. This is in keeping with its function as the essence of the Sabbath, when God rests and refrains from creating. In the passage below we can see that the seventh day corresponds to the seventh "Double," Tav (ת). Its correspondence to the Sabbath is verified in the Book of Creation.

4.14 *He made the letter Tav (ת) king over Grace*
  And He bound a crown to it
  And He combined one with another
 And with them He formed
  Jupiter in the Universe
  The Sabbath in the Year
  The mouth in the Soul,
   male and female.

:1	:2	:3	:4	:5	:6	:7	:8	:9	:10	:20
1:1=d	1:2=d	1:3=a	1:4=d	1:5=f#	1:6=a	1:7=c	1:8=d	1:9=e	1:10=f#	1:20=f#
2:1=d	2:2=d	2:3=a	2:4=d	2:5=f#	2:6=a	2:7=c	2:8=d	2:9=e	2:10=f#	2:20=f#
3:1=g	3:2=g	3:3=d	3:4=g	3:5=b	3:6=d	3:7=f	3:8=g	3:9=a	3:10=b	3:20=b
4:1=d	4:2=d	4:3=a	4:4=d	4:5=f#	4:6=a	4:7=c	4:8=d	4:9=e	4:10=f#	4:20=f#
5:1=bb	5:2=bb	5:3=f	5:4=bb	5:5=d	5:6=f	5:7=ab	5:8=bb	5:9=a	5:10=d	5:20=d
6:1=g	6:2=g	6:3=d	6:4=g	6:5=b	6:6=d	6:7=f	6:8=g	6:9=a	6:10=b	6:20=b
7:1=e	7:2=e	7:3=b	7:4=e	7:5=g#	7:6=b	7:7=d	7:8=e	7:9=f#	7:10=g#	7:20=g#
8:1=d	8:2=d	8:3=a	8:4=d	8:5=f#	8:6=a	8:7=c	8:8=d	8:9=e	8:10=f#	8:20=f#
9:1=c	9:2=c	9:3=g	9:4=c	9:5=e	9:6=g	9:7=bb	9:8=c	9:9=d	9:10=e	9:20=e
10:1=bb	10:2=bb	10:3=f	10:4=bb	10:5=d	10:6=f	10:7=ab	10:8=bb	10:9=c	10:10=d	10:20=d
20:1=bb	20:2=bb	20:3=f	20:4=bb	20:5=d	20:6=f	20:7=ab	20:8=bb	20:9=c	20:10=d	20:20=d
30:1=eb	30:2=eb	30:3=bb	30:4=eb	30:5=g	30:6=bb	30:7=db	30:8=eb	30:9=f	30:10=g	30:20=g
40:1=bb	40:2=bb	40:3=f	40:4=bb	40:5=d	40:6=f	40:7=ab	40:8=bb	40:9=c	40:10=d	40:20=d
50:1=gb	50:2=gb	50:3=db	50:4=gb	50:5=bb	50:6=db	50:7=fb	50:8=gb	50:9=ab	50:10=bb	50:20=bb
60:1=eb	60:2=eb	60:3=bb	60:4=eb	60:5=g	60:6=bb	60:7=db	60:8=eb	60:9=f	60:10=g	60:20=g
70:1=c	70:2=c	70:3=g	70:4=c	70:5=e	70:6=g	70:7=bb	70:8=c	70:9=d	70:10=e	70:20=e
80:1=bb	80:2=bb	80:3=f	80:4=bb	80:5=d	80:6=f	80:7=ab	80:8=bb	80:9=c	80:10=d	80:20=d
90:1=ab	90:2=ab	90:3=eb	90:4=ab	90:5=c	90:6=eb	90:7=gb	90:8=ab	90:9=bb	90:10=c	90:20=c
100:1=gb	100:2=gb	100:3=db	100:4=gb	100:5=bb	100:6=db	100:7=fb	100:8=gb	100:9=ab	100:10=bb	100:20=bb
200:1=gb	200:2=gb	200:3=db	200:4=gb	200:5=bb	200:6=db	200:7=fb	200:8=gb	200:9=ab	200:10=bb	200:20=bb
300:1=cb	300:2=cb	300:3=gb	300:4=cb	300:5=eb	300:6=gb	300:7=bbb	300:8=cb	300:9=db	300:10=eb	300:20=eb

Table 6 – The 462 Musical Paths which Must Be "Closed" to Reveal 231 Numerical Gates

	2	3	4	5	6	7	8	9	10	20
1	2	3	4	5	6	7	8	9	10	20
2	4	6	8	10	12	14	16	18	20	40
3	6	9	12	15	18	21	24	27	30	60
4	8	12	16	20	24	28	32	36	40	80
5	10	15	20	25	30	35	40	45	50	100
6	12	18	24	30	36	42	48	54	60	120
7	14	21	28	35	42	49	56	63	70	140
8	16	24	32	40	48	56	64	72	80	160
9	18	27	36	45	54	63	72	81	90	180
10	20	30	40	50	60	70	80	90	100	200
20	40	60	80	100	120	140	160	180	200	400
30	60	90	120	150	180	210	240	270	300	600
40	80	120	160	200	240	280	320	360	400	800
50	100	150	200	250	300	350	400	450	500	1000
60	120	180	240	300	360	420	480	540	600	1200
70	140	210	280	350	420	490	560	630	700	1400
80	160	240	320	400	480	560	640	720	800	1600
90	180	270	360	450	540	630	720	810	900	1800
100	200	300	400	500	600	700	800	900	1000	2000
200	400	600	800	1000	1200	1400	1600	1800	2000	2200
300	600	900	1200	1500	1800	2100	2400	2700	3000	6000

Table 7 – The 231 Numerical Gates which Must Be "Opened" to Reveal 462 Musical Paths

In Part 2, we will examine how the legacy of Abraham's theology evolved within the three faiths. We have seen the solution to the wonderful riddle of how 231 numerical "Gates" open, to lead mankind toward 462 musical "Paths" to God. It is more accurate to say, however, that there are 462 musical steps from which the three musical paths are derived. The musical steps are notes, while the paths are musical scales. These tables provide a cross walk between Abrahams book of number (*Sephar*) and his book of sound (*Sippur*). The musical table is the harmonic matrix of divine light created by God on the first day of Creation. The preceding table provides details, to be explained later, of how these tables were developed by Abraham for all subsequent acoustical constructions within the Book of Creation as well as for the entire Tanakh.

In the Torah, God's first Utterance "Let there be light," manifests Abraham's two mathematical tables in a sort of biblical "Big Bang" of divine light. In Part 3, we will see that the Word of God, *Yahweh*, "reorders" this matrix of light to "engrave" the multitude of objects and beings in Creation. Rediscovering the acoustical basis of Abraham's writings puts us in a position to understand the theological foundation of the Tanakh, the New Testament, and the Koran.

Figure 6– Day 1 Descent of Divine Light
(Robert Fludd: utriusque cosmi)

PART II. THE SONG OF THE NATIONS

Figure 7a– Seven Circuits Around the Sukah

Figure 7b– The Tefillin:
Seven Circuits Around
the Sacred Cube

Firgure 7c -
Seven tone circles
heralding the Descent
of the "foursquare"
New Jerusalem

Figure 7d -
Seven
Circumambulations
Around the Ka'bah

Rediscovering the Lost Practice

The Seven Noahide Laws

The Jewish oral tradition tells us that when Adam was cast out of Eden, God had compassion and sent him the Archangel Raziel, whose name means "secrets of God," to give him the *Sefer Raziel* (Book of Raziel), containing all the secrets of existence. The book and teaching were handed down to the "sons of God," i.e., to Adam's son Seth, to Enoch, and so on, until it reached Abraham.[61]

Although kabbalistic legend speaks of a book called the *Sefer Raziel*, perhaps it wasn't actually a book, per se. If this knowledge existed in some form before Abraham, it was probably transmitted orally, or, perhaps this mathematical cosmology and cosmogony were transmitted to later generations on the "Pillars of Seth," as the historian Josephus chronicles. Whatever the actual method of transmission, the secrets of God are said to have been passed down from Adam to Seth, to Enoch, to Noah, to Shem, to Melchizedek, and finally to Abraham. It is this same body of knowledge that became the legacy of secrets encrypted in Abraham's Book of Creation.

God's Covenant with Noah revealed seven Noahide Laws. We will come to understand that these seven laws defined a secret practice of the High Priests. Shem, the son of Noah, was the most honored of Noah's children. Shem was also "a priest of God, the Most High." Melchizedek, who was the King of Salem (Jerusalem), was also "a priest of God, the Most High." In fact, Jewish sages have identified Melchizedek as the reincarnation of Shem.[62] Ten generations after God's Covenant with Noah, God established a Covenant with Abraham. That Covenant resulted from Melchizedek's initiation of Abraham into what the New Testament calls the "order of Melchizedek," or the "eternal priesthood."

61 *Zohar*, 37b, 55b; Z'ev ben Shimon Halevi, *Kabbalah and Exodus* (Boulder Colorado: Shambhala, 1980), 15, 30.
62 *Chumash*, Genesis 14:18-19 fn. 18.

This secret practice of High Priests is still accessible to mankind thanks to Abraham's Book of Creation. The Book of Creation is the only extant record of the transcendental meaning and explanation of how to execute the seven laws of the eternal priesthood. Later Talmudic explanations of these laws must defer to Abraham's explanation.

Abraham reveals them as "seven circuits around the sacred cube." Melchizedek initiated Abraham into what I have called the "Song of the Nations," which must ultimately be learned and "sung" by everyone in order to "bind" to God. Within the Hebrew Scriptures: Enoch, Noah, Shem, Melchizedek, Abraham, Isaac, Jacob, Joseph, Moses, the High Priests, and the great prophets, were all initiated into the transcendental meaning and pronunciation of the Word of God, *Yahweh*, embodying the secret practice of seven laws that purify the body and liberate the soul.

The following passage explains the origins of this secret practice. It is taken from *A New Encyclopedia of Freemasonry*, by Arthur Waite:

> From year to year no longer did the High Priest pass behind the veil and pronounce the Great Word on the other side of the curtain of palms and pomegranates. It came about in the course of the centuries that the true way of its pronunciation passed even from the memory of the elders. Therefore "until time and circumstances should restore the genuine," they continued to do of necessity... the substitution of Adonai for Jehovah...the Tradition with its whole heart looks for that day to come when Israel shall be taken out of exile and the palladium of the elect people shall be declared in the hearing of all who have come out of great tribulation into the inheritance of Zion. [63]

The exile of Israel can finally come to an end with the revelation of the "secret tradition in Israel." Abraham's original definition of that secret tradition establishes that all human beings are proud owners of their very own set of harmonic vibrations, which comprise the inner vibrations of their divine soul. With absolutely no effort on their part, all people possess eternal and divine souls – souls that are held earthbound by what the Hebrew Scriptures calls sin. Man must learn to properly "sing" God's <u>Great Name in</u> order to raise his soul up to God, in the manner of the

63 Waite, 416-419.

ancient prophets. To quote the *Zohar*, "From a word of Torah is formed a sound... that sound ascends and breaks through the heavens.[64]

With no understanding of the Book of Creation's "Song," Aryeh Kaplan still manages to conclude that the Book of Creation focuses on meditation. He writes;

> What we therefore have in the Book of Creation appears to be an instruction manual, describing certain meditative exercises. There is some evidence that these exercises were meant to strengthen the initiate's concentration, and were particularly helpful in the development of telekinetic and telepathic powers. It was with these powers that one would then be able to perform feats that outwardly appeared to be magical.[65]

Without an understanding of string theory, the enormous depth of meaning that is buried in the text is lost. Kaplan, however, was able to use the following grammatical analysis to determine that the Book of Creation takes the form of an instruction manual;

> Hebrew is written without vowels, and therefore, the third person and the imperative are written exactly the same... "[Yah] engraved it" can also be read in the imperative, "Engrave it..."[66]

According to Kaplan, the Book of Creation's use of the imperative serves as a set of instructions to mankind. We read from Kaplan's translation in Stanza 6.7:

> *And when, Abraham our father, may he rest in peace, looked, saw, understood, probed, engraved, and carved, He was successful in creation....*

Despite the inability of the rabbinical establishment to understand the Book of Creation's mathematical riddles, the book still played a role in keeping some knowledge of Abraham's techniques alive over the

64 *Zohar,* part III, 31b, 121b.
65 Kaplan, *Sefer Yetzirah,* xi.
66 Kaplan, *Sefer Yetzirah,* 90.

centuries. One of the most well known examples of its influence was the
development of Abraham Abulafia's (1240-1292) practice of "prophetic
Kabbalah." Scholem writes;

> The techniques of "prophetic Kabbalah" that were used
> [by Abbulafia] to aid ascent of the soul, such as breathing
> exercises, the repetition of the Divine Names, and meditations
> on colors, bear a marked resemblance to those of both Indian
> Yoga and Muslim Sufism. The subject sees flashes of light
> and feels as though he were divinely "anointed."[67]

Tanakh and New Testament miracles were therefore not considered
tricks but rather true magic – mind over matter – presumably possible
when a man "binds himself to God" through Abraham's practice. The
assumption is that after years of undistracted meditation one begins to
develop "divine gifts." Some, who practice meditation for many years,
without knowing Abraham's acoustical details or specific techniques, may
get close enough to his core practice to realize certain "gifts."

The True Birthright

Within Genesis, the first book of the Hebrew Scriptures, each of the
founding fathers of Israel passed on Abraham's teachings to the "anointed
one" of the next generation by awarding the all-important birthright to the
son considered divinely worthy, rather than to the firstborn, as Hebrew
law of the time prescribed. The Torah taught what kind of behavior was
deemed worthy of God and what was not. This lesson begins with the
children of Adam and Eve: Cain and Abel, and extends to Isaac and
Ishmael, Jacob and Esau, Joseph and his brothers, etc. A comparison of
good and bad behavior was intended to reinforce the Torah's message
characterizing good and evil.

God favored and rewarded those who were "good" and most
spiritual, often creating resentment and hatred in the sibling who was
effectively cast aside. The siblings of Genesis who were known to have
received the precious birthright determined the ancestral lineage of the
Jewish people while those siblings who were not chosen went on to

---

67 Scholem, *Kabbalah,* 180-181.

populate other nations. For example, Ishmael fathered the Arab people, while Jacob's brother Esau was considered progenitor of the Edomite Romans. Sibling rivalries for the birthright were characterized by both good and bad behavior. Since several of these siblings were considered the founders of nations, their characteristic behaviors sometimes became associated with the nations they founded.

A patriarch's choice between rival siblings was divinely influenced, intended to convey the necessary righteousness worthy of receiving the birthright. Once the Book of Creation's explanation of that birthright had been lost, all that seemed to remain within the Torah was the notion that God takes sides, not only in sibling rivalries, but presumably in cultural and national conflicts as well.

The biblical notion that Jews were the "chosen people" played an important role in characterizing the world's relationship to them. Once an understanding of the true birthright was lost, the biblical legacy was debased to a perpetuation of the rivalry for the good graces of God. The biblical allegories of sibling rivalry and their establishment of exclusivity has left a stigma of resentment and divisiveness that has become culturally ingrained in the monotheistic world, and has undermined the peaceful development of Western civilization. This age-old psychology of divisiveness might justifiably be considered the root cause of many wars fought throughout history, as well as the foundation for much anti-Semitic behavior.

Jews, Muslims and Christians are geographical neighbors within the Holy Land, and especially in Jerusalem, where a single site can play host to all three faiths. Ironically, despite their close geographic proximity, their shared theological roots, although identical, were abandoned. The Jewish rejection of both Jesus and Mohammed as prophets can be attributed to the common belief that the days of the prophets were over. They were, in fact, over — but only because the "Word of God" and the secret practice were lost. The two most notable exceptions to this rule were Mohammed and Jesus. We know that Mohammed had a lifelong meditation practice, and from Abraham's perspective, Jesus' spiritual accomplishments tell us that Jesus had one as well.

Understanding Abraham's legacy will teach mankind how to pray in the manner of the prophets. This teaching was inherited by all three monotheistic faiths, as the Ka'bah, the tefillin, and the New Jerusalem. But each faith proceeded in its own isolated direction, driving additional wedges of doctrine between them. There was no longer a spiritual common ground to nourish theological discussion. As a result, each of the three faiths tends to believe that it alone holds the true path to God.

Abraham's explanation of the "Lost Word" enabled Abraham's direct heirs to successfully embark on the path to God, and each successive generation was therefore assured of an "anointed one" to lead the way. Without that birthright, all that remained was the polarizing effect of God's favoritism toward a "chosen" sibling. It is all too obvious that religious tensions play a major role in today's world politics. It is arguably the most significant root cause of strife throughout the history of civilization.

Considering the long history of bloodshed in the name of religion, it is natural to wonder whether it might be too late for Abraham's great teaching to help modern civilization return to the state of harmony and peace envisioned by the framers of Scripture. Mankind has waited in anguish and suffering for deliverance, while the faithful cling to the Messianic hope that discovering and disseminating the true meaning of the Bible would enable mankind to transcend ego, and to transform the psychology of exclusivity and divisiveness into one of peace and understanding.

We will hopefully come to realize that the mathematics of the Lost Word is the essence and foundation of Scriptures, while the Creation allegory of the Torah can be understood as step-by-step instructions to help reconstruct that knowledge. Taken together, the Torah and the Book of Creation form a cohesive framework that enables the individual to develop a direct relationship with God, at a level that was previously attained by the great prophets and the High Priests of Solomon's Temple.[68] The Jewish people can be considered the book's caretakers, but the Book of Creation belongs to all the descendants of Abraham. The Lost Practice was taught directly to both Isaac and Ishmael, demonstrating that Arabs share in the true birthright. Abraham's practice, however, should be shared with all his descendents, and all of mankind.[69]

The Lost Word is quite literally the soul of the Bible and without understanding how the Lost Tables lead us to the Lost Word and Abraham's

68 Zalman, 279. During the Day of Atonement only the High Priest was allowed to enter the Holy of Holies where the Ark of the Covenant contained the original Ten Commandment tablets.

69 One can infer that Abraham's teaching was intended for all of mankind from a Talmudic teaching explaining that "He taught mysteries to the children of his concubines." "Abraham gave gifts, and he sent them away ... to the lands of the east" - Genesis 25:6; Zohar 1:99b-100b.

Lost Practice, civilization has no way to heal itself, and as a result, it has been torn apart by divisiveness and violence for thousands of years.

Common Spiritual Ground

The need to create a Palestinian state within the borders of Israel may be a modern reflection of a long-standing resentment over the right to inhabit what Arabs view as common ground: the land of Israel. The denial of Arab entitlement to inhabit Israel is chronicled in the Bible, beginning around 1700 BCE when Abraham's wife Sarah couldn't conceive. She then offered her hand servant, Hagar, to Abraham for a wife. Hagar conceived Abraham's firstborn son, Ishmael, but then a miracle occurred. At 90 years old, Sarah was finally able to conceive, and she gave birth to Isaac. The Bible describes the uncomfortable relationship between Hagar and Sarah, with Sarah ultimately insisting that Abraham send Hagar and Ishmael away. Sarah didn't want Ishmael to share in Abraham's inheritance with her son Isaac. Abraham was upset with Sarah's demand, but God told the grieving Abraham that a nation with 12 princes would descend from Ishmael, and Abraham should not grieve, but should grant Sarah's request.

Hagar and Ishmael wander in the wilderness with only bread and water. This appears terribly cruel and unjust, and it has resulted in centuries of indignation on the part of Arabs over the right of firstborn Ishmael to claim Abraham's inheritance as prescribed by Hebrew law. The biblical story of Abraham, Isaac and Ishmael plays a central role in the history of Islam, and was revisited in the Koran from a Muslim perspective.

Long before Mohammed's revelations began ca. 610, the pilgrimage of Arab tribesmen to circle the Ka'bah was already an ancient tradition. Local Arab tradition maintains that Hagar and Ishmael settled in Mecca, and that Abraham had visited and rebuilt the Ka'bah, at God's command, together with Ishmael. Abraham is said to have observed the construction of the Ka'bah standing on a stone which God caused to soften leaving his footprint. Today the stone is enclosed in copper and glass, and it is known as the "station of Abraham." "This was music to Mohammed's ears. It seemed that the Arabs had not been left out of the divine plan after all, and that the Ka'bah had venerable monotheistic credentials."[70] Mohammed believed that Allah and the God of the Hebrews and Christians were the same.[71]

70 Karen Armstrong, *Islam: A Short History* (New York: Random House, 2002), 17.
71 Armstrong, *A History of God,* 135.

Perhaps Mohammed came to understand the importance of meditation from the local Jewish population of Mecca and Medina. In any case, there can be no doubt that he developed a great vision as a result of his lifelong meditation practice. Mohammed's "gift of vision" is evident by his appreciation of the historical and theological significance of the Ka'bah. Mohammed tied Islam to the ancient cult of the Ka'bah and made sense of the Arab legends about Abraham.

The Koran extols the sacred duty of each Muslim to meditate, kneel, and prostrate himself at the holy mosque of the Ka'bah and pay respects to the revelations of Abraham by kissing or touching the stone where he stood. It is the greatest privilege in life for a Muslim. After Mohammed's revelations, his new Muslim followers had trouble gaining access to the Ka'bah, which had been controlled for over two millennia by non-Islamic Arab tribesmen. Only after Mohammed conquered his own Quraysh tribesmen very late in life did Islam not only gain access, but from that point forward, controlled access to the Ka'bah.

The true birthright that is Abraham's legacy has little to do with the physical land of Israel inherited by Isaac, and everything to do with the most ancient of spiritual practices, handed down to Abraham, and then passed on to both Isaac and Ishmael. That ancient spiritual practice is defined by the Arab cult of the Ka'bah, which is tied directly, through the Book of Creation, to a similar tradition of worship within Judaism, the Jewish mitzvoth (commandment) of putting on tefillin every weekday morning.

Tefillin, or phylacteries, consist of two small boxes, sacred cubes, with black leather straps attached to them. One box is placed on the head and the other on the arm, opposite the heart. The straps are wrapped seven times around the arm to represent the seven aspects of the soul being bound to God. Inside the sacred cubes are four sets of handwritten scrolls with verses from the Torah about love. One of the most powerful of the tefillin prayers, from the prophet Hosea, is often used as a commitment statement at Jewish weddings:

V'eirastikh li l'olam	I betroth you to me forever.
V'eirastikh li b'tzedek	I will betroth you to me in righteousness,
U'v'mishpat	and with judgment
U'v'hessed	and with loving-kindness
U'v'rahamim	and with compassion.

v'eirastikh li b'emunah I will betroth you to me in faith
v'yadat et Adonai. So that you will know God.

A couple being wed stands beneath a chuppah, which is also a sacred cube, while the groom is circled seven times by the bride, her mother, and mother-in-law. During the ceremony the bride and groom often recite the tefillin prayer quoted above. The intent of this ceremony is to bind all of one's being to God. It is, in effect, a marriage to God. Clearly, this is also the meaning of the Ka'bah and the Mecca pilgrimage.

The Jewish holiday of *Sukkoth*, the Festival of Tabernacles, also refers to the sacred cube (tabernacle) that Jews are commanded to live in for seven days during this holiday. On the seventh day of Sukkoth, seven circuits are made around the sacred cube. These processions commemorate similar processions around the sacred cube of the Ark of the Covenant in Solomon's Temple, as well as seven circuits around the tabernacle in the desert during the Exodus. Thus we can see that this most ancient of spiritual teachings, "seven circuits around the sacred cube," represents the true birthright, and was shared between Isaac and Ishmael. Abraham's teaching was later inherited by Christianity and can be found in the Book of Revelation as the seven trumpet tones (seven "tone circles") heralding the descent of the sacred cube of the New Jerusalem.

Abraham was the first to imply that man's free will allows him to choose his soul's direction toward either good or evil. Abraham also teaches us that choosing good requires us to remain undistracted from God by any longings of the ego, in order to perform "seven circuits around the sacred cube." A battle between man's "inner" and "outer" nature manifests within Scripture as the need to atone for Adam's sin.

A Jew who is able to "do good" and "refrain from evil" by performing 613 commandments is ultimately transformed into a *tzadek* (righteous one). Mohammed introduced biblical morality to Muslims requiring that they undergo an "inner struggle" or *"greater jihad"* to ultimately attain the ranks of the righteous. Both Jews and Muslims are empowered to approach God through their good works. Christians, however, are not empowered in this manner. They don't have a direct relationship with God, the Father, and must wait for Christ's return to separate believers from nonbelievers on Judgment Day and determine who will be sent to heaven and who will be sent to hell.

The Storm on the Mountain

Figure 8 - Meeting God on the Mountain

Within Scripture, thunder, lightening and the sound of trumpets at crucial moments is a repetitive theme. For example, it accompanies God's presence on Mount Sinai when Moses was about to receive the Torah:

> *...as the morning dawned, there was thunder, and lightening, and a dense cloud upon the mountain, and a very loud blast of the horn...Now Mount Sinai was all in smoke, for the Lord had come upon it in fire; the smoke rose like the smoke of a kiln, and the whole mountain trembled violently. The blare of the horn grew louder and louder.*[72]

The most significant biblical description of the "storm on the mountain," other than Moses on Mount Sinai, occurs after Elijah fasted 40 days and nights during his walk to Mount Horeb (God's other mountain);

> *"Come out," He called, "and stand on the mountain before the Lord." And lo, the Lord passed by. There was a great and mighty wind, splitting mountains and shattering rocks by the power of the Lord; but the Lord was not in the wind. After the wind – an earthquake; but the Lord was not in the earthquake. After the earthquake — fire; but the Lord was not in the fire. And after the fire – a soft murmuring sound. When Elijah heard it, he wrapped his mantle about his face and went out and stood at the entrance of the cave. Then a voice addressed him...*[73]

The "soft-murmuring sound" that Elijah heard comes in the quietude of meditation, only after the "storms" of the body's physiology quiesce. In Isaiah 30:15 we read;

> *For thus said my Lord God, the Holy One of Israel,*
> *"You shall triumph by stillness and quiet;*
> *Your victory shall come about*
> *Through calm and confidence."*[74]

---

72 Exodus 19:15-19.
73 I Kings 19:11-12.
74 Isaiah 30:15.

Abraham's ancient practice is also embedded in the allegories of the New Testament's Book of Revelation. In the "preparatory visions" before the peace and tranquility of the descent of the sacred cube from heaven (the New Jerusalem), seven angels descended with seven golden bowls, full of the wrath of God. In the prophecy, all seven bowls were poured out:

> *And there were flashes of lightening, rumblings and peals of thunder, and there was a great earthquake such has never been seen since men were first upon the earth, so great an earthquake was it...and great hail, heavy as a talent came down from heaven upon men...*[75]

There were also seven angels with trumpets (seven tone circles). The seventh angel sounded the trumpet heralding the New Jerusalem's descent from heaven:

> *And the temple of God in heaven was opened, and there was seen the ark of his covenant in his temple, and there came flashes of lightening, and peals of thunder, and an earthquake, and great hail.*[76]

Understanding the sound of horns or trumpets as Abraham's seven "tone" circles was made more literal in the Hebrew Scriptures by the seven circumambulations around Jericho made by Joshua's priests, while each priest held a trumpet. The Lord had just gathered the waters of the Jordan River together, splitting the waters to fashion a path for the Israelites to cross over into the Promised Land after wandering in the desert for 40 years.[77] God then delivered Jericho to the Israelites with these instructions to Joshua:

---

75 Revelation 16:19-21.

76 Revelation 11:19

77 Many recurring biblical allegories have an acoustical basis that will be explained in Part 3. For example, the "separation of the waters from the waters" occurred in the very first words of Genesis, as well as the splitting of the Red Sea for Moses, and the Jordan River for Joshua. Similarly, the Israelites wandered 40 years in the desert; Elijah fasted 40 days before hearing God; the temptations of Christ also occurred during 40 days in the wilderness.

*Let all your troops march around the city and complete one
circuit of the city. Do this six days, with seven priests carrying
seven ram's horns preceding the Ark. On the seventh day, march
around the city seven times, with the priests blowing the horns.
And when a long blast is sounded on the horn – all the people
shall give a mighty shout. Thereupon the city wall will collapse,
and the people shall advance, every man straight ahead.*[78]

Like seven circuits around the sacred cube of the Ka'bah, the tefillin,
and the New Jerusalem, this allegory describes Abraham's lost practice
of seven "tone circles" around the sacred cube that will tear down the
walls separating the Israelites from the city God promised them. With
the Lord's instructions to Joshua *"people shall advance"* and, to use St.
Paul's words, *reach behind the veil...*[79] between life and death.

Similarly, in Hindu allegory, the most powerful God, Indra, hurls
thunderbolts off Mount Meru (the Eastern version of Mount Sinai). From
this we can surmise that the appearance of lightening in these ancient texts
is associated with man's contact with God on the mountain – always a
metaphor for ascending to God through meditation. Biblical references
to the "Storm on the Mountain" were given their original context within
Abraham's Book of Creation. Abraham describes his meditation practice
amidst references to the primordial elements of wind, fire and water and
an *"appearance of lightening"* on the mountain.

The Temple Within

Within the Book of Revelation, the Beast of the Sea will gather the
forces of evil to face the forces of good in the final battle at Armaggedon.
The forces of evil will all wear the "mark of the Beast" on their right hand
or forehead. The Divine Warrior will sit on a white horse and:

*he has a name written which no man knows except himself...
his name is called the Word of God. And the armies of heaven,*

---

78 Joshua 6:3-5.
79 Hebrews 6:20..

clothed in fine linen, white and pure, were following him on white horses.

Leading these forces of good in the final battle will be the Lamb (Christ) standing on Mount Sion with 144,000 followers with his name (Christ) and the name of the Father on their foreheads, playing on their harps and singing *"a new song before the throne."* *"And no one could learn the song except those one hundred and forty-four thousand, who have been purchased from the earth..."* [80] One should not miss the musical allusion in this passage that derives from the Book of Creation.

The Holy City of the "New Jerusalem," which will descend foursquare, as a sacred cube from heaven, was constructed to contain these 144,000 pure souls. The number 144,000, comprising the forces of God, is reaffirmed in a different passage of Revelation, where an angel having the seal of the living God instructs other angels:

> *Do not harm the earth or the sea or the trees, till we have sealed the servants of God on their foreheads. And I heard the number of those who were sealed, a hundred and forty-four thousand sealed out of every tribe of the children of Israel; of the tribe of Judah, twelve thousand sealed; of the tribe of Rueben, twelve thousand; of the tribe of Gad, twelve thousand...*

In Revelation, a man holding a measuring line was asked where he was going. "To measure Jerusalem, he replied, to see how long and wide it is to be." In the Book of Revelation "the angel's measure" showed that:

> *the city stands foursquare...twelve thousand stadia: the length, breath, and height of it are equal. And he measured its wall, of a hundred and forty-four cubits.* [81]

In the Hebrew Scriptures the prophet Zechariah tells us that Jerusalem shall be measured and "peopled as a city without walls," and those who populate the Holy City will be the 144,000 that were "sealed" from among the 12 tribes of the spiritual Israel. If the city has no walls, but only its edges, i.e., the 12 diagonal boundaries that contain the divine light, then

80 Revelation 14:1-4.
81 Revelation 21:16-18

by adding the contribution of each of the twelve tribes, we arrive at our 144,000 inhabitants.

Rabbi Kaplan tells us that there are two ways to order the 12 tribes of Israel. The first appears at the beginning of Exodus 1:2-4. The second way results after Levi was given the priesthood and removed from the order of the tribes. To complete the 12, Joseph was divided into Ephraim and Manasseh. Figure 9 depicts the arrangement of camps in the desert according to this second method:

Revelation 7:5-8, however, in a bit of revisionism, "seals the spiritual Israel" with its own unique order that omits Dan and Ephraim but includes both Joseph and Manasseh. Most important, however, is that the New Jerusalem's gates will be populated by the 12 tribes of the spiritual Israel:

> *And it had a wall great and high with twelve gates, and at the gates twelve angels, and names written on them, which are the names of the twelve tribes of the children of Israel. On the east are three gates, and on the north three gates, and on the south three gates, and on the west three gates.*[82]

The 12 tribes of Israel, the 12 apostles of Christ, 12 Arab princes, etc., originally derive from the 12 diagonals of the sacred cube, which, according to Abraham, comprise the boundaries of the Universe. They manifest within the three faiths as the 12 diagonals of the Ka'bah, the tefillin and the New Jerusalem. The Book of Creation describes them as follows:

5.2 Twelve Elementals
HVZ ChTY LNS OtzQ (הוז חטי לנס עצק)
Their foundation is the twelve diagonal boundaries:
The east upper boundary
The east northern boundary
The east lower boundary
The south upper boundary
The south eastern boundary
The south lower boundary
The west upper boundary

82 Revelation 21:12-14.

The west southern boundary
The west lower boundary
The north upper boundary
The north western boundary
The north lower boundary
They extend continually until eternity of eternities
And it is they that are the boundaries of the Universe

Figure 9 – Twelve Tribes Camped in Desert

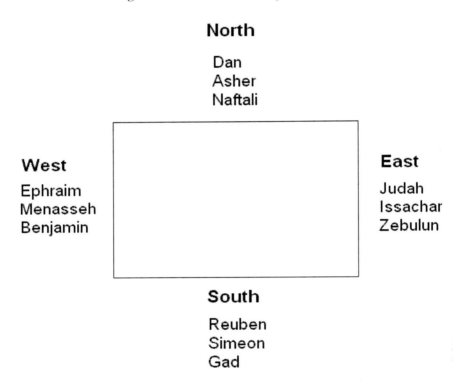

In this passage, Abraham provides a configuration for the 12 Elementals as 12 diagonal boundaries of the sacred cube. This is then reflected in both the Tanakh and the New Testament as the 12 tribes of Israel. Rabbi Kaplan corroborates:

> The ordering of directions is also the same as that of the four camps in the desert. The twelve diagonal boundaries thus correspond to the twelve tribes. It is for this reason that our

(Gra) version gives three boundaries for each of the four sides. These correspond to the three tribes in each of the four camps.[83]

The 12 diagonals clearly play a central role in Abraham's teaching, and a detailed acoustical explanation in Parts 3 and 4 will provide a much deeper understanding of their transcendental meaning and significance. In brief, however, the mind learns to make 7 tone circles around the 12 diagonals of the sacred cube in order to fill the 12 directors of a man's soul with divine light that will purify the body. Knowing the details of this ancient practice will enable us to purify our body, and ultimately to liberate our soul. This practice is the foundation doctrine of the Tanakh, the Koran, and the New Testament. It is reflected in the seven wraps around the twelve diagonals of the tefillin; the seven circumambulations around the twelve diagonals of the Ka'bah in Mecca; and the seven trumpet tone circles that herald the descent from heaven of the twelve diagonals of the New Jerusalem in the Book of Revelation.

With a proper understanding of Abraham's text we can help fulfill the prophecy of the "world to come" by learning how to "pronounce" the Lost Word like the High Priests of Solomon's Temple and, in so doing, bind our soul to God in eternal life. As each one of us learns to reenter Paradise while still living and breathing, civilization can quickly evolve toward a time when *"God Shall wipe away all tears from their eyes; and there shall be no more death, neither sorrow, nor crying, neither shall there be any more pain; for the former things are passed away."*[84]

---

83 Kaplan, *Sefer Yetzirah*, 203.
84 Revelation 21:4.

Figure 10 – Moses Receiving the Law on Mount Sinai
(Gustave Dorè: Moses)

Judaism

Sin & Redemption

Two trees grew right next to one another in the Garden of Eden. Adam and Eve were cursed for eating the fruit taken from the Tree of the Knowledge of Good and Evil. Only by partaking of the second tree, the Tree of Life, could they atone for their sin and save themselves from death and suffering;

> *And the Lord God said, "Now that the man has become like one of us, knowing good and bad, what if he should stretch out his hand and take also from the tree of life and eat, and live forever!" So the Lord God banished him from the Garden of Eden...*[85]

Adam and Eve's bite of the fruit of the Tree of Knowledge of Good and Evil brought the duality of good and evil into their nature. And with that bite, their nakedness was revealed to them and they were ashamed before God. As a result "original sin" is often associated with sexuality. Adam and Eve's unworthiness to remain in paradise, forced mankind, from that point forward, to endure death, the pain of giving birth, physical labor, and the spiritual struggle against temptation. Adam and Eve's hope for redemption, and thus the hope of their descendants, was to also partake of the Tree of Life, which, according to kabbalistic tradition, is equated with the Torah and the purification process of the Torah's commandments.

Each Jew is therefore responsible for fulfilling each of the Torah's commandments in order to compensate for Adam's fall from grace. When Moses received the law on Mount Sinai, it is interesting to note the horns that appear to be coming from Moses' head in Gustave Dorè's rendering (figure 10).

85 *Tanakh: The Holy Scriptures* (Jerusalem: Jewish Publication Society, 1985), *Genesis*, 3:22-24.

Michelangelo's Moses also has horns. This is derived from a mistranslation of the Hebrew phrase "karnu panav" קרנו פניו. The root קרן may be read as either "horn" or "ray," as in "ray of light." "Panav" פניו translates as "his face." In other words, Moses' face was aglow with enlightenment as he came off Mount Sinai — neither Moses nor the devil had horns!

The law of Moses can be found within the Five Books of Moses, otherwise known as the Torah. It contains 613 commandments, each of which must be accomplished with the appropriate *kavanah* (meditative intent). Kavanah is necessary for the words of Torah to rise and stand before God. The 613 commandment are all said to derive from the Ten Commandments.[86] "The Ten Commandments are the 'All-embracing principles of the whole Torah,' which comes from the Higher Wisdom that is far higher than the world of manifestation."[87]

The Torah's 613 commandments are comprised of 365 prohibitive commandments and 248 positive commandments. Violation of the prohibitive commandments results in sins of commission, while disobeying the positive commandments results in sins of omission. Once all the commandments have been successfully accomplished with the appropriate levels of kavanah, tradition maintains that God will bestow a "crown" on a righteous man, causing the *Shechinah* (the Divine Presence) to "hover" overhead. In the Tanya it states that: "every soul of Israel needs to be reincarnated in order to fulfill all the 613 commandments."[88] However, even after all 613 commandments have been fulfilled, Jews are taught never to put the "crown" of divinity on their own head, i.e., to believe that they could ever consider themselves "One with God." Jews are taught that they need to remain humble and "as low as the dust … or a grain of sand."

The desire to remain humble and "low as the dust" should be understood in the context of prostrating one's ego to God. The Jewish posture of humility is related to a Muslim's repeated prostrations before God to help facilitate the death of the ego and begin the migration toward God. We might think of ourselves as a great artist, a powerful politician or the richest person in town. While being great, powerful or rich may not be inherently wrong, we are undermined all too often by the superficial longings of ego. If fame, fortune, and power happen to result in the course of events, then one can remain untarnished. However, to the degree that

86 Zalman, *Tanya*, 83.
87 Zalman, 277; Zohar II, 85a; 121a.
88 Zalman, 429.

these things become someone's identity or goal, then it is theologically clear that this person was distracted from God.

Most of us are familiar with the distinction between an "outer me" described by occupation, wealth, physical appearance, etc., and a spiritual "inner me." Trying to find "the real me" is a lifelong quest for most of us. Abraham Lincoln referred to "the better angels of our nature" in his first inaugural, and modern literature is replete with references to "the real me," the "inner me," the "self," etc. By engaging in Abraham's unique practice of prayerful meditation, the clouds of confusion will begin to disappear, and the "real me" will begin to express itself.

Magic & Mysticism

Before we can understand this inner reality from the Jewish perspective it is important that we clarify a few key kabbalistic concepts. The terms *Shechinah, crown, kavanah,* and *golem* are not currently understood in a way that is consistent with Abraham's metaphysics.

- Today's kabbalistic tradition equates the term *Shechinah* with the term *crown.* The Shechinah is believed to "hover" above the head of a *tzadek* (righteous one) as a divine reward, or *crown,* for completing all of the Torah's commandments.
- The act of completing each of the 613 commandments requires the "meditative intent" of *kavanah* to be successful.
- The term *golem* usually carries the negative association of a Frankenstein-like android magically created by man.

Before we provide Abraham's perspective on these terms, we should be aware that the Book of Creation has long been associated with magic:

> This is supported by the Talmudic references, which appear to compare the use of the Book of Creation to a kind of white magic. [89]

Kaplan continues:

---

89 Kaplan, *Sefer Yetzirah,* xi.

The Talmud relates that "Rava created a man" and sent him to Rava Zeira. When the latter saw that this android would not answer his questions, he realized that it was a Golem, and told it to "return to the dust." The Bahir remarks that the Golem could not speak because Rava was not completely free from the taint of sin, and as long as man sins [not yet deemed "righteous" by God] he cannot partake of the powers of the Creator... the expression "Rava created a man" in Hebrew is RaBha BaRA GaBhRA, which is reminiscent of the Hebrew expression ABRA K'ADaBRA, which literally means "I will create as I speak. [90]

The Bible's allegory of Creation is based upon the Book of Creation's mathematical description of the Creation process. Following Abraham's methods are believed to give man the ability to create in the manner of God. The performance of miracles, such as those performed by Moses, Elijah, Jesus, and those described in the golem stories, is rooted in the Book of Creation. But, one may wonder why a tzadek might ever want to create an android?

The term "golem" (literally: shapeless mass) has taken on the meaning of an android or artificial human being within Hebrew folklore. According to Kaplan, the golem didn't always have negative connotations. "In a number of places prophecy is defined as the experience wherein a man sees the form of his own self standing before him and relating the future to him."[91] According to Scholem,

The study of the book [Book of Creation] was considered successful when the mystic attained the vision of the golem, which was connected with a specific ritual of remarkably ecstatic character. Only in later times did this inner experience assume more tangible forms in popular legend.[92]

What both Kaplan and Scholem attempt to describe here using language is more accurately described by Abraham's mathematical explanation for the liberation of a tzadek's prophetic soul from his

90 Kaplan, *Sefer Yetzirah,* xxi.
91 Scholem, *Kabbalah,* 181; Aryeh Kaplan, *Meditation and Kabbalah* (York Beach, ME: Samuel Weiser, 1978), 109.
92 Scholem, *Kabbalah,* 40.

purified body. Within that context the golem is a very positive concept that is closely related to the Shechinah hovering over the head of a tzadek. A golem's lingering "taint of sin" might be compared to the Buddhist concept of an "impure illusory body," whereas the Shechinah would be comparable to Buddhism's "pure illusory body." Abraham's core practice of binding to God through deep prayerful meditation will purify the body and liberate the soul as a golem. Continuing this practice will ultimately purify the golem until it is the Shechinah that hovers overhead.

Abraham's mathematics reveals that the crown corresponds to the letter *Heh* (ה = 5). It should not be thought of in the traditional manner of God crowning a tzadek the way a king might be crowned, because it has a very specific mathematical meaning within the Book of Creation. The crown can be characterized by a "divine influx" physically experienced during meditation,[93] and it is most closely related to the kabbalistic concept of kavanah, since "meditative intent" is what induces the divine influx to bind the letter *Heh* (ה) to our mind, body and soul.

Biblical allegory depicts God adding the letter *Heh* to the name of Abram, calling him Abraham, once he was deemed righteous. It is Abraham's meditation practice of "seven circuits around the sacred cube" that invokes the "divine influx" of the crown ("ה") to irradiate the body, mind and soul. Abraham describes this process as "binding the crown." God does not "crown" the tzadek with a Shechinah, the tzadek's meditative intent invokes the crown's "divine influx" to irradiate and purify the body, clearing the way for the tzadek's creation of a golem, i.e., the initial liberation of one's soul. With continued deep meditation, the tzadek's initial creation of the golem stabilizes into the Shechinah, which then hovers over the head of the tzadek.

Confusion between the concepts of the crown and the Shechinah may have resulted from stories about a crown or "halo" that existed over the head of a tzadek. "*Aggadah* [stories] about the rays of light that shone from Moses' forehead fathered the kabbalistic notion of a special halo [or 'crown'] that circled above the head of every righteous man. This belief became widespread, although the halo was sometimes considered to appear only shortly before a tzadek's death."[94]

---

93 One can safely speculate that experiencing this "divine influx" is somehow related to the nervous system's electrical energy. Electrical energy, and all electromagnetic phenomena, are consistent with the mathematics of the harmonic series.
94 Scholem, *Kabbalah*, 188.

Humility is a desirable virtue, but the idea that only God can "crown" a tzadek distorts Abraham's use of the term "crown" to inappropriately characterize this virtue, i.e., "never put a crown on one's own head." Actually, Abraham teaches us that "binding a crown" to our mind, body, and soul, is indeed a proactive act rather than a passive one. Even a renowned tzadek, for example, would never admit to being a tzadek, nor would they admit to being in close proximity to God. This immobilizing preoccupation with humility may have resulted from wild claims being made by Christianity that Christ was God. It is reasonable to speculate that Jesus understood Abraham's practice, and used it to "transfigure" his corporeal body into his "heavenly body." Without knowledge of Abraham's lost practice, Jews and Christians had no frame of reference to understand how this "miracle" was possible without Jesus being the Lord Himself.

When viewing the biblical passage of how Abram became Abraham, through the lens of Abraham's writings, we can see that the Torah considerably shortens the time frame between the time Abram began his meditation practice of irradiating himself with the "divine influx" of the letter "ה", to when Abraham is deemed righteous, receiving a "ה" permanently into his name. Abraham's meditation practice began immediately after Melchizedek blessed him, saying: "Blessed be Abram of God, the Most High."[95] This marked Abram's initiation into the secret practice, and in the very next section of the Torah, Abram had his "vision of the Lord," in which God established His Covenant with Abraham.

God deems Abram righteous and simply rewards him with the letter *Heh*, but within the Book of Creation we can closely examine all steps within the process of spiritual evolution. One must first bind the letter *Heh* within God's Great Name (יהוה = *YHVH*) to all 22 aspects of one's mind, soul, and body (3 + 7 + 12, respectively). The meditation process of binding a *Heh* to one's being and the subsequent liberation of the soul is all described in great mathematical detail in Part 3.

For Mohammed, the word *Sakinah* is closely related to the Hebrew word Shechinah. In the Koran we read that when Mohammed meditated in his cave, the "tranquility" or "Sakinah" descended upon him.[96] Within the Book of Genesis the Shechinah is described as the divine "cloud of prophecy" that situated itself over the Ark of the Covenant within the Holy of Holies; it was also the "cloud" that hovered over Moses' tent in the desert.

95 *Tanakh*, Genesis 14:18-19.
96 *The Koran*, Repentance 9:40 (London: Penguin Books, 1999), 137.

It has always been assumed that there was only one divine cloud that alternated between the Ark of the Covenant and Moses' tent. A proper understanding of Abraham's teachings reveals that this cloud is more accurately interpreted as the liberated divine soul of a highly evolved mortal – a tzadek. Long before the resurrection of Jesus, the Torah tells us that neither Enoch nor Elijah died; Enoch "walked with God" and Elijah was lifted to heaven "in a whirlwind." Abraham's teachings suggest the possibility that it was the liberated soul of Enoch that hovered over the ark in the Holy of Holies as the "cloud of prophecy," while the cloud over Moses' tent was the Shechinah of Moses that resulted from his evening meditation.

For any Jew, Christian or Muslim to believe that any man or woman can accomplish what Moses, Jesus and Mohammed accomplished is unthinkable from the current theological perspective of the three faiths. Jews are often blocked from spiritual progress because remaining humble is believed to be mutually exclusive with thinking of oneself as Godly. A Jew wears a skull cap so the Shechinah (Divine Presence) can "rest on his head," but the skull cap usually takes on the function of a psychological wall between man and an unapproachable God – between the sacred and the profane.

The original theology of monotheism found within the Book of Creation teaches us that the higher force we pray to as God actually lives within us as our soul. Abraham's method of prayerful meditation requires us to look within with no need to look elsewhere. This "new" method of prayer allows us to transcend sin and to heal its negative effects on our body. Abraham's legacy can empower us to transcend our negative self-image and our corporeal body to enter the heavenly realm – while the physical body remains earthbound. For Abraham, we are saints when our lives focus on undistracted meditation that "binds us to God" and we are sinners when we are distracted from that practice.

Prophecy was only one of the divine gifts that resulted from liberating the soul. It also afforded a way to heal oneself and others – even to conquer death. Within the Jewish kabbalistic tradition, the Messianic Era will bring about the Resurrection of the Dead for all the souls of Israel. This tradition maintains that once all 613 commandments have been completed there is no longer a need to reincarnate, enabling the tzadek to conquer death. Once again, there are two examples of this phenomenon within the Tanakh: Enoch did not die, he "walked with God," and Elijah did not die, he "went up to heaven in a whirlwind" on "a fiery chariot with fiery horses."

Figure 11 – Raphael's Transfiguration of Christ

Christianity

Gnosticism & the Book of Creation

In 1945 several "Gnostic Gospels" were found in Nag Hammadi, Egypt, written in the Coptic language, dating to approximately the fourth century. There are important scholars who categorize the Book of Creation as just another fourth century Gnostic text. It will be conclusively demonstrated that this cannot be the case, because the Book of Creation predates the oldest pages of the Torah, and provides its theological framework.

Gnostic schools are characterized by the belief in a special knowledge (gnosis) of God. In 325 CE, Christianity's First Ecumenical Council rejected Gnosticism as one of the main Christian heresies. If Abraham's Book of Creation were considered Gnosticism by the Church, it would be rejected out-of-hand. What the Church Fathers rejected as heresy, however, was a mélange of conflicting gnostic ideologies that were believed to derive from either the pantheism or humanism of the ancient Greeks (most notably Pythagoras and Plato); the polytheism of Hinduism or Buddhism; or some other even less desirable gnostic source. We will show that Abraham's gnosticism became the theological framework for Judaism, Christianity, and Islam.

How would Church fathers feel if the Book of Creation was actually authored by Abraham and therefore not only provides the structural framework of the Tanakh, but can also be shown to provide the framework for the Book of Revelation and the "Order of Melchizedek" or the "eternal priesthood" as described in the Epistle to the Hebrews.[97] In other words, Abraham's monotheistic gnosticism is defined in purely biblical terms to solve what St. Paul described as "God's great mysteries,"[98] including the Holy Trinity, the Incarnation, and the Transfiguration. Revelation of

97 Hebrews, 7:8.
98 Romans 16:25-26; Ephesians 2:8-10

the meaning of these riddles corresponds to the "increase of knowledge" prophesied in Daniel 12:4 during the "Last Days."

Although many argue that Plato's writings are the original source of Gnosticism, Philo of Alexandria (20 BCE-50 CE) believed that both Pythagoras and Plato learned their theology from the Torah. In the early centuries of Christianity there were also well-respected Church fathers, such as Origen (ca. 185-254) and Clement of Alexandria (ca. 150-215), who were Platonists. "Clement had no doubt that Yahweh and the God of the Greek philosophers were one and the same..."[99] In a detailed comparison of both Abraham and Plato's string theory I have been able to conclusively demonstrate that both Abraham and Plato use identical mathematical constructions to define God and the soul. From this we will be able to conclude that Philo, Origen, and Clement were correct in many of their assumptions.

The Book of Creation is the original source of all monotheistic gnosticism, while polytheistic gnosticism can trace its roots back to the earliest Vedic text, called the Rig Veda. The Rig Veda is roughly contemporary with the Book of Creation and appears to provide the string theory and metaphysical foundation for both Hinduism and Buddhism.

The First Ecumenical Council

In the early years of the Christian Church a great debate raged. This debate would be played out at the First Ecumenical Council at Nicea on May 20, 325 CE, where the bishops gathered together under the watchful eye of the Emperor Constantine. The two opposing sides were represented by the Gnostic and Arian positions. The Word of God figured prominently in this debate.

Christian Gnostics maintained that Jesus was god by nature. Saint Paul's theology initiated this position, but it was "set in stone" in the Gospel of John the Apostle, which is considered the most gnostic of the four Christian gospels. The Gospel of John begins: "*In the beginning was the Word, and the Word was with God: and the Word was God...*" The gospel continues by describing Jesus as the "Word Incarnate": "*And the Word was made flesh, and dwelt among us. And we saw his glory – glory*

---

99 Armstrong, *A History of God*, 98.

as the only-begotten of the Father." For Saint Paul and Saint John, the Word of God, *Yahweh*, became the Word of God, Christ.

Christian Gnostics, like Clement and Origen, believed that the God of the Greeks was also the God of the Hebrews, but they still believed in Christ.[100] "Clement believed that Jesus was God... If Christians imitated Christ, they too would become deified..."[101] Christian Gnosticism, as practiced in the first few centuries of the Church, had evolved from the gnosticism of the Hebrews. Following in the theological tradition of Saint Paul and Saint John, it was no longer *Yahweh*, but rather Christ, who was the Word incarnate according to Christian Gnostics.

The word "logos" is simply Greek for "word." In the Gospel of John, Jesus was said to preexist Creation itself: *"Father, glorify me with thyself, with the glory that I had with thee before the world existed."*[102] Armstrong describes its significance within the Gospel of John as follows:

> The Logos had been the instrument used by God to call other creatures into existence…St. John made it clear that Jesus was the Logos; he also said that the Logos was God…He was different from the rest of us, because God created him directly but all other things through him.[103]

At the First Ecumenical Council, Bishop Athanasius (ca. 293-373) believed that Christ, as the Word of God incarnate, belonged to the divine realm. Armstrong believes there would be serious consequences for mankind: "If Jesus had not been a human being, there would be no hope for us... nothing for us to imitate."[104] According to Armstrong, Arius' concept of salvation required an exemplary life of good works. This was close to the thinking of Plato and other Greek philosophers: "The Stoics, for example, had always taught that it was possible for a virtuous human being to become divine"[105]

Most held a position somewhere between the opposing views of Athanasius and Arius, but the perceived divinity or mortality of Jesus

---

100 Armstrong, *A History of God*, 108.
101 Armstrong, *A History of God*, 98.
102 *New Testament* (New York: Catholic Book Publishing Co., 1952), St. John 17:5.
103 Armstrong, *A History of God*, 109.
104 Armstrong, *A History of God*, 110.
105 Armstrong, *A History of God*, 109.

lay in the balance. Athanasius imposed his theology on a majority of the delegates: "Only he who had created the world could save it, and that meant that Christ, the Logos made flesh, must be of the same nature as the Father."[106] Armstrong states:

> "...the term *homoousion* (literally, 'made of the same stuff') was highly controversial because it was unscriptural and had materialistic association... Athanasius' creed begged many important questions. It stated that Jesus was divine but did not explain how the Logos could be 'of the same stuff' as the Father without being a second God."[107]

Arius' theology of man becoming divine through virtuous works was too easy — God was too accessible. Athanasius used a Greek explanation against Arius: God's essence (*ousia*) was considered unknowable, however, we can know God through three expressions (*hypostases*): the Father, Son, and Holy Spirit.[108] Saint Jerome, and many others, thought that ousia and hypostases were roughly equivalent, concluding that the Greeks, therefore, believed in three divine essences.[109]

In the Greek tradition, salvation and divinity could only be achieved through what Plato called *theoria* (contemplation).[110] Christian Platonists such as Clement and Origen followed this tradition.[111] According to Armstrong, Augustine was also a Platonist who defined the Trinity for the Latin Church based on this more contemplative Greek notion of hypostases. For the Greeks, retaining the mystery of God was important, and that mystery could be preserved in the complexity of the hypostases.[112] "God, therefore, was not an objective reality but a spiritual presence in the complex depths of the self."[113] The Trinity was meant to resonate within the complexities of the self. It was not meant to become oversimplified as three equivalent divine beings.

106 Armstrong, *A History of God*, 110.
107 Armstrong, *A History of God*, 111-112.
108 Armstrong, *A History of God*, 116; Abraham, of course, teaches us that the essence of God is knowable as the harmonic series.
109 Armstrong, *A History of God*, 116.
110 Armstrong, *A History of God*, 114.
111 Armstrong, *A History of God*, 113.
112 Armstrong, *A History of God*, 121.
113 Armstrong, *A History of God*, 121.

There is a long tradition of oversimplification of the Trinity in the West. Making God too understandable was not the intention of Augustine, or of its ancient Greek origins. The Greeks started with the hypostases, but could not fathom God's unity.[114] The Western Church started with God's unity, but had trouble understanding how there could be three divine persons in one God.[115]

This difference of approach in understanding God was the underlying reason for the split between the Eastern and Western Church. What precipitated the split, however, was a new controversial clause that was added to the Nicene Creed in 796 called the *filioque* (and the Son). The East felt that the clause made the Trinity too simple and rational.[116] The Greeks, and the Eastern Church, preferred to contemplate the nature of their God, and the filioque implied that there was no need for such contemplation. French philosopher, Peter Abelard (1079-1147), later tried to steer Christians away from any confusion by stressing unity at the expense of the Three Persons.[117]

Saint Augustine had seen the Holy Spirit as the principle of unity in the Trinity, maintaining that he was the love between Father and Son.[118] The following passage follows Saint Augustine's interpretation of the Holy Spirit as the love that binds the Father and the Son together. It is taken from a nineteenth-century *General History, Cyclopedia and Dictionary of Freemasonry* by Robert Macoy, explaining the relationship of the doctrine of the Holy Trinity to the actual Logos, i.e., the Holy Trinity of letters in the Word of God, *Yahweh*:

> יהוה. This word contains the mystery of the Trinity, as the ancient Jews who lived before Christ testify in their traditions. For by י they understand the origin of all things. By ה they mean the Son, by whom all things were made. By ו which is a conjunction copulative, they understand the Holy Ghost, who is the love which binds them together, and proceeds from them. And further that ה refers to the two natures of Christ, the divine and human.[119]

114 Armstrong, *A History of God*, 200.
115 Armstrong, *A History of God*, 201.
116 Armstrong, *A History of God*, 200.
117 Armstrong, *A History of God*, 203.
118 Armstrong, *A History of God*, 200.
119 Macoy, 554

Platonists Clement of Alexandria and Origen were trying to build the Church's foundation on stronger ties to the past. Armstrong tells us that, "He [Origen] did not believe that we were "saved" by the death of Christ, but that we ascended to God under our own steam."[120] By the time of the First Ecumenical Council, some time had past since Origen and Clement taught their Christian Platonism. The early Church was still evolving and had not established an official policy or doctrine. That policy only developed as a result of two centuries of struggle regarding the Word of God, finally culminating at Nicea with the Gnostic and Arian heresies.

Only Arius and two supporters would not sign the Nicene Creed, but the battle was not completely resolved. Arius continued it for another sixty years.[121] Eventually his position became heresy. The Church's orthodox position established Jesus as both "true God and true man," but Abraham defined every man that way. Abraham would have no problem with Athansius' statement that "the Word became man in order that we could become divine."[122] What is the dual nature of Jesus within Christianity is the dual nature of all men within the Book of Creation.

Through the Eyes of Abraham

From Abraham's perspective, "the Word" (Logos) did not preexist Creation. The four Hebrew letters that comprise the Word of God, YHVH, gradually came into existence letter by letter, day by day. In the Creation allegory, on the first day, God says, "Let there be Light," and divine light was created as Ten Utterances contained by the letter *Yud* (׳ = 10), the first letter of the Word, *Yahweh*. Just as the white light of God contains the diversity of the rainbow, the letter *Yud* (׳ = 10) contained the diversity of divine vibrational energy that was, as the Freemasons believe, the origin of all things. Those Ten Utterances echoed across the universe creating Abraham's divine light matrix in two mathematical tables. "And there was evening and there was morning, a first day."

Only the first letter of the Word, *Yud* (׳ = 10), existed on the first day of Creation. Beginning with Day 2 and lasting through Day 7, the divine light was reordered to create the multitude of objects and beings, including man's soul in the image of God on Day 4. This reordering process is known

120 Armstrong, *A History of God*, 100-101.
121 Armstrong, *A History of God*, 110-111.
122 Armstrong, *A History of God*, 110.

within the Jewish tradition as *Tikun* (literally: reordering). On the Fifth Day, the letter *Heh* (ה = 5) was reordered into the vibrational essence of all "creatures that moveth" – but the Logos still did not fully exist! On the Sixth Day, the letter *Heh* (ה = 5) harmonized with the letter *Vav* (ו = 6), creating Adam's body as a vessel to contain the divine light of the letter *Yud* – and with that, the "Holy Trinity" of letters, *YHV* (יהו), within the Lost Word, *YHVH* (יהוה), gradually came into existence, unfolding over the first six days of Creation, as its vibratory essence and sustenance.

Jews and Muslims humble themselves in prayer directly before God as part of their soul's "inner struggle" to achieve righteousness, but Christians can reach the Father only through the Son, and so it might therefore appear that Christians have no direct relationship with God. However, many Christians believe that the Holy Trinity equates the Son with the Father. Having a direct relationship with the Son would therefore imply having a direct relationship with the Father. As already discussed, many of today's Christians oversimplify the Trinity and equate each of the three "divine persons" with the Godhead.

Differentiating the Father from the Son would require clarification of the Nicene's Creed's expression "Light from Light, True God from True God." In addition, it would help clarify the controversy regarding Psalm 110:

> [1]Of David. A psalm.
> [2]The LORD says to my Lord: "Sit at my right hand until I make your enemies a footstool for your feet."
> [3]The LORD will extend your mighty scepter from Zion; you will rule in the midst of your enemies.
> [4]Your troops will be willing on your day of battle. Arrayed in holy majesty, from the womb of the dawn you will receive the dew of your youth. The LORD has sworn and will not change his mind: "You are a priest forever, in the order of Melchizedek."
> [5]The Lord is at your right hand; he will crush kings on the day of his wrath.
> [6]He will judge the nations, heaping up the dead and crushing the rulers of the whole earth.
> [7]He will drink from a brook beside the way; therefore he will lift up his head.

In the line "The LORD says to my Lord" the Hebrew Scriptures differentiate between the word "LORD" and the word "Lord" since the first "LORD" is translated from the Hebrew *YHVH* (*Yahweh*), while the second "Lord" translates from *Adonai* as "my master." The common Christian interpretation of Psalm 110 reads "The Lord said to my Lord," creating an ambiguity that is consistent with Christian ambiguity about the roles of the Father and the Son. The Church maintains that distinguishing "Light from Light and True God from True God" is part of a "sacred mystery" that can never be explained, except perhaps at the end of days.

In that case, perhaps this is the end of days, since a proper reading of the Book of Creation will demonstrate how Abraham's mathematical detail differentiates "light from light, and True God from True God." Abraham would describe "the Son" as the spiritual principle of a liberated soul that is "in the image of the Father," while the Transfiguration of Jesus into "the Son" would have been a specific manifestation of that principle. Christians believe that only Jesus was capable of a "transfiguration" from his mortal, corporeal body into his "heavenly body," enabling him to function as the intermediary between mortals and God for all eternity. But for Abraham, every man is capable of liberating his soul, i.e., "transfiguring" into his "heavenly body." The acquisition of that ability would be the defining characteristic of "the Son."

When the Son's liberated soul hovers above, it becomes the "wellspring of prophecy" wherein a man "sees his own image standing before him, speaking to him and telling him of the future."[123] The Book of Creation therefore implies that liberated souls hovered over the heads of all the great and righteous prophets of the Hebrew Scriptures, in the form of a "cloud of divinity," exactly like the one that hovered over Moses' tent in the desert, and over the Ark of the Covenant in Solomon's Temple.

In days two through six of Creation, the divine light of the Ten Utterances "descended" into matter, creating multiple layers of concealment, one of them being man's corporeal body. This differentiates the Father from the Son because the Son, i.e. the liberated soul, contains a tiny subset of God's vast rainbow of light. One could correctly say that there is no substantial difference between them in the literal sense of the term *homoousion* (of the same substance as). However, the Father defines divine light itself, whereas any realized "Son of God" would also be a "Son of Man," containing a tiny but complete subset, miniaturization,

123 Kaplan, *Meditation and Kabbalah*, 109; Scholem, *Kabbalah*, 181.

or "image of" the Father. Although the liberated soul that defines "the Son" corresponds to the highest level of evolution for a man, it is the manifestation of just one soul's harmonic series. It does not represent the defining global law of the harmonic series itself that corresponds to the omnipresence of the Father.

The "layering" or progressive "containments" of divine light also account for the difference between the Son (the liberated soul) and the Holy Ghost (the soul exiled within the corporeal body). As we can see, Abraham's mathematics implies separate roles for each member of the Holy Trinity as distinct from the other two, and each fulfills its own unique and critical function.

Abraham believed that all men were capable of becoming "Sons of God." The Gospel of Luke states that there will be many Sons of God in the "world to come": *"For neither shall they be able to die anymore, for they are equal to the angels, and are sons of God, being sons of the resurrection."* From Abraham's perspective, the "world to come" will be at hand only when all men practice his method of prayer as defined by "seven circuits around the sacred cube."

Christians are baptized in water, as Jesus was by John the Baptist. In Part 4 we will see that it is Abraham's ancient practice that creates the "true baptism of the spirit" spoken about in the New Testament.[124] From Abraham's perspective, Jesus could become *Christos* (Greek: "Anointed One") only because he learned to "transfigure" or liberate his soul using "seven circuits around the sacred cube."

Faith versus Works

Abraham lived seven generations before the Torah was revealed to Moses, yet the rabbis tell us he naturally followed the Torah's commandments.[125] How is this possible and how is it possible that Abraham's writings explain the Torah's inner meaning, considering that the Torah had not yet been revealed to mankind?

This is the same question asked by Saint Paul in his Epistle to the Romans. If God could deem Abraham righteous before the Law of Moses

---

124 St. Mark 1:8.
125 Zalman, 563-564. The *pnimiyut* of Torah is the esoteric, deeper and sublime root of the Torah observed by Abraham, i.e. its vibrational essence.

ever existed, why couldn't gentiles, who were never given the Law of Moses, follow Abraham's example.

> *When the Gentiles, who have no Law by nature, do what the Law prescribes, these having no Law are a law unto themselves. They show the work of the Law written in their hearts.* [126]

Since Moses and Mosaic Law did not yet exist, Abraham's "grace" before God appeared to be "the work of the Law written in his heart." Paul therefore declared that Abraham was to be the model of Christian faith. [127] Paul wanted to evangelize beyond the Jewish community to gentiles as well. To accomplish this he wrote of Christians as *"set free from the Law... so that we may serve in a new spirit and not the outworn letter* [of the Law]." [128] Paul writes further that *"man is justified by faith independent of the works of the Law."* [129]

Not all the Church Fathers agreed with Paul on the faith versus works issue. The New Testament's Epistle of Saint James states exactly the opposite: "For just as the body without the spirit is dead, so faith also without works is dead." But neither Saint Paul's Jewish mentors nor Paul himself could possibly have known Abraham's lost secret, which would have revealed that Abraham's merit before God was not simply reckoned by "his trust in the Lord." Abraham's faith was not "blind faith"; it was based on the mathematics of *Yahweh,* the ancient and secret practice described by the Epistle to the Hebrews as the "order of Melchizedek." [130] In the New Testament's Epistle to the Hebrews 7:11-12, it was the "order of Melchizedek" (the High Priests), and not the "order of Aaron" (the Levite priests who were keepers of the Law), that accounted for Melchizedek being *"likened to the Son of God* as a high priest forever." [131]

The discovery of the Dead Sea Scrolls in the 1940's taught us more about a small group of very conservative, secretive, Jewish ascetics who appear to have broken off from the Jewish Essene sect and settled in

---

126 Romans 2:14-15
127 Romans 4.
128 Romans 7:6
129 Romans 3:28-29.
130 Hebrews, 6:20.
131 Hebrews 7:3.

Qumran near the Dead Sea.[132] Within the Essene hierarchy, the "Sons of Aaron" were priests who ranked beneath the *Christos*, or High Priest. The word Christ derives from the Greek word *Christos*, which means "anointed one." *Christos* derives from the Hebrew word *Meshiah*, which also means "anointed one." This is the derivation of the English word, Messiah.

There is speculation that this breakaway group of ascetics may have included both John the Baptist and Jesus. It is possible that this group may have been able to reconstruct, or partially reconstruct, the meaning of the Lost Word, or at least reconstruct Abraham's lost practice. If Jesus was able to master this secret practice, it is certainly plausible that the other two major Jewish sects of that time, the Pharisees and the Sadducees, had no knowledge of it, and therefore could not fathom the nature of Jesus' "works."

Just as Seth, Enoch, Noah, Shem, Melchizedek, Abraham, Isaac, Jacob, the "anointed ones" of each generation, the great prophets, and the high priests of Solomon's Temple, all received initiation into this secret practice; and just as Enoch and Elijah "conquered death" within the Hebrew Scriptures, the Epistle to the Hebrews leads us to believe that Jesus was also initiated into this *"superior covenant"*[133] and *"reached behind the veil... having become a high priest forever according to the order of Melchizedek."*[134] The high priest who could conquer death could therefore always mediate between man and God.[135] After reviewing the mathematical details of *Yahweh* in Part 3, we should realize that God's Covenants with Noah, Abraham, and Jesus must necessarily consist of the same core practice of seven circuits around the sacred cube. The secret "order of Melchizedek" that was taught to Abraham, and explained in all its mathematical detail within the Book of Creation, is the only practice capable of going *"behind the veil"* within the context of monotheism.

Abraham naturally aligns with the Torah's commandments, not because of blind faith, but because the mathematics of *Yahweh* describes the vibrational essence of the Torah's commandments themselves. "Abraham merited this [God's Grace] by reason of his works and his advancing in holiness from degree to degree, as it is written: 'And Abram

---

132 The Jewish sects mentioned in the New Testament only include the Pharisees and the Sadducees.
133 Hebrews, 7:22-23.
134 Hebrews, 6:20.
135 Hebrews 7:22-25

journeyed, going on and on.'"[136] This degree-by-degree ascent to God is made possible by the "pronunciation" of the Word *Yahweh,* as a two-step meditation process of the eternal priesthood that will ultimately be shared and learned by all Abraham's descendants. The first step incorporates the essence of the Torah's 365 negative commandments to purify the body, while his second step incorporates the essence of the 248 positive commandments of the Torah to liberate the soul.

Only this ancient practice can fulfill the biblical prophecy marking the "End of Days" and the building of the "third temple" within our own bodies, enabling all of mankind to become "anointed ones." The transcendental meaning and pronunciation of the Lost Word will be explained, in all its mathematical and theological detail, in Part 3.

Yahweh and Christ

In the New Testament there is much discussion about "the Name." The English translation of God's Great Name, YHWH, is "Lord." The elders and high priest of the Sanhedrin spoke to the arrested apostles of Christ, saying, "We strictly charged you not to teach in this name [of Christ]."[137] After Peter and John's arrest for teaching in the name of Christ, Peter stated: "there is no other name under heaven given to men by which we must be saved."[138] In his Epistle to the Ephesians, Paul states that Christ's name was set "above every name that is named, not only in this world, but also in that which is to come."

The New Testament tells us that Paul was taught Mosaic Law by one of the great elders of Sanhedrin, Gamaliel.[139] This implies that Paul was well aware of the significance of the "unspeakable Name." If this were true, by teaching in the name of Christ, one has to wonder how Paul felt justified to violate this strictest of all Jewish taboos when he replaced the Word of God, *Yahweh,* with the Word of God, Christ. No longer did he teach in the Name of *Yahweh,* but rather in the name of Christ.

If Paul did study with Gamaliel then he was aware of God's great mysteries embeded within the Word, *Yahweh.* This is verified in Romans

---

136 Zalman, 247.
137 Acts 5:28.
138 Acts 4:7-12.
139 Acts 22:3. Sanhedrin was the tribunal of Hebrew elders. One of the most distinguished members of this tribunal, Gamaliel, was said to be Paul's teacher.

16:25-26, where Paul describes the preaching of Jesus Christ "according to the revelation of the mystery which has been kept in silence from eternal ages," while in Ephesians 2:8-10 Paul claims that he is able to "enlighten all men as to what is the dispensation of the mystery which has been hidden from eternity in God." To those who have come to understand that the great mysteries of God are mathematically encrypted only in the Word of God, *Yahweh*, and not in the Word of God, Christ, Paul's claim does not ring true.

As Paul shaped Christian theology, the resurrection is its defining moment. He believed that even Adam's sin could be atoned for by the crucifixion of God's "sacrificial lamb": "He [Jesus] died to sin once for [the benefit of] all."[140] The sacrificial lamb is an important biblical concept representative of man's plea to God for atonement of his sins. Within the Torah, God stopped Abraham at the moment he was to sacrifice Isaac, and a lamb was sacrificed in his place; within Mosaic Law animal sacrifices on the "four-horned altar" were intended to replace the need for human sacrifice. Ishmael fulfills Isaac's role within Islam, and Jesus fulfills it within Christianity. The Torah's four-horned altar had its theological origins within Abraham's acoustical process of purification that "burned away" tonal impurities within the vibrational essence of the body.

Paul, however, was more interested in the future than the past. He did not want Christians exposed to the "outworn letter" of Mosaic Law. The most profound way to distance Christianity from Mosaic Law was to replace the heart of monotheistic theology, the unspeakable Name, *Yahweh,* with the name of Christ. The transcendental meaning of *Yahweh* was long lost, and one could ascribe its transcendental meaning to Christ with no fear of being substantially contradicted. In Paul's new approach, the great divine mysteries associated with *Yahweh* would now be considered part of the "Mystical Body" of Christ. Neither Paul nor his mentor Gamaliel, the great Sanhedrin elder, understood the mysteries of the Lost Word; therefore, Paul's nontraditional approach could not be proven wrong from a theological perspective — at least not at that point in time. Paul successfully convinced the early Church Fathers that simple faith in the name of Christ would hold the same meaning for Gentiles that the name *Yahweh* held for Jews. But, Paul's radical approach violated Judaism's most sacred taboo. It profaned the name of *Yahweh*. It would

---

140 Romans 6:10

require a complete break with Judaism — a position strongly opposed by Saint Peter. Paul persisted, ultimately convincing Church Fathers (who were all fellow Jews) that gentiles did not need to be Jews first, in order to believe in Christ. As a result, he created the foundation for a new religion: Christianity. Paul's position implied that Jesus was more than just an "eternal priest" in the secret tradition of Abraham, it implied that Jesus was God. From Abraham's perspective, however, becoming "One with God" was not equivalent to becoming God.

The transcendental meaning and pronunciation of the Word, *Yahweh,* defined a secret practice capable of returning the souls of all Israel to God from its exile within the body. Once it was lost, all of Israel would have to remain in exile within the dense human body. Rediscovering this great secret implies that the exiled souls of Israel finally have a way to return to Eden and God. The divine gifts of wisdom, prophecy, magic, healing, and even resurrection, are among the divine gifts of someone who can liberate their soul.

Christians believe that Jesus was unique in his divinity and unique in his Messianic gifts. However, if Jesus' gifts could not be acquired by mere mortals then why would Jesus try to tutor Peter on how to walk on water? During this passage, Jesus was in his "heavenly" (transfigured) body tutoring Peter. Peter must have been partially successful in his transfiguration effort, because he attempted a few steps on the water. Peter was then distracted and "fell in" due to either a momentary lapse in faith, or, as Abraham might say, from a lapse in his meditative concentration.

Before Christ became "the Word" within the writings of the New Testament, there is precedent within both the Jewish kabbalistic tradition and ancient Hebrew writings for man to "become" the Logos. That man was Enoch. Biblical scholars generally agree that when the Old Testament was canonized[141] the most important writings among the Apocrypha and Pseudopigraphia were the Books of Enoch. According to III Enoch, the Hebrew Book of Enoch, Chapter IV, God took Enoch to become Metatron, His highest-ranking angel.[142] Metatron is referred to in the Hebrew

141 J.R. Porter, *The Lost Bible* (Chicago: University of Chicago Press, 2001), 6-9. The Old and New Testaments were selected compilations from a large body of ancient scriptures.
142 Hugo Odeberg, ed., *Hebrew Book of Enoch* (New York, KTAV, 1973) Chapter IV; Halevi, 30; Harry Sperling and Maurice Simons, trans., *Zohar* (London: Soncino Press, 1984), 37b, 139 fn. 1. 223b.

Scriptures (Proverbs 22.6 and Job 32.6). The Torah tells us that Enoch didn't die, that "he walked with God." Within the Jewish kabbalistic tradition the Holy Tetragrammaton, *YHVH*, is embodied by Metatron – and Enoch "became" Metatron, ergo Enoch "became" the Logos within the Tanakh. Both Elijah and Jesus, like Enoch, similarly "conquered death," and so we ask ourselves, how is it that three men could have been united with the Logos, yet still not have actually become the theological God.

The scholar Gershom Scholem provides us with some insight into this question by referencing "certain stages" within the Jewish meditation tradition called "prophetic Kabbalah" begun by Abraham Abulafia (1240-1292):

> In certain stages [of meditation] he lives through a personal identification with an inner spiritual mentor or guru who is revealed to him and who is really Metatron, the prince of God's countenance, or in some cases, the subjects own true self."[143]

It is clear that Abulafia had some understanding of Abraham's methods of "becoming one with" or "binding to" the holy letters of the Logos that defines being. All men should aspire to this eternal priesthood because all men are meant to follow Abraham's methods to purify the body and resonate with the image of God that lives within. However, this is not the same as saying man is capable of uniting with the vibratory essence of a rock, or a tree, or of "becoming" the harmonic series itself. It is important to reexamine the meaning of Logos within the Gospel of John from Abraham's scientific perspective.

As the Logos itself, John's Jesus became the theological "God of Abraham." John follows through on this line of reasoning when Jesus declares: *"...before Abraham came to be, I am."*[144] In his book *Jesus and Yahweh,* Harold Bloom regards Saint John's use of this last phrase as a Christian revisionist interpretation of the Exodus 3 passage "And God said to Moses, '*Ehyeh Asher Ehyeh*'(I AM WHO I AM)."[145] Bloom speaks about a play on words between *Yahweh* and *Ehyeh,* and he cites a Christian obsession with Exodus 3, culminating in "Augustine's endless preoccupation with that passage, since for Augustine it was the deepest

143 Scholem, *Kabbalah*, 180-181.
144 St. John 8:58-59
145 Exodus 3:14

clue to the metaphysical essence of God."[146] Augustine's effort to explain *Ehyeh* may have been an effort to tie the Gospel of John to the metaphysical essence of God embedded in *Yahweh*. However, we will show beyond any doubt that the "Lost Practice" and the "Blueprint of Creation" are both encrypted in the word *Yahweh* – not in the word Christ, not in the word *Ehyeh,* and not in the word *Yeshua* (Jesus).

The replacement of *Yahweh* with Christ as the "Word of God" is the most significant example of Christian revisionism. It was the most taboo of all possible acts, necessitating a break with Judaism. Another significant example can be found in the terms "Old Testament" and "Old Covenant," which are Christian designations for the Hebrew Scriptures and God's Covenant with Abraham, respectively. They imply fulfillment of the "Old" by the "New"; Christianity's New Testament would replace the Old Testament, while the New Covenant would replace the Old Covenant. The "Old Testament" also reorders the books of the Hebrew Scriptures in a way that creates what Bloom calls "a prism through which the precursor text is to be read, revised, and interpreted."[147] The reordering of the books of the Hebrew Bible does provide a smoother transition between the Old and New Testaments, but not without impact to the original Hebrew text. For example, within Hebrew Scriptures, Daniel was not even included in the Book of Prophets. However, within the New Testament he became a major prophet. In addition, ending the "Old Testament" with Malachi sets the stage for the emergence of Christianity, rather than the Tanakh's actual conclusion in II Chronicles, which calls for a return to Jerusalem to rebuild the Temple.[148]

The Impact of Revisionism

Each attempt at revision runs the risk of widening the gap that exists with the original theology of Abraham. Revisionism was also the root cause of the split between Catholics and Protestants. The crux of the Catholic-Protestant conflict revolves around the relationship between Scripture and religious tradition, as represented by papal decrees and council proclamation. *Sola scriptura* – the statement that the Scripture is the sole

---

146 Harold Bloom, *Jesus and Yahweh: The Names Divine* (New York: Riverhead Books, 2005), 73-75.
147 Bloom, 6, 44-45.
148 Bloom, 49-51.

infallible authority – was the rallying cry of the Protestant reformation, denying that authority to the Church and tradition and councils.

Typifying this debate are two separate doctrines that are not explicit in Scripture and are often confused in the minds of the faithful: the Immaculate Conception and the Virgin Birth. The Immaculate Conception is a Roman Catholic doctrine asserting that Mary, the mother of Jesus, was free of Original Sin from the first moment of her conception. This doctrine was debated by theologians during the Middle Ages and was ultimately rejected by Saint Thomas Aquinas. However, in 1854 Pope Pius IX issued a solemn decree defining the Immaculate Conception for all Roman Catholics, but the doctrine has not been accepted by Protestants or by the Orthodox churches.

Pope Pius IX was also the pope who issued the decree defining indulgences and papal infallibility. "Catholicism puts tradition on an equal footing with both the Old and New Testaments."[149] Many within the Protestant reformation felt that the Roman Catholic Church had made its traditions superior in authority to the Bible, resulting in practices still questioned by the Protestant and Orthodox churches. These practices include prayer to saints and/or Mary, the Immaculate Conception, indulgences, and papal authority. Martin Luther, the founder of the Lutheran Church and father of the Protestant Reformation, challenged the Catholic Church for its unbiblical teachings and was eventually excommunicated.

A further example of the revisionist approach to theology can be found in the long-standing debate between Christians and Jews regarding the Virgin Birth. The Greek word *parthenos* can mean either a young woman or a virgin, while the Hebrew word *alma* signifies a young woman, unmarried as well as married, and thus distinct from *bethulah*, "a virgin." The *Septuagint,* the Greek translation of the Hebrew Scriptures, used the word *parthenos* to translate the Hebrew word *alma* in Isaiah 7:14.

The New Testament's use of the Septuagint as its source for Hebrew Scriptures has therefore been the subject of hotly contested debate. Matthew 1:23 quotes Isaiah 7:14 as, "Behold, a virgin will be with child and bear a son, and she will call His name Immanuel." The Hebrew version of Isaiah 7:14 reads, "Behold, the young woman is with child, and shall bear a son, and she shall call his name Immanuel." In this case, altering the translation

149 Gary DeMar, "Denying Sola Scriptura: The Attempt to Neutralize the Bible," *Biblical Worldview*, December 1993.

of a single Hebrew word is consistent with the theology of Church Fathers who want to characterize Jesus as divine by nature.

The Nicene Creed marked an important crossroad for Christianity in which the beliefs of Clement of Alexandria and Origen were rejected in favor of those of Saint Paul and Saint John. Once Abraham's legacy was lost, the "theological compass" he provided was also lost, and there was no way to distinguish between revisionism and revelation. Clearly one should not revise an eternal truth. The logic of the Protestant argument is the belief that eternal truth can be found only within Scripture, and if Scripture was no longer used as the sole arbitor of Church policy, then Church edicts and papal rulings might all be untruths. On the other hand, Catholic revelations are believed to bring new insights to a "living" Scripture, while Protestant literalism often flies in the face of modern science. Without Abraham's theological compass one can only speculate about the direction of true north.

The Church's belief in only one "Son of God" is in direct contrast to Abraham's belief that man's liberated soul is the "Son of God." Once we can accept that the Book of Creation is the authentic basis of monotheistic theology, then the Nicene Creed can be reexamined from that perspective. Christian belief in only one Son of God would deny the "eternal priesthood" to Enoch and Elijah, who, like Jesus, had also "conquered" death.

The great legacy of Abraham's self-realization teaching embedded within the word *Yahweh* transformed Jesus into an "anointed one," and although monotheism's last great prophet was Mohammed, rediscovering Abraham's writings once again makes it possible for all men to become annointed ones, and follow in the footsteps of the great prophets. The eternal truths of Abraham's mathematics and teaching makes *Yahweh* unique and irreplaceable as the Word of God. Abraham's "compass" also teaches Protestants that eternal truth lies well beneath the surface of Scripture's literal interpretation.

The beliefs of Saint Paul and Saint John still resonate with Christians today because the Book of Creation has never been properly understood, and could therefore never provide the perspective to correct Paul's theology regarding the Word of God. To give Saint Paul his due, however, we must look deeper than the letter of the law to realize the deepest meaning of freedom from exile. Paul felt very strongly that there was something greater than the letter of the law, i.e., Mosaic Law. He saw that something manifest in Jesus Christ. What Paul couldn't see was that the great mystical secret that accounted for the ascension of Christ was the purity of his kavanah — his meditative intent — as he fulfilled the commandments. The mystical secret to establish that kavanah is encrypted in the Word of God, *Yahweh*. One can only become an "anointed one" by learning Abraham's deep meditation practice. Without access to this lost knowledge, Paul assumed that Abraham's faith must have accounted for his grace before God, since the Torah did not yet exist.

For peace and understanding to gain a foothold between monotheistic religions and sects, it is imperative that religious scholars and clergy within the three faiths understand that the Book of Creation is the authentic source of monotheistic theology. All Abraham's descendants must realize that Abraham's core teaching – the seven circuits around the sacred cube – is central to all three faiths, and derives from the only Word of God that mathematically embeds Abraham's cosmology, cosmogony, and secret practice.

The theology of the Synoptic Gospels appears consistent with the spiritual principles in the Book of Creation. As a learned rabbi Jesus would have known about an ancient text as important as the Book of Creation. We will show that the book existed at the time of Jesus, and that Jesus must have engaged in Abraham's practice. As a result of that practice, Jesus would have been able to heal illness that resulted from the body's "sinful" abuse. This ability to heal enabled him to effectively forgive himself any sins that manifested within his own body, as well as the ability to heal others and effectively "forgive" their sins.

Abraham's writings explain how each of us can purify our bodies and balance our divine energies in order for the Holy Ghost (the soul) to liberate into the "Son" (the Divine Presence or Shechinah). Abraham's explanation of *Yahweh* does not require blind faith. It stands on its own as the foundation of monotheistic theology and the first scientific "theory of everything." Abraham's lost practice provides mankind with a practical, hands-on, experiential solution that is the very definition of the "works" which mankind must accomplish to liberate the soul, and be "reborn" as pure spirit.

Figure 12 – Mohammed's Night Journey

Islam

The Lesser Jihad

In the post-9/11 world there is much anxiety about whether or not the West's Judeo-Christian traditions are somehow preventing us from understanding and relating to the mind of Islam. The fear exists that there is no basis for substantial dialogue between these vastly different cultures; that whatever the West stands for is repudiated before any discussion can even begin. The violence that confronts the West has a name — *jihad*. It is a religious term that is, paradoxically, also a military term. If for no other reason than to understand the root cause of this military threat, those of the Judeo-Christian tradition are compelled to get a better understanding of Mohammed and Islam.

> Constantly the Quran points out that Mohammed had not come to cancel the older religions, to contradict their prophets or to start a new faith. His message is the same as that of Abraham, Moses, Davis, Solomon, or Jesus.[150]

If this were true then how do we explain the evolution of Muslim contempt for the West as characterized by jihad?

Jihad is one of the most significant and misunderstood terms in Islamic culture. Linguistically it simply means "struggle," but the term is often used as fuel to ignite Muslim hatred toward their "oppressors." Jihad is widely understood in the Arab world as any sincere striving or sacrifice in the way of Allah but has become a characteristic mode of relating to the non-Muslim world, emphasizing a military posture. The historical use and hidden meanings of this important word must be further explored in order to gain insight into the Muslim mind and tradition.

The *Hadith* is a collection of the sayings and actions of Mohammed. After the Koran, the Hadith is considered the most important source of

150 Armstrong, Islam, *A Short History*, 8.

Islamic law. The authenticity of certain collections of Hadith is more respected within the Islamic community then others. In a popular reference in a Hadith, Mohammed addresses Muslims returning from battle:

> We have come home from the lesser sacred struggle [*al-jihad al-asghar*].
> We are returning to the greater sacred struggle [*al-jihad al-akbar*]

Within this context the *greater jihad* refers to the sacred struggle with the lower self (*jihad an-nafs*). We will later demonstrate exactly how this derives from Abraham's religious practice of seven circuits around the sacred cube.

Muslim use of this term today frequently associates the *lesser jihad* (*al-jihad al-asghar*) with the battlefield, and often characterizes its warlike posture as somehow comparable, from a religious perspective, to the peaceful inner struggle of the greater jihad. Many within the Islamic community don't differentiate between these two types of "struggle" since they are both considered to be within the path of Allah. Abraham, however, clearly differentiates between these two types of jihad.

Muslims understand the lesser jihad to be a posture against perceived external injustice, oppression and evil, justified as the right to self-defense.[151] Since the lesser jihad is often the face that Muslim's present to the non-Muslim world, it will be helpful to explore the historical context of Mohammed's life, and then view the early years of Islam against the backdrop of Abraham's religious practices.

In the years immediately preceding the rise of Islam, Bedouin tribalism dictated that "the social unit is the group rather than the individual." A sheikh or sayyid was then elected by the tribal elders.[152] Bernard Lewis describes the evolution of the Arabic political organization from its nomadic tribal roots to a more urban form that serves as a context for Mohammed's early years in Mecca;

> The function of the Sheik's "government" was arbitration rather than command. He possessed no coercive powers and the very concepts of authority, kingship, public penalties,

---

151 John Renard, 54,61.
152 Bernard Lewis, *The Arabs in History* (New York: Oxford University Press, 2002), 24.

etc., were abhorrent to the Arab nomad society…[153] He was advised by a council of elders called the Majlis, consisting of the heads of the families and representatives of clans within the tribe…[154] Here and there settled nomads established towns with a rather more advanced stage of society. The most important of these was Mecca…where a council known as the Mala', drawn from the Majlises of the clans, replaced the simple tribal Majlis. [155]

Lewis also describes how both political and religious cohesion in Mecca centered on the Ka'bah;

> The religion of the tribes had no real priesthood; the migratory nomads carried their gods with them in a red tent forming a kind of ark of the covenant, which accompanied them to battle. Their religion was not personal but communal. The tribal faith centered around the tribal god, symbolized usually by a stone, sometimes by some other object…[156] In the town each clan still had its Majlis and its own stone, but the union of the clans forming the town was outwardly expressed by a collection of stones in one central shrine with a common symbol. The cube-shaped building known as the Ka'ba was such a symbol of unity in Mecca. [157]

The concept of authority was totally alien to the Bedouin nature and Mohammed understood religion to be the only acceptable authoritative force.[158] Perhaps the greatest "revelation" of Mohammed was recognizing the powerful political and religious significance of the Ka'bah. Mohammed's Koranic revelations boldly married "church and state" by recognizing the Ka'bah's potential as the most powerful symbol of unity in Arabia.

---

153 Lewis, 24.
154 Lewis, 25.
155 Lewis, 26-27.
156 Lewis, 25.
157 Lewis, 26.
158 Lewis, 41.

Just as Saint Paul brought biblical morality to the gentiles, Mohammed's Islam brought biblical morality to Bedouin tribalism and established God as a politically cohesive force. The brutality of tribal life was a reality of the political structure which Mohammed inherited and attempted to mold. One of the hallmarks of tribal society was the blood vengeance imposed on the kin of a murdered man. With the changes brought about by Mohammed, "faith replaced blood as the social bond." The source of authority was no longer the consensus of the Majlis, but was now God speaking through Mohammed.[159]

The Meccan government was a successful model of trade and commerce that began to feel threatened by the fledgling religious movement. The Quraysh tribe went so far as to forbid marriage and trade with the Muslims.[160] In the nearby city of Medina, there were several large Jewish tribes who were having trouble living amicably with the pagan population. Word of Mohammed's open-minded approach to community and social justice resulted in an invitation for Mohammed and his Muslims to come to Medina and establish a functional community of monotheists and pagans. This migration became known as the *hijrah*, marking the first significant date in Islamic history: 622 CE.

To forge this community, Mohammed oversaw interactions between Muslims, pagans, and Jews, and established a unique sort of "supertribe," bound together by ideology rather than blood. "It proved to be an inspiration that would bring peace to Arabia before the death of the prophet in 632, just ten years after the *hijrah*."[161] Members of this new type of hybrid community (*ummah*) promised not to attack one another, and even offered each other protection. Besides setting the communities guidelines, he presided over regular meetings to discuss and resolve problems.

In these early years the Jews of Medina functioned well within the ummah, and "he adopted a number of Jewish practices, including the fast of Kippur and the prayer toward Jerusalem...The Jews, however, rejected the pretensions of this gentile Prophet and opposed him on precisely the religious level where he was most sensitive."[162] "By 624 it was clear that most of the Jews of Medina would never be reconciled

159 Lewis, 40.
160 Armstrong, *Islam: A Short History*, 12-13.
161 Armstrong, *Islam: A Short History*, 14.
162 Lewis, 39.

with the Prophet."[163] Around this time, Mohammed, in the middle of a prayer, turned his face from Jerusalem to Mecca, and his followers did the same. Turning to face the Ka'bah in Mecca was also a test of faith for Muslims, as the Koran points out:

> *We decreed your former qiblah only in order that We may know the Apostle's true adherents and those who were to disown him. It was indeed a hard test, but not to those whom God has guided.*[164]

Armstrong offers the following observations on Mohammed's bold act:

> By turning away from Jerusalem towards the Ka'bah, which had no connection with Judaism or Christianity, Muslims tacitly demonstrated that they were reverting to the original pure monotheism of Abraham, who had lived before the revelation of either the Torah or the Gospel and, therefore, before the religion of the one God had been split into warring sects.[165]

For Islam, Abraham is clearly the most important prophet of the Hebrew Scriptures, and appears to have been important to Arabs even before the time of Mohammed. A historian named Sozomenos tells us that Arabs in Syria believed that they had rediscovered the authentic religion of Abraham, who existed before Judaism and Christianity.[166] Armstrong relates a story from Mohammed's first biographer, Muhammad ibn Ishaq (d.767), in which four Quraysh tribesmen were seeking the *hanifiyyah*, the true religion of Abraham. One of them, who later became the second caliph after Mohammed's death, was Zayd ibn Amr. Zayd later found out that his prayer's for revelation were fulfilled on Mount Hira in 610 on the seventeenth night of Ramadan, when Muhammad was awakened by an angel who commanded him to: 'Recite!' (iqra!).[167] Mohammed's Koranic revelations had begun

163 Armstrong, *Islam: A Short History*, 17.
164 Koran, *The Cow*, 2:142.
165 Armstrong, *Islam: A Short History*, 18.
166 Armstrong, A History of God, 136.
167 Armstrong, A History of God, 136-7.

when he uttered his first words of Scripture. Muslims understand this to be the Word of God.[168]

Paying homage to Abraham and his legacy of seven circumambulations around the Ka'bah became one of the five pillars of Islam. Mohammed wanted to take the Ka'bah out of the hands of pagans and reestablish it as the center of monotheism that he knew it to be. Any future attempts to take it from the amoral and oppressive hands of his own Quraysh tribesmen would be considered a righteous use of force.

Mohammed also justified the use of force for economic survival. Lacking adequate means of producing income, the recent Meccan emigrants resorted to *ghazu*, the "raid." This practice "was a sort of national sport in Arabia," as long as no one was killed, which would begin a vendetta. Not only did these raids bring in booty as income, but it offered the Muslims a way to strike back at their own Quraysh tribesmen who oppressed them and forced them to leave their homes in Mecca and emigrate to Medina.[169] Therefore "raids on merchant caravans were seen as a natural and legitimate act of war."[170]

In 624, under Mohammed's leadership, a band of Muslims surprised a large Meccan caravan at Badr. The outraged Quraysh sent an army in response with hopes of wiping out the Muslims and stopping the raids that had been going on. The Muslim success at Badr against much greater numbers is mentioned in the Koran. This victory helped strengthen the ummah, and according to Armstrong:

> In Medina, the chief casualties of this Muslim success were the three Jewish tribes of Qaynuqah, Nadir, and Qurayzah, who were determined to destroy Mohammed and who all independently formed alliances with Mecca.[171]

The three Jewish tribes were eventually destroyed, because they were believed to have allied themselves with Mecca's pagan leaders against Mohammed. The *Sirah*[172] gives an account of the destruction of

---

168 Armstrong, A History of God, 137.
169 Armstrong, *Islam: A Short History*, 19.
170 Lewis, 41.
171 Armstrong, *Islam: A Short History*, 20.
172 Mohammed's companions wrote about the prophet's life, personality, and behavior in different situations.

the last of the three Jewish tribes in Medina, after they were said to have plotted Mohammed's assassination. Despite Mohammed's problems with the three Jewish tribes, Armstrong points out that this did not affect Mohammed's attitude toward the Jewish people:

> The struggle did not indicate any hostility toward Jews in general, but only towards the three rebel tribes. The Quran continued to revere Jewish prophets and to urge Muslims to respect the People of the Book. Smaller Jewish groups continued to live in Medina, and later Jews, like Christians, enjoyed full religious liberty in the Islamic empires.[173]

In the years that followed some still fought against the growing Islamic movement. "But after the Battle of the Trench, when Mohammed had humiliated Mecca and quashed the opposition in Medina, he felt that it was time to abandon the jihad and begin a peace offensive." In 628 he made the hajj with about 1000 Muslim pilgrims bearing no arms. The Quraysh sent troops out to attack Mohammed before he reached safe haven, but Mohammed managed to evade the troops with the help of some Bedouin allies, and the Quraysh were eventually pressured by this peaceful demonstration into negotiating a treaty that granted Muslims access to the Ka'bah.[174]

Then, in the year before Mohammed's death, a Meccan murdered a Muslim, breaking their treaty, and triggering Mohammed's final attack on Mecca. Mohammed's lifetime mission was eventually completed after securing the Ka'bah for Islam by defeating his own Quraysh tribesmen and capturing Mecca.

It is important to understand that the biblical doctrine of "an eye for an eye," often quoted to justify a military jihad, derives from Hammurabi's Code[175] and not from the religion of Abraham. However, Mohammed was a practical man, who believed that a militaristic lesser jihad, to secure the Ka'bah for his Muslim followers, was a justifiable means to an end. The end that he sought, his lifelong strategic goal, was to secure the Ka'bah for his Muslim followers and lead them to the light of the greater jihad, symbolized by the Ka'bah.

173 Armstrong, *Islam: A Short History*, 21.
174 Armstrong, *Islam: A Short History*, 22-23.
175 In contrast to the New Testament's call "to turn the other cheek."

Armstrong describes Mohammed's perspective on war and peace as follows:

> The Quran teaches that war is such a catastrophe that
> Muslims must use every method in their power to
> restore peace and normality in the shortest possible
> time. Arabia was a chronically violent society, and
> the ummah had to fight its way to peace.[176]

According to Armstrong, Muslim hatred of Jews is a more recent development:

> Anti-semitism is a Christian vice. Hatred of the Jews became
> marked in the Muslim world only after the creation of the state
> of Israel in 1948 and the subsequent loss of Arab Palestine.[177]

Mohammed's justification to engage in a lesser jihad was either for survival or to secure the Ka'bah, but the Ka'bah has been controlled by Muslims for almost 1400 years. Today, any perceived oppression in no way threatens the Ka'bah as the focal point for Islam's sacred practice. Modern Muslims struggle against what is perceived as encroaching materialism threatening their devout way of life. From Abraham's point of view, resorting to hatred and violence as a means to eliminate the threat of materialism is just as sinful as the attachments and materialism it seeks to avoid. Abraham's perspective makes it clear that today's militaristic call for lesser jihad distracts Muslims from God and the greater jihad. The authentic religion of Abraham teaches us that man must rise above both his material attachments and his anger to stay focused on God and the greater jihad.

---

176 Armstrong, *Islam: A Short History*, 22.
177 Armstrong, *Islam: A Short History*, 21.

Surrendering the Self

The Koran states:

Whoever leaves home in God's cause will find on earth
frequent and ample place of refuge. If death should overtake the
one who leaves home and migrates to God and His Messenger
[Mohammed], God is certain to reward that person.[178]

The Imam Ruhallah Khumayni interprets this passage as follows:

If a person departs from the home of egohood and migrates
toward God and His Messenger, and then reaches a state where
he is "overtaken by death," where nothing remains of his self
and he sees all things as coming from God — if he engages
in such a migration, then it is incumbent upon God to reward
him... there is a class of people who have accomplished this...
there are others who have migrated but not yet reached the
goal of being "overtaken by death." And there is still another
group — to which you and I belong — that has not even begun
to migrate. We are still caught up in the darkness; we are
captives in the pit of attachment to the world, to nature, and
worst of all to our own egos. We are enclosed in our home of
selfhood, and all that exists is ourselves … As time goes on we
become more and more distant from the point of origin, that
place toward which we are supposed to migrate.[179]

According to the Imam, being "overtaken by death" should not be
taken literally, but rather as death of the "self" in which one leaves one's
ego behind. This passage describes the internal struggle within each of
us in which the enemy to be vanquished is one's own ego. This critical
passage from the Koran is often quoted by Muslims who believe that
martyring themselves for a perceived cause (lesser jihad: *al-jihad al-
asghar*) is the only prerequisite for divine reward. The Imam Ruhallah
Khumayni tells us that most of today's Muslims find themselves "caught

178 Koran, *Women* 4:100; Renard, 53.
179 Renard, 53-54.

up in the darkness … captives in the pit of attachment to the world, to nature, and worst of all to [their] own egos." From this description it appears that Muslims can join Christians and Jews, all laboring in the same "pit" of ego, sin and worldly attachments.

The word *Islam* means surrender. Muslims prostrate themselves before God five times each day. Armstrong describes the significance of these prostrations for the first Muslims living within a thriving mercantile and pagan Mecca:

> The prostrations were designed to counter the hard arrogance and self-sufficiency that was growing apace in Mecca. The postures of their bodies would re-educate the Muslims, teaching them to lay aside their pride and selfishness, and recall that before God they were nothing.[180]

This is the first in a two-step process. One must first "leave home" (vanquish the ego) before one can begin "migrating to God." Abraham teaches us that it is only through the prayerful meditation of a greater jihad (*al-jihad al-akbar*) that one can begin one's migration toward God. Without the esoteric meaning of the Book of Creation to shed light on the meditative techniques symbolized by the Ka'bah, the Muslim, like his Jewish and Christian brothers, must remain in exile from paradise.

The Greater Jihad

Once the ego dies, one's thoughts and emotions are no longer wrapped up in one's own hatreds and attachments and one begins the process of migrating toward God. *Hajj* is the term that symbolizes the second step of this process. It is the pilgrimage to Mecca, to circumambulate the Ka'bah seven times. These seven circuits represent the meditation process that purifies the body in order to liberate the soul. It should not be characterized by emotional or religious fervor of any sort.

Abraham describes twelve body organs that "stand in war," manifesting as dualistic biological imperatives of love and hate, that lead man to procreate and kill. We can see from the following stanza how Abraham characterizes man's internal struggle:

180 Armstrong, *Islam: A Short History, 6.*

6.5 *Twelve stand in war:*
> *Three love,*
> *three hate,*
> > *three give life*
> > *and three kill*
> *Three love: the heart and the ears.*
> *Three hate: the liver, the gall, and the tongue.*
> *Three give life: the two nostrils and the spleen.*
> *Three kill: the two orifices and the mouth.*

The practitioner struggles with his thoughts and emotions to seek a balanced state of calm that will enable him to transcend this dualistic mind. Once a state of calm can be maintained for relatively long periods of time the practitioner should begin to experience a divine influx of energy that will irradiate the body, marking the beginning of the purification process. If man is to reenter Paradise during this "marriage to God," it is only the ego, with all its hatreds and attachments, which must die. When this inner energy assumes more importance to the practitioner than the day-to-day activities of the material world, it is a good indication that the attachments and hatreds of the ego have died, and the soul has begun its migration toward God. That is the meaning of the Hajj as originally defined by Abraham.

It bears repeating that Abraham's method of attaining paradise does not require the practitioner to physically die. Physical death is not only unnecessary but counter to spiritual progress. The undistracted practitioner performing the Hajj according to Abraham's instructions will learn to ascend to Paradise at will, while the living body remains earthbound.

If a person dies who's life was ruled by attachments to material things, or who was consumed by anger and hatred, one can be sure that they did not even begin the first of this two-step process, and would not be entering Paradise any time soon. Abraham's "science of transfiguration" tells us that no matter how noble a martyr's death might appear, if they have hatred or vengeance in their heart, or if their time is spent striving after land, money, or other sorts of worldly things, then they have succumbed to idolatrous distractions and departed from the path toward God.

In order to liberate the soul, spiritual judgment requires more than just judiciously deciding whether or not, and to what extent, the body's appetites are indulged. We can see from Abraham's meditation instructions that man must rise above his inner turmoil by not allowing it to rule his thoughts or speech.

Bridle your mouth from speaking
And your heart from thinking

Abraham also tells us that heaven is not all about love and hell is not all about hate. Attachments and anger can both keep the human spirit earthbound. The "divine influx" of meditation will create a judicious mind that is capable of harmonizing the twelve who "stand in war," purifying the body as a prerequisite to liberating the soul.

We know Mohammed had a meditation practice. We have already mentioned the Sakinah, God's "tranquility descending" on Mohammed as he meditated in the cave.[181] For Mohammed to lead the pagan world "toward the light of the Ka'bah" required a vision that could only have been a gift from god. Armstrong states that Mohammed's divine guidance resulted from his meditation:

> When faced with a crisis or dilemma, Mohammed had entered deeply into himself and heard a divinely inspired solution. His life had thus represented a constant dialogue between transcendent reality and the violent, puzzling and disturbing happenings of the mundane world. The Quran had, therefore, followed public and current events, bringing divine guidance and illumination to politics. Mohammed's successors, however, were not prophets, but would have to rely on their own human insights.[182]

The Book of Creation's clear assertion is that no man could have become a prophet without the meditation process that binds man to God. The irony of Mohammed's revelations and prophecy is that he was probably unaware that seven circumambulations around his cherished Ka'bah were actually Abraham's instructions for deep meditation — the very practice that accounted for the prophet's divine "gifts."

---

181 *Koran*, Repentance 9:40.
182 Armstrong, *Islam: A Short History*, 24.

The Middle East crisis can be solved only when men learn the wisdom of choosing Oneness with God over squabbles about land, material possessions, and vengeance. The land of Israel and Abraham's material possessions may belong to Isaac and his descendants, but Abraham's true birthright, seven circuits around the sacred cube, was equally shared between Isaac and Ishmael as evidenced by the existence of the Ka'bah and its tradition. Imams and rabbis must recognize that Abraham's core religious practice is the shared basis of both religions, and represents a profound common ground between the two cultures. This sharing of the true birthright between Isaac and Ishmael implies that the Book of Creation rightfully belongs to Muslims as much as it does Jews. I believe that Abraham's teachings need to be shared by all his descendants – by all three faiths who call him their patriarch.

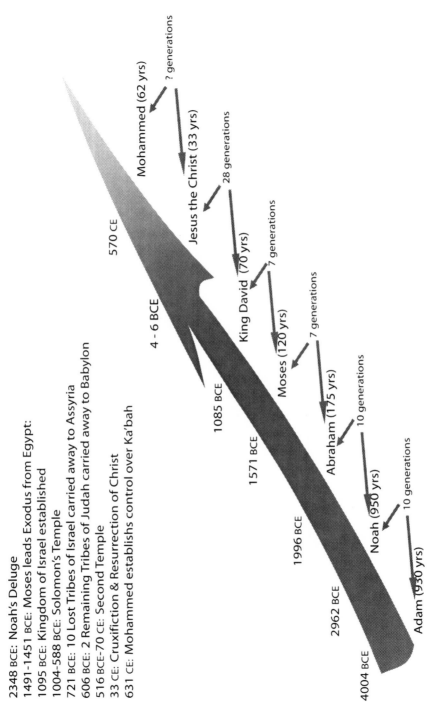

2348 BCE: Noah's Deluge
1491-1451 BCE: Moses leads Exodus from Egypt:
1095 BCE: Kingdom of Israel established
1004-588 BCE: Solomon's Temple
721 BCE: 10 Lost Tribes of Israel carried away to Assyria
606 BCE: 2 Remaining Tribes of Judah carried away to Babylon
516 BCE-70 CE: Second Temple
33 CE: Cruxifiction & Resurrection of Christ
631 CE: Mohammed establishs control over Ka'bah

Figure 13 – The Patriarchal Lineage

Abraham's Legacy of Peace

Polytheism & Gifts that Traveled East

According to Aryeh Kaplan, there is a Talmudic teaching that after Abraham's wife Sarah died, Abraham took concubines. He then taught "mysteries" to the children of his concubines. This is based on the verse "to the sons of the concubines that Abraham had, Abraham gave gifts, and he sent them away ... to the lands of the east."[183] Kaplan continues, "These gifts consisted of occult mysteries, which then spread in eastern Asia,"[184] presumably to become the basis of Eastern religions. If it is true that Abraham's techniques of prayerful meditation made their way to the Far East with either Ishmael's descendants or the children of the concubines, then Abraham's teachings may have had a wider influence than is generally believed.

Buddhist cosmology appears to have theological roots in the ancient string theory of Vedic Hinduism, but striking similarities between Taoism and the religion of Abraham indicate that Taoism either originated with, or was greatly influenced by, Abraham's "gifts that traveled East." If one draws lines of perspective backwards in time, we arrive at what appears to be the oldest extant metaphysical texts based on string theory: the Book of Creation and the Rig Veda. If we continue to extend even further, our lines of perspective will converge at their place of origin ca. 4000 BCE in Mesopotamia, Sumer and Egypt.

If Abraham's teachings did travel East in this manner, one may wonder how polytheism developed, and how it relates to monotheism in terms of string theory. And at what point does the deification of each individual become consistent with polytheism? For example, if Jesus was able to realize his inner divinity and even went so far as to overcome death through resurrection, should he be considered God, and if so, would that make Christianity polytheistic? There is no Christian explanation

183 Genesis 25:6; Sanhedrin, 91b; Zohar 1:99b, 1:133b, 1:233a.
184 Aryeh Kaplan, *Meditation and Kabbalah,* 32-33.

for the three divine "persons" within the Holy Trinity. It may be easier for Abrahamic monotheists to relate to a polytheistic approach because in that approach all people are capable of uniting with their inner divinity, exactly the way Jesus did.

A sticking point for some monotheists is whether prayer to a spiritually evolved entity (or to some symbol of them) constitutes idol worship. When a polytheist prays to one of the five evolved Dhyani-Buddhas, or to one of the legendary Indian mahasiddhas, is it any different than a Roman Catholic praying to Mary or to Saint Anthony; or is it necessarily different than the contact of Jesus with Moses and Elijah on Mount Tabor; or the contact of Mohammed with Gabriel? Who is to say that the spiritual entities, who we believe have ascended, can't respond to our prayers and help us in our own spiritual journey?

In the East, "deity yoga" is a visualization technique in which the meditator imagines himself or herself as one of the divine saints, living where they would live, speaking as they would speak, etc., merging their very beings together as one being. Soon enough, there is the awakening that one's own essence is similarly divine. Of course, practitioners of deity yoga must also be able to negate ego so that worldly things do not distract them. Realizing the divinity of one's inner self is, or should be, common to both monotheists and polytheists. The desire to become "One with everything" reflects the attempt to unite with the divine essence that exists within all beings and things. Abraham would call this the omnipresence of God as defined by the harmonic series.

Monotheism implies the unification of both realized and unrealized souls into the white light of God. For unrealized souls one has to die to "give up the ghost," whereas realized souls have learned to liberate their soul at will into the "clear light." That unity should not be mistaken for love. Transcendence is more profound than any emotion.

Healing the Three Faiths

Understanding the Book of Creation brings a fresh perspective to religious conflict within the three faiths. Once the complexities of the Book of Creation are understood, one can see that God does not take sides. Any religious culture that claims ownership of the only true path to God will be seen as contrary to the egalitarianism and scientific objectivity of Abraham's approach.

Soon after Mohammed's death: "Muslims began to assert that Mohammed had been the last and greatest of the prophets, a claim that is not made explicitly in the Quran..."[185] The Koran does state, however, that Mohammed is the "Seal of the Prophets."[186] Muslims often interpret this to mean that Mohammed was meant to supersede all Old and New Testament prophets (including Moses and Jesus). Within this interpretation, those who don't follow Mohammed's ways, including all Jews and Christians, could never attain the ranks of the righteous and are therefore considered infidels. This tendency toward exclusivity is also prevalent among Jews who number themselves among God's only chosen people and discount any possibility that Jesus and Mohammed were prophets who offer their adherents a path to God. Similarly, Christian dogma maintains that anyone who doesn't believe in Jesus will go to Hell. Each of the three faiths tends to believe that God is exclusively on their side – a paradox! – and the root cause of countless wars.

Taking issue with this type of interpretation has been difficult up until now because the Koran, the Torah, and the New Testament, are all considered the Word of God. It must be clearly stated, however, that the divine inspiration of the Torah, the New Testament, and the Koran, cannot be literally understood to be the Word of God. We will see that the religion of Abraham was established by the Word of God, *Yahweh*, which encrypts the Blueprint of Creation and the secret practice of the eternal priesthood.

Jews, Christians and Muslims believe that the recorded words of their prophet are divinely infallible and, further, that reason can have no sway over blind faith or what they consider to be the "Word of God." Although the three faiths may not listen to each other beyond superficial acknowledgment, is it possible that they might listen to the only writings of their patriarch? Even those who stubbornly cling to religious dogma might subscribe to Abraham's objective and scientific truth about God.

One can anthropomorphize God as an old man with a beard, as depicted on the ceiling of the Sistine Chapel, while polytheism might then be described as many old men with beards. This type of literal interpretation ignores the coalescing "rainbow principle" (the harmonic

185 Armstrong, *Islam: A Short History*, 26.
186 Koran, Surah 33:40

series) that mathematically defines God and Creation for Abraham. Each definable entity of Creation corresponds to its own individualized rainbow, and each rainbow entity is capable of coalescing into the "white light of God." In some forms of polytheism, each "rainbow" entity, or even each color might be defined as a different god. For Abraham, each color and each tone circle becomes a different angel. The vibrational essence of the multitudes, whether symbolized by gods or angels, mathematically coalesces into *Yahweh*.

The *En Sof*, the Father, and Allah are all names of God that can be understood within the mathematical framework of divine light provided by Abraham. Only the Word, *Yahweh,* is defined by Abraham as a self-contained and all-inclusive mathematical encryption of the transcendent and omnipresent God. The three faiths each demonstrate the following tripartite structure of *Yahweh,* in which man approaches God through an intermediate state:

- The En Sof, the Shechinah, and the soul
- The Father, the Son, and the Holy Spirit
- Allah, the prophet, and greater jihad

Yahweh encompasses all of these. The question we must really ask ourselves is whether the religion of Abraham is compelling enough to gather all his descendants "from the four corners of the earth" and bring them together under one scientific and theological umbrella, or, whether the evolution of sectarian dogma will prevent Abraham's descendents from recognizing the truth.

During the time of the great Hebrew prophets, Abraham's meditation practice was still understood and practiced. One is reluctant to suggest that any of the three faiths have erred in their theological evolution. It might be better to say that they have traveled, to a lesser or greater extent, away from the writings of Abraham. The distance a faith has traveled from its theological point of origin will impact the ability, or at least the time it takes, for the faithful to arrive at their "final reward." For example, an evangelist will have surrendered his ego in identification with Christ's death on the cross and will be "born again" in Christ's resurrected spirit. No one would question this person's spirituality, but from Abraham's perspective, this person's very real focus of energies would be concentrated not within, but rather on the spirit of Christ, who is an external entity. Within the context of Abraham's writings, this displaces one's focus from the body's purification process, which is a prerequisite to liberating the soul.

A proper reading of the Book of Creation will give us a better understanding of how our current set of beliefs impact our thoughts, our prayers, and our inner energies. It will also demonstrate, in a very practical way, how a theological course correction from Abraham can improve our daily lives, and ultimately enable us to heal our bodies and liberate our souls in this lifetime. One can speculate that if Abraham's teachings had never been lost, Jesus and Mohammed might both have been accepted as prophets, and neither Christianity nor Islam might have felt the need to break with Judaism. For that matter, if Abraham's knowledge of *Yahweh* was never lost to his descendants there would have been no need for a Torah, and Judaism would never have had to break with pure Abrahamism.

The Book of Creation is the cradle of religion and science. For Abraham, the metaphysics of God and nature is written in the terms of civilization's earliest scientific disciplines — arithmetic, music, geometry, and astronomy — the Quadrivium. Rediscovering Abraham's theology will put men of faith on a level playing field with men of science, and the three faiths on a level playing field with each other. Only the writings of Abraham have the religious, cultural, moral, and scientific authority to create an egalitarian world capable of evolving into a true and lasting peace.

PART III. THE DIVINE LIGHT OF YAHWEH

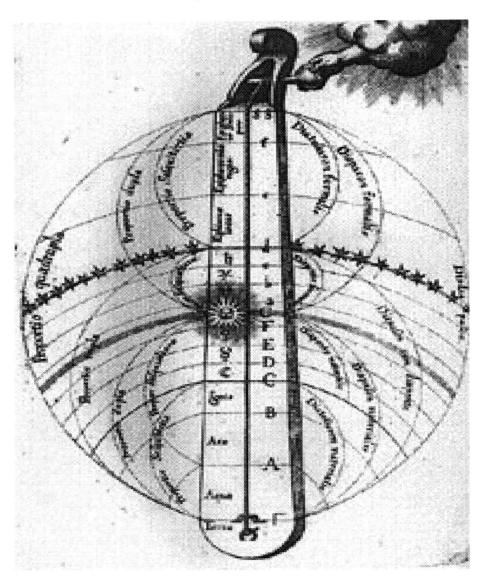

Figure 14 - God Tuning the Monochord of the World
(Robert Fludd: The Mundane Monochord)

An Overview of Creation

The Foundation of Scripture

The motto of the United States, *E Pluribus Unum* (From Many One), is a political maxim defining a unified nation of component states. It could also be considered the deist motto of America's founding fathers. Deism was popular during the Enlightenment, a time when modern science would have been most aligned with Abraham's "theory of everything." If this maxim was applied to Abraham's mathematics, it would define God as the natural unifying principle of Creation's diversity. Abraham mathematically defined God as the most fundamental universal law — a law that scientists later defined as the harmonic series. It unites the diversity of colors in the rainbow into what Abraham might call the "white light of God." Abraham's two mathematical tables (Tables 6 and 7) extend this harmonic series into a matrix of divine light that become the essence and sustenance of Creation.

In Genesis, from Day 2 forward, God begins to "reorder" and contain His light. We must remember that the divine light matrix is based on the theory of vibrating strings, and it might therefore be helpful to continue our musical explanation by thinking of God as a violinist playing on only one string; or perhaps think of Him setting the stops on an ancient monochord as depicted in the Robert Fludd painting of Figure 14. With each new Day of Creation, God divides His string into as many sections as there are days. For example, on Day 1 Abraham has the one undivided string with undifferentiated harmonics defining the complete spectrum of divine light. On Day 2 He would divide His string into two equal parts, creating a very specific mathematical and musical structure essential to Creation. On Day 3 this heavenly string would be divided into three equal parts, supplementing Day 2's structure and adding another layer of complexity to Creation. This complexity continues to grow with the string's division into four parts; then five parts; six parts; and finally seven parts.

D
1

x 2 =

D
2

4 .16 Two stones build 2 houses
Three build 6 houses
Four stones build 24 houses
Five stones build 120 houses
Six stones build 720 houses
Seven stones build 5040 houses
From here on go out and calculate
that which the mouth cannot speak
and the ear cannot hear.

D
1

x 3 =

D
3

x 4 =

D
12

x 5 =

G
A
4

x 4 =

G   A
A   G
16   18

x 5 =   x 5 =

x 3 =

D
6

x 4 =

D
24

x 5 =

	e♭		f		G	A	b♭		c		
D	c#		b		A	G	f#		e		D
60	64		72		80	90	96		108		120

x 6 = x 6 =   x 6 =   x 6 =   x 6 = x 6 =   x 6 =   x 6 =

	e♭	e	f	f#	G	A	b♭	b	c	c#	
D	c#	c	b	b♭	A	G	f#	f	e	e♭	D
360	384	400	432	450	480	540	576	600	648	675	720

x 7 = x 7 = x 7 = x 7 = x 7 = x 7 = x 7 = x 7 = x 7 = x 7 = x 7 = x 7 =

	e♭	e	f	f#	G	A	b♭	b	c	c#	
D	c#	c	b	b♭	A	G	f#	f	e	e♭	D
2520	2688	2800	3024	3150	3360	3780	4032	4200	4356	4725	5040

Figure 15a – Musical Counting and Mathematical Means

The seven Days of Creation in Genesis derive from the mathematics of Abraham's seven integer *"stones"* as a subset of God's Ten Utterances. In the Book of Creation, God uses these stones to construct musical *"houses"* of varying numeric ratios. In Genesis, God "engraves" Creation during each successive day, based on stones which build Abraham's increasingly complex musical structures. In Part 3, as we explore the acoustical details for each successive day of Creation, we will be referencing the corresponding musical construction within figures 15b and 15c.

In Stanza 4.16 Abraham is telling us to use *stones... to calculate.* In other words, he wants us to use "pebble arithmetic," an ancient device usually associated with Greek mathematicians, to calculate the complete paths to God. We already know that the 231 Gates table can point us toward the appropriate "gate." This gate becomes our musical starting point in the 462 Paths table to help us determine the appropriate next steps along the paths to/from God. In this manner, Abraham's mathematical tables resemble a treasure map. We are given just enough musical and mathematical material to determine the steps along the path, as per Abraham's instructions: *"From here on go out and calculate that which the mouth cannot speak and the ear cannot hear."* The musical path to God contains the inaudible sounds of the spirit, as described in Psalm 19:

> *The heavens declare the glory of God,*
> *The sky proclaims His handiwork.*
> *Day to Day makes utterance,*
> *night to night speaks out.*
> > *There is no utterance, there are no words,*
> > *their sound is not heard.*

Those calculations will ultimately show that God "engraved" three types of musical scales in their ascending and descending form: the Greek Phrygian mode (Figure 32a), the diatonic scale (Figures 15 and 43), and the chromatic scale (Figures 15 and 65). It is through these symmetrical musical "paths" that God's essence descends into matter to bless and sustain Creation, and it is through reciprocal paths that man's prayerful meditation ascends to God, ultimately liberating his soul. After God's Ten Sefirot of Nothingness are "reordered" (*Tikun*) in the second step of Creation, the scales generated become the vibratory essence and sustenance for the multitude of various objects and beings in Creation. We will provide a detailed analysis of the Book of Creation's step-by-step account of Creation and compare it to the Torah's day-to-day account. It will also demonstrate how the Book of Creation and the Torah are interdependent complements of one another – both necessary to properly illuminate the Word of God.

It is important to realize that the Word of God does not preexist Creation, it is tied to the act of Creation itself. As the Word of God is revealed, Creation occurs. In the Book of Creation, *Yahweh* gradually reveals Himself, letter by letter, "engraving" new categories of things and beings with each new "stone" and each new letter of His Name. "Each new stone" in the Book of Creation translates to "each new day" in the Creation allegory of the Torah. The first letter of the Tetragrammaton, *Yud* (י = 10), completely reveals the divine light of God's Ten Utterances on Day 1, and "reorders" divine light on Days 2 through 4 to create time and the heavenly bodies. On Day 5, the Tetragrammaton's letter *Heh* (ה = 5) is revealed as the container of divine light that would contain the essence and sustenance of all "creatures that moveth" – but the Logos, i.e., the Word of God – still did not fully exist! On the Sixth Day, the revelation of the letter *Vav* (ו = 6) created the soul of man within the container of his body. With man as God's final creation on Day 6, the Word of God, *Yahweh*, was fully revealed.

God's Utterance on Day 7 was designated God's day of rest, therefore no new objects or beings were created after Day 6. Since only prime numbers create new musical tones; and since God's remaining Utterances beyond the number 7 were not prime numbers, they also did not generate the vibrational essence of any new objects or beings. For Abraham, God was the Transcendent "One," i.e., the Monad, which was extended by the acoustical ratios of the next ten Hebrew numerals. They form a harmonic series, which Abraham calls the Ten Sefirot of Nothingness, and are encapsulated within the letter *Yud* (י = 10), the first letter of the Tetragrammaton. God reordered the divine light of these ten numerals as the fully revealed Word, *YHVH* (יהוה), to form the vibrational essence and sustenance of Creation.

By the end of Day 7 we will see exactly how the Book of Creation defines the musical framework for the Bible's creation allegories, encoding

God's use of three different musical tuning systems, Pythagorean tuning, Just tuning and Archytas tuning. Using these three tuning systems, God *engraves* three types of musical scales in their ascending and descending form. It is through these symmetrical musical "Paths" that God's spiritual waters descend into matter to bless and sustain Creation, and it is through the rising spiritual waters that man's meditational prayers, and the soul itself, ascends to God.

They comprise three of the four tunings and temperaments named by McClain as the essence of Plato's dialogues, the Republic, Timaeus, Criteas, and Laws. "Plato's four model cities — Callipolis, Ancient Athens, Atlantis, and Magnesia — were each associated with a specific musical-mathematical model, with individual algebraic yantras and related tone-mandalas."[187] Athens is associated with Pythagorean tuning; Atlantis with Just tuning; Magnesia with Archytas tuning; and Callipolis with Equal temperament.[188] Of these, only equal temperament is not defined by Abraham. Later in Part 3 we will see that the use of equal temperament eliminates the need to atone for the musical "imperfections" of sin that differentiates the pantheistic Greek culture from the Levant's religious culture.

187 McClain, *The Myth of Invariance,* 161.
188 McClain, *The Pythagorean Plato,* 14.

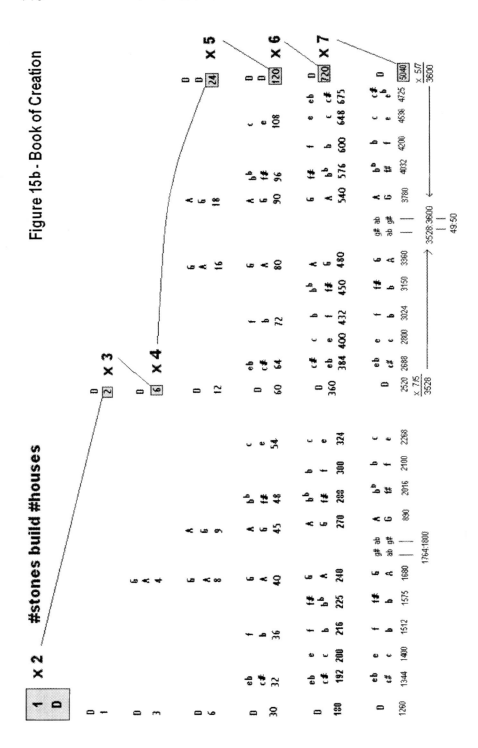

Figure 15b - Book of Creation

Figure 15c - Torah

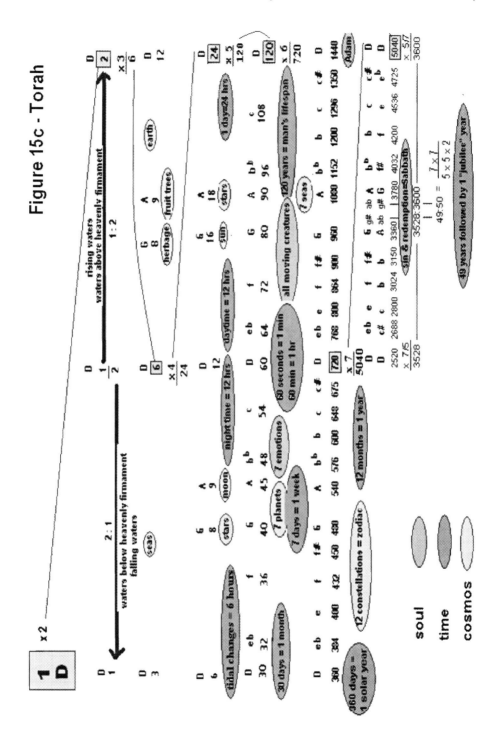

On Day 1 of Creation God created light:
God said, "Let there be light," and there was light.

On Day 2 of Creation, God's second creation was the Heavenly Firmament:
God said, "Let there be a firmament in the midst of the waters, and let it seperate between water and water."

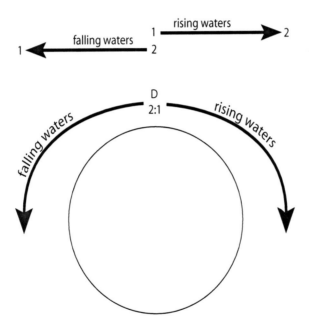

The Heavenly Firmament is the "octave container" (1:2) of all other vibrations
The opposing waters are the musical reciprocals of frequency and wavelength

Figure 16 – Creating the Heavenly Firmament on Day 2

The Second Day of Creation

The Heavenly Firmament

Within the Creation allegory, from Day 2 forward, God begins to "reorder" the divine light of Day 1.

God said, "Let there be a firmament in the midst of the waters, and let it separate between water and water." So God made the firmament, and separated between the waters which were beneath the firmament and the waters which were above the firmament. And it was so. God called to the firmament: "Heaven." And there was evening and there was morning, a second day.[189]

As Day 2 begins, God, the violinist, puts His finger directly in the middle of the heavenly string in order to generate the most basic musical creation: the octave. The upper half of the string would become the upper Firmament, while the lower half of the string would become the lower Firmament. On the Second Day God created the Heavenly Firmament as two reciprocal octaves, 1:2 and 2:1, which would ultimately "give birth to" all the tones of Creation. The "waters above*"* and the "waters below*"* equate the flow of spiritual waters with the flow of musical "waters" going up or down in pitch. This is the key to understanding all Scriptural allegory that pertains to a splitting of the waters. Moses' splitting of the Red Sea to lead the Israelites out of Egypt is pure mathematical allegory, as is the allegory of Joshua leading the Israelites across the Jordon River into Israel, in which, "The waters of the Jordan River were cut off because of the Ark of the Lord's Covenant.*"*[190] The division of the waters from the waters has been characterized within various kabbalistic writings as: *"running and returning,""waxing and waning,"* and *"advance and retreat.*[191]

---

189 Genesis 1:6 – 1:8.
190 Joshua 3:14-17.
191 Zalman, 215.

To understand what it means to have a heavenly *"firmament in the midst of the waters,"* we must first understand that Abraham viewed numbers and musical ratios as the vibratory essence of Creation's objects and beings. In both the ancient Greek and Hebrew traditions the number 1 corresponds to God, the number 2 is symbolic of woman, and the number 3 is symbolic of man. On the second day of Creation the relationship of the Kav's second integer, the number 2, is taken in relation to the number 1, producing the octave ratio of 1:2. In this acoustical manner, woman (the number 2) "gives birth" to an octave container of all tones within the musical scales created by God over the next six days, which serve as the vibratory essence of Creation, thus fulfilling woman's function as the symbolic womb of Creation.

The Book of Creation tells us, however, that God wasn't playing a violin; He was playing an instrument that somehow bent the string around into a circle. Abraham hints that it is a circle because its *"end is embedded in* [its] *beginning."* As God begins to play this circular instrument, He adds a new numerical tone generator with each passing day, which becomes the essence of that day's creations.

1.6 Ten Sefirot of Nothingness
       Their vision is like an "appearance of lightening"
       Their limit has no end
  And His word in them is "running and returning"
  They rush to His saying like a whirlwind
       And before His throne they prostrate themselves.

1.7 Ten Sefirot of Nothingness
       Their end is imbedded in their beginning
       and their beginning in their end
          like a flame in a burning coal
  For the Master is singular
      He has no second
  And before One, what do you count?

2.4 Twenty-two Foundation letters
      He Placed them in a circle
        like a wall with 231 Gates.
  The Circle oscillates back and forth.
  A sign for this:
      There is nothing in good higher than Delight (Oneg - ﬠ נ ג)
      There is nothing evil lower than Plague (Nega - ﬠ ג נ).

Abraham describes a construction in which the "*running*" and "*returning*" musical waters are also spiritual waters that "*whirl*" this way and that around the tone circle. We might foresee, from Stanza 2.4 above, that the 22 Foundation letters will ultimately produce 22 tonal ratios, "*like a wall with 231 Gates,*" that are also "*Placed in a circle... The Circle oscillates back and forth.*" The riddle that we might paraphrase from this stanza is "when can a wall be like a vibrating circle?" The answer is: when we toggle between a multiplication table of 231 Gates and a musical tone circle of 22 tones, derived from a musical subset of the 462 Paths table.

The tone circle, or mandala, is an ancient symbol common to many religions and cultures. The association of time with a circular object can be found in the Sefer Bahir. A *galgul* (Hebrew: sphere) is spoken of in the Sefer Bahir as a womb, that is, a cycle of time from which the future is born.[192] Like time, a circle has no beginning or end. Nothing can precede that which has no beginning, therefore Stanza 1.7 states "... *before One, what do you count?*" Isaiah 17:13 relates the galgul to the whirlwind: "*Like a sphere* (galgul) *before the whirlwind* (sufah)."

All tones transpose up or down in pitch by the eight notes that make an octave,[193] spinning one complete revolution around the tonal mandala with every multiplication or division by 2 – "*like a whirlwind*" – into their new vibratory rates, in which these tones must "*prostrate themselves before His throne,*" in order to relocate their frequency to the desired place on the circle. In the case of the mandala in Figure 16, if one doubles string length (multiplication by 2), one "spins" in a counterclockwise direction. Conversely, when one divides by 2, one "spins" in a clockwise direction, halving string length. We should note that a complete spin will never change the name of the tone, because one always winds up exactly where one started on the tone circle. As an exercise for our musical muscles, if we can find the ratio 2:3 = A on the 462 Paths table, and then multiply it by two octaves (2^2), we would get $2/3 * 2^2 = 8/3$. If we then look up 8/3 on the 462 Paths table, we will once more see an A, but this A will be two octaves lower in pitch than the last one – because it spun *like a whirlwind* twice around the tone circle until it arrived at its destination *prostrating*

---

192 Aryeh Kaplan, *Bahir* (York Beach, ME: Samuel Weiser, 1979), 164.
193 Western musical practice typically divides the musical interval 1:2 into seven notes plus a repeating tonic note. However, different scalar quantities can produce different divisions of the octave, such as ancient Chinese pentatonic scales, which divide the octave into five notes.

before His throne. In other words, all soon to be created tones other than D will be "prostrating" themselves at various points around the tone circle.

Since the fundamental tone, D, corresponds to the number 1, we read that *"the Master is singular,* [therefore] *He has no second."* In other words, when our meditation enables us to ascend the circle in a clockwise direction, or to descend in a counterclockwise direction, we may be said to be descending from God to incarnate as a newborn or ascending to God through either prayerful meditation or death; we will always return to God = D.

According to Plato, only the Dorian and Phrygian modes were "retained as promoting the virtues of courage and temperance respectively."[194] This particular scale can be roughly approximated by playing all the white notes on the piano beginning and ending with the note D.[195] The Greek concept of ethos states that playing in other modes would be detrimental to the body, mind and soul.

Creation of the Heavenly Firmament as a tone circle occurs within the microcosm of the soul, as well as within the macrocosm of the heavens. Today, the heavens appear to rotate in a circular motion around the north star, but due to a slight wobble in the motion of the earth's axis[196] during the time of Abraham, a star in the tail of the constellation Draco, named Thuban, functioned as the north star around which all the other stars rotated. Draco traveled in a complete circle around the heavens as the only constellation with stars in every house of the zodiac. In the chapter on meditation, we will learn more about Draco's importance to Abraham, and how the microcosm of the soul vibrates to the same "Music of the Spheres" as the macrocosm of the cosmos. In summation, circular tonal mandalas are based on a musical octave of ratio 1:2; corresponding to the heavenly firmament from which time and all the rest of Creation is born.

---

194 Grout, 8.

195 Today's equally tempered piano is slightly "out of tune" with nature, since its pitches are not in the integer ratios of the harmonic series.

196 Astronomers refer to this wobble as precession. You can see an example whenever you spin a top – the top rotates about the axis while the axis "wobbles."

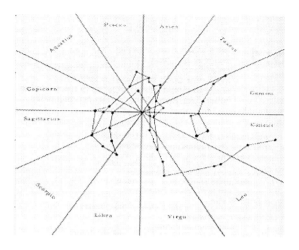

Figure 17a – Draco and the Constellations

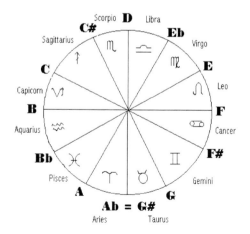

Figure 17b – Mandalla or Tone Circle Depicting the Zodiac[197]

---

197 McClain, *The Myth of Invariance*, 10.

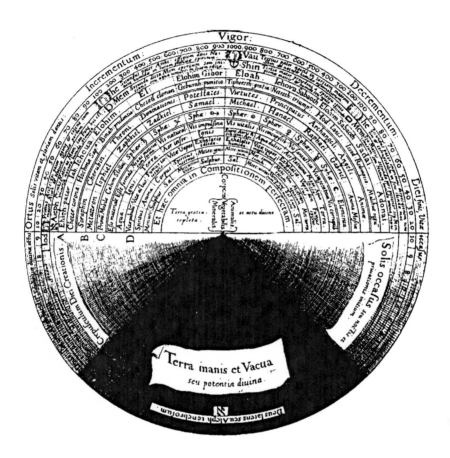

*Figure 18 – Tone Circles of God Gathering the Waters into Seas
(Robert Fludd: Integrum morborum mysterium)*

The Third Day of Creation

The Doctrine of Opposites and the Mean

Within Abraham's numerology, "threeness" derives from the mathematical opposites of woman's number (2) and man's number (3) united in God (1). God resides in the Heavenly Firmament at the apex of the tone circle. God is both the source and destination of the rising fires and falling waters, which manifests in nature as the reciprocity of frequency and wavelength.

The doctrine of opposites fulfills a similar function within other religions. For example, within Taoism, the polarity of yin and yang sums up all of life's basic opposites – good-evil, light-dark, male-female – while the Taoist "pivot point" mediates between them. One hundred years after Pythagoras, Philolaus stated that Pythagorean opposites were combined by a harmonic process "making them capable of interrelationship while without it they would not be clear either in themselves or in relation to one another."[198] It must also be said that harmony is not fusion. The components maintain their individuality.[199] Now, instead of two distinctly different elements, we have a blended group, with the elements in relation to one another.[200] The Quadrivium's doctrine of "opposites and the mean" is the mathematical and metaphysical foundation of "threeness" that is so prevalent in Abraham's theology.

Day 3 of Creation presents us with a pendulum like motion of the Triple Progression, rising and falling in musical fifths, with God at the center, creating the seas, the earth, and its vegetation. On the third day of

198 Curt Sachs, *Our Musical Heritage* (New York: Prentice Hall, 1948), 42-3.
199 Plato, *The Republic*, trans. by G.M.A. Grube (Indianapolis: Hacket Publishing Company, 1974), 107, Book IV:443d.
200 Edward Lippman, *Musical Thought in Ancient Greece* (New York: Columbia University Press, 1964), 14.

Creation, the number 3 enables us to rise and fall in pitch by the musical interval of a fifth (five notes) from the starting point D:

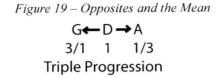

Figure 19 – Opposites and the Mean

G←D→A

3/1   1   1/3

Triple Progression

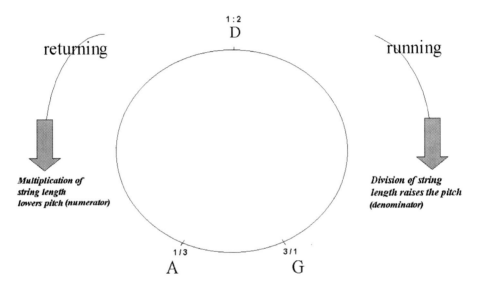

A ratio of 1/3 would mean that we divide the string length by the denominator 3, causing us to start spinning clockwise on our tone circle. As we spin we can begin to count integers. We start at the number 1 and spin past the number 2, making a complete circle. As we continue to spin past the number 2 and continue on to number 3, we add a partial spin of five more notes, until we arrive at our final destination of A. Our final resting place on the tone circle would be an octave plus a fifth higher than the starting pitch.

Conversely, a ratio of 3/1 would mean that we multiply the string length by 3 and start spinning in a counterclockwise direction. As we go from 1 to 2 we have completed spinning an octave lower in pitch. As the numerator continues to change from 2 to 3, we add a partial spin of five more notes, until our final resting place on the tone circle would be the note G, an octave plus a fifth lower than the starting pitch.

Multiplying or dividing by 2 simply spins us "like a whirlwind" into a higher or lower octave. The number 2 provides an octave container, while the number 3 is the first to generate a tone other than D within the octave. When we superimpose this pendulum like motion around D onto our tone circle, we can see that the male number 3 produces musical intervals of a fifth above and a fifth below D.

One helpful way to navigate the tone circle without getting confused is to first decide whether to think in terms of frequency or wavelength. Since units of length may be easier to visualize than units of time, I suggest thinking in terms of wavelength (which is really a tiny string length). With this decision out of the way, we can begin to think of any fractional ratio in terms of the denominator (implying division of a string length) or the numerator (implying multiplication of a string length). Division of the string will cause us to go clockwise around the tone circle, shortening string length and raising pitch. Multiplication of string length, however, will cause us to go counterclockwise around the circle, effectively lengthening the string and lowering the pitch.

It is important to realize that all tones must be understood in relation to God, and that musical relationships are defined by a ratio of integers. If we start with an octave double of ratio 1/2, and multiply both the numerator and denominator by the number 2, we would "spin around" to the tone circle octave double 2/4; traveling two octaves clockwise (the denominator of 4) and then one octave counterclockwise (the numerator of 2) until our final resting place puts us one octave higher. Once our numerosity has been increased our new frame of reference has been transposed up one octave. The benefit of working with a 2:4 octave as opposed to a 1:2 octave is the room it allows us to squeeze in the number 3, which then generates a new musical tone, in this case the interval of a musical fifth.

In the following figure, we can use our spinning method to determine that the musical interval of a perfect fifth (2/3) and a perfect fourth (4/3) both arrive at the note A (one octave apart). The first fraction spins an octave plus a fifth in the clockwise direction (the denominator 3), and then spins one octave in the counterclockwise direction (the numerator 2). The second fraction spins an octave plus a fifth in the clockwise direction (the denominator 3), but then spins two octaves in the counterclockwise direction (the numerator 4). To check if you are spinning correctly just consult Table 6. We can look in the table for 2/3 and 4/3 to determine that both ratios generate an A measuring from the reference tone (D):

Figure 20a – The Arithmetic Mean within the Endpoints of the Octave

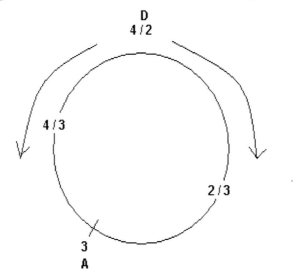

Another tricky thing about understanding tone circles is that musical distances on the circle are not linear, they are logarithmic. In other words, musical distances on the tone circle are not the same as the physical distances that we perceive visually. For example, a tone circle cannot be cut up like a piece of pie; 1/3 of a tone circle will wind up looking like 2/3 of a pie. Tone circle ratios are visually counterintuitive.

We can generate arithmetic and harmonic means only when the octave container is large enough to contain the necessary arithmetic. Remember, larger numerosity has no effect on the ratios between these large numbers. For example, both 6:12 and 1:2 contain only one octave. Although prime numbers are the only generators of tone, a higher numerosity that maintains ratio relationships, will allow us to squeeze more notes or number operations between the octave's two endpoints. This ability to increase complexity with higher numerosity is the basic mathematical tool that enables God's prime number Utterances to extend into matter.

Figure 20b – Increased Numerosity With Equivalent Ratios

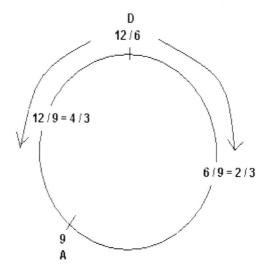

If we calculate whole-number values for both the arithmetic and harmonic means within the octave double 6:12, we generate the four notes shown in the diagram below. The figure below gives us an idea of how the harmonic and arithmetic means produce complementary intervals of perfect fifths (diapente) and fourths (diatesseron) within the octave (diapason).

Figure 21 – Complementary Arithmetic and Harmonic Means

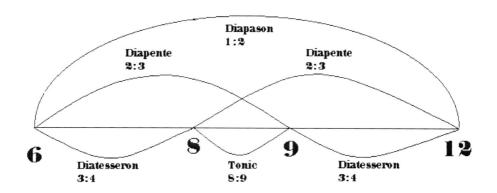

Engraving Opposites and the Mean

Now that we have more confidence generating tones with the number 3, we can better understand the creation allegory for Day 3 within the Book of Genesis. We can follow along in Figure 15c as we try to make acoustical sense out of Day 3. The challenge here is to determine whether the textual layer of biblical allegory seamlessly fits over the Book of Creation's acoustical framework, as we compare figures 15b and 15c. To simply apply the textual layer of biblical allegory over Abraham's acoustical layer may initially seem a bit forced, but I can promise that this process will make more and more sense as we progress through a detailed analysis of all Seven Days of Creation.

> *In the Biblical allegory of the third day, we read:*
> *God said, "Let the waters beneath the heaven be gathered into one area, and let the dry land appear." And it was so. God called to the dry land: "Earth," and to the gathering of the waters He called: "Seas." And God saw that it was good. God said, "Let the earth sprout vegetation: herbage yielding seed, fruit trees yielding fruit each after its kind, containing its own seed on the earth." And it was so. And the earth brought forth vegetation: herbage yielding seed after its kind, and trees yielding fruit, each containing its seed after its kind. And God saw that it was good. And there was evening and there was morning, a third day.*[201]

On the third day, God gathers the waters together into one place and "*dry land*" appears in the upper octave, while the "*seas*" are gathered into the lower octave (see Figure 18). The earth then, "*brought forth* [two types of] *vegetation: herbage yielding seed after its kind, and trees yielding fruit, each containing its seed after its kind.*" Within the context of Abraham's approach, the two types of means: arithmetic and harmonic, can be understood as the vibrational essence for the two types of vegetation. We can see from the rising and falling triple progression how both means can be created around the D. However, within the two adjacent octaves (3:6:12) that define the upper and lower spiritual waters,

201 *Chumush*, Genesis 1:9-13.

it is possible to calculate a whole-number harmonic mean of 4 in the lower octave (3:6), but since there is no room for a whole-number arithmetic mean, the Book of Genesis somewhat arbitrarily chooses to move both means to the higher octave. The biblical text tells us there are two types of vegetation that grow in the earth, even though it would be mathematically possible to also plant one type of vegetation in the seas.

The principle of procreation is expressed in the biblical passage: *"each containing its seed after its kind."* Training in the ancient Quadrivium informs us that the "genetic" principle of musical string theory uses only prime numbers to generate musical tones around the tone circle. In other words, all compound numbers must be reduced to smallest factors in order to gauge their true musical value. We may recall that larger numbers provide us with more space on the tone circle to squeeze in all sorts of different tones. For example, to squeeze an integer between the endpoints of ratio 1:2 is impossible, but raising the ratio's numerosity to 6:12 retains the fundamental ratio of 1:2, while giving us the flexibility to insert harmonic and arithmetic means (8 and 9, respectively). You might say that the larger numbers cover or disguise the smallest factor (genetic) ratio, but they also provide us with greater possibilities for the creation of new tones.

As we can see from the overview diagram, the acoustics for the Creation allegory of Genesis on Day 3 takes place across two octaves 3:6:12, which is a higher numerosity extension of God's separation into the upper and lower spiritual waters on Day 2.

> **2.4** *Twenty-two Foundation letters*
> *He Placed them in a circle*
> *like a wall with 231 Gates.*
> *The Circle oscillates back and forth.*
> *A sign for this:*
> *There is nothing in good higher than Delight*
> *(Oneg - ג נ ע)*
> *There is nothing evil lower than Plague (Nega - ע נ ג).*

In Stanza 2.4 of the Book of Creation, Abraham provides a self-checking riddle, presumably intended to tell us if we're on the right track as we begin to generate tones around the tone circle: A circular rotation of Hebrew letters within the word "Delight" yields its opposite: the word "Plague." The three letters can be used to describe the proximity to God.

With the phrase "*A sign for this*," Abraham is suggesting that we are on the right track acoustically if our various rotating oscillations around the tone circle of God's heavenly firmament for the arithmetic and harmonic means also cycles the letters of the tones produced.

On Day 3 we generate arithmetic and harmonic means using the number 3. In terms of wavelength, the triple progression generates an A ascending to God along the x axis and a G descending from God along the y axis. However, if we reverse our approach, and change terms of wavelength to terms of frequency then 1/3 the string length (=A) would turn into 1/3 the frequency (=G). In other words, the G would now be generated descending from God along the x axis while an A would be generated ascending to God along the y axis. It would reverse the pitch's letter names as well as the direction to/from God. Ascent toward God (Delight) would now become descent away from God (Plague) along the axis of the 231 Gates table, as well as around the tone circle. This cycling of letters and directions constituted Abraham's criteria for a self-check.

The Three Mothers

The acoustical principle of "opposites and the mean," otherwise known as the harmonization process, forms a superset of "threeness," that extends beyond the specific creations of Day 3. God imposes this superset over all of Creation; therefore the remainder of this chapter will need to provide a preview of some of the more advanced acoustical concepts that will be covered in later chapters on Days 4, 5, 6 and 7, but all from the perspective of "threeness."

The basic mathematical principle of opposites and the mean forms the primordial "stuff" that God uses to fashion Creation. The Book of Creation calls this balanced set of primordial elements the *Three Mothers*: air, water and fire.

> **3.4** *Three Mothers, AMSh (אמש),*
>   *in the universe are air, water, fire.*
>   *Heaven was created from fire*
>   *Earth was created from water*
>   *And air from Breath decides between them.*

Over the next several days of Creation, God, symbolized by the note D at the apex of the circle, can be considered the midpoint or mean of all the other notes, which will wax and wane around it. The note D therefore corresponds to the *"air from Breath [that] decides between them."* God's Heavenly Firmament is the octave tone circle, which provides the acoustical context to separate the rising spiritual waters of "fire" from the falling spiritual waters of "water." The three primordial elements – air, water and fire –will become the ethereal, vibratory essence of all objects and beings. Air, water and fire are three of four primordial elements within the ancient world. Earth, the fourth element, is not included among them, because the Book of Creation focuses on the spiritual realm of the Three Mothers, and its vibrational structure, rather than its dense earthly reflection in the physical world.

The *Three Mothers* provide us with three "gates" (*AMSh* אמש), locating where the three primordial elements can be found on the 231 Gates table. They define the first, middle and last "gates" of the table. Once we learn to find and open these gates, we have positioned ourselves at the beginning of three well-worn paths to God; the same paths traveled by the great prophets. We must learn exactly how our mind, body, and soul can partake of this "fruit of the Tree of Life" in order to begin our migration toward God. The paths themselves are the specific vibratory paths of the primordial elements of air, water, and fire. They are not audible musical scales, but they do serve as vibrational paths for our meditative consciousness.

As we construct these three musical scales, we will learn to construct the necessary subsets of Abraham's divine light matrix of 231 Gates and 462 Paths. These three paths are necessary components for the meditator to master in order to travel the return path to God and Paradise. Although it sounds very complicated — and fully understanding it all is complicated — when all is said and done, anyone can be taught Abraham's practice. Ultimately, the practitioner will learn to ascend and descend the seven heavens facilitated by these three paths.

The gate to the first row of the 231 Gates table (*Alef* א) leads to the construction of the musical path that corresponds to the mastery of the element air; the gate to the middle row of the table (*Mem* מ) leads to the construction of the musical path that corresponds to mastery of the element water; while the gate to the final row (*Shin* ש) leads to the construction of the musical path that corresponds to the mastery of fire.[202]

It is important to remember that we are talking about elements that exist within us, and that need to be understood and mastered as they exist within us. Of course, sound and the primordial elements exist in the physical world, but they manifest in unique ways within the inner world of body, mind and soul. Abraham is not suggesting that we start playing with matches to learn about fire. His writings, and the writings of Scripture, need to be understood as mathematical allegory, and must be interpreted within the context of the ancient Quadrivium. Just as God can be said to live within us as our soul, so does Heaven and Hell exist as the soul's dwelling place — within — perhaps in other dimensions of reality that we are not yet aware of. The primordial elements, therefore, need to be harmonized within us, in order to learn how to pray in the manner of the prophets.

Uncovering the Three Mothers

Abraham's riddle of the *Three Mothers* holds the key that will enable us to solve a *great mystical secret* that has been deeply encrypted and inaccessible through the centuries. Solving that riddle is crucial to our understanding of the Creation process:

> 3.2 *Three Mothers: Alef Mem Shin (אמש)*
> *A great mystical secret*
> *covered and sealed with six rings*
> *And from them emanated air, water and fire*
> *And from them are born Fathers,*
> *and from the Fathers, descendants.*

---

202 It is interesting to note a similarity of the Three Mothers (אמש) with the Hebrew word for truth (אמת) with a difference of only the last letter being exchanged for the second to the last letter (to accommodate the 231 Gates table). A classic rabbinical interpretation of the word truth (אמת) encompasses Time with the beginning, middle, and end corresponding to the first (א), middle (מ), and last (ת) letters of the Hebrew alphabet.

3.3   *Three Mothers: Alef Mem Shin (אמש)*
He engraved them, He carved them,
He permuted them, He weighed them,
He transformed them,
And with them He depicted
Three Mothers AMSh (אמש) in the Universe,
Three Mothers AMSh (אמש) in the Year,
Three Mothers AMSh (אמש) in the Soul,
male and female.

The *Three Mothers* are a *great mystical secret covered and sealed with six rings.* Numerically, *Alef Mem Shin (אמש)* translates to 1, 40 and 300, and they can be located on the y axis of the 231 Gates table as the gate to the first, middle and last rows. Once we have solved the riddle, the first gate will open to reveal the Air (or Wind) Path to God; the second gate will open to reveal the Water Path; and the third gate will open to reveal the Fire Path.

Our musical perspective informs us that the expression *six rings* relates to the musical tone circles formed by God's Ten Utterances. However, the question still remains that if God corresponds to the number 1, and His Ten Utterances include the numerals 2, 3, 4, 5, 6, 7, 8, 9, 10 and 20, then why does Abraham only speak about six rings and not ten? What are the six tone circles in question?

The Torah and kabbalistic tradition provide us with the answer. They tell us that God's Ten Utterances (the Kav) created the world in six days,[203] and God rested on the seventh. If the six days of Creation creates the limiting subset we are looking for, then the musical tone circles created by the first six integers would account for the *six rings* in question. Levarie and Levy offer evidence that favors this approach:

> The first six numbers are known as the senarius. There is a special formative power inherent in the senarius — a force that sets limits and thereby shapes the given elements... Crystallography operates primarily with ratios based on the senarius. Snowflakes that deviate from the norm of the hexagon are rare exceptions. The senarius becomes manifest again and again in affinity calculations of chemical elements,

203 Zalman, 287.

in chromosome numbers, in plant structure, et cetera. The number of faces, edges, and vertices of the five regular polygons, which are the perfect forms in three dimensional space, are all determined by senaric values.[204]

Now that we have some idea of what the six rings are, we need to discover how they *cover* and *seal* the *great mystical secret* of the Three Mothers.

The mathematical disciplines of the Quadrivium inform us that musical tones can only be generated by prime numbers. One way to conceal or "cover" numbers that correspond to musical ratios would be to multiply them against one another to produce a compound number. When we apply this principle to God's Ten Utterances, the subset of prime numbers includes: 1, 2, 3, 5 and 7, while the remaining integers 4, 6, 8, 9, 10, and 20, are all compound numbers that would not be able to generate a new tone during God's creation process. Since God rested on the seventh day, only the first six rings were used by God during the Creation process. The seventh prime number tone circle was therefore not used as a tone generator to create new objects or beings on the Sabbath. When we "uncover" the prime factors of the Three Mothers: 1, 40 and 300, we get the following:

- $1 = 1$
- $40 = 2^3 \times 5$
- $300 = 2^2 \times 3 \times 5^2$.

This result corroborates our thinking thus far, since the genetic material produced: 1, 2, 3, and 5, are prime number tone generators that fall within the range of senaric values (six rings) used by God during the Creation process. The next question we must ask is whether the Three Mothers "gave birth" to these four Fathers?

Of these prime numbers we know that God's number (1) is the Father of all tone circles, and could not be considered one of the Fathers born of the Three Mothers. We also know from Day 2's construction of the Heavenly Firmament, that powers of 2 are associated with female octave doubles. The prime number 2, therefore, appears to function as the lone female born to the Three Mothers, along with male *Fathers,* 3 and 5. It is significant to note that this riddle provides us with a single

---

genetic female to procreate with two genetic males to produce the next generation's "descendants."

Even with two males and a female ready to procreate the next generation, there is still a problem. Since the first six utterances of God are discrete and transcendent tone circles, i.e., the *six rings*, the riddle tells us they need to be *unsealed* before they can harmonize with one another to procreate musical descendants. Unsealing the rings is metaphor for reordering (*Tikun*) the divine light within the acoustical constructions of Day 2 through Day 6, to harmonize all musical ratios created by tone circles 2, 3 and 5.

On the Sabbath, we have already established that the prime number 7 does not generate any new tones during the Creation process. However, in the chapter on Day 7 we will see that multiplication by the numeral 7 does raise the numerosity of the Day 6 Water Path, transforming it into Day 7's Fire Path. Use of the prime number 7 is therefore limited, but it still plays a very significant role during the Creation process. Since only three male number primes — 3, 5 and 7 — can generate (or in the case of the number 7 "raise the numerosity of") musical *descendents*. Each of them are considered Fathers (although the number 7 might be better characterized as a foster father) and each is identified with a tone circle representing one of the primordial elements: air or wind (powers of 3), water (powers of 5), and fire (powers of 7). We will see this verified in the Book of Ezekiel, where woman's number (2) corresponds to the primordial element earth. The four "wheels of Ezekiel" are the tone circles: 2, 3, 5 and 7, representing the four primordial elements.

The Seven Doubles

4.1 *Seven Doubles:*
  Bet (ב), Gimel (ג), Dalet (ד),
  Kaf (כ), Peh (פ), Resh (ר), Tav (ת).
They direct themselves with two tongues
  Bet-Bhet, Gimel-Ghimel, Dalet-Dhalet,
  Kaf-Khaf, Peh-Pheh, Resh-Rhesh, Tav-Thav,
A structure of soft and hard,
  Strong and weak.

4.6 *Seven Doubles: BGD KPRT (בגד כפרת) of Foundation*
He engraved them, He carved them,
He permuted them, He weighed them,
He transformed them,
And with them He formed,
Seven planets in the Universe,
Seven days in the Year,
Seven gates in the Soul,
male and female.

Abraham lists the *Seven Doubles* as the numerals 2, 3, 4, 20, 80, 200, and 400. The concept of Doubles has been encrypted within Hebrew linguistics as a sort of double entendre: *two tongues...soft and hard...strong and weak: Bet-Bhet, Gimel-Ghimel, etc.* This duality in linguistic articulation is a perfect metaphor for octave duplication of the tonic note. Abraham's octave Doubles sound the same note, but their 1:2 ratio makes them sound an octave apart.

Once the Three Mothers are located on the 231 Gates table, they are framed by the three sets of octave doubles, all created from female powers of 2. Six of the seven Doubles listed by Abraham in Stanza 4.1 are genetically female (powers of 2), they are: *Bet (ב)* =2; *Dalet (ד)* = 4; *Kaf (כ)* = 20; *Peh (פ)* = 40; *Resh (ר)* = 200; *and Tav (ת)* = 400. These three sets of "female" octave doubles can only generate musical tones and scales with a male seed, and the only male seed included within this list of Doubles is *Gimel (ג)* = 3. Abraham's inclusion of the number 3 as one of the Doubles makes procreation possible once the six rings are unsealed as part of the reordering process. This reordering is described in Stanza 4.6.

On Day 4 of the Torah's Creation allegory, the Book of Creation provides the acoustical "genetics" of how the female octave double (2:4) harmonizes with male powers of 3 to generate the seven vibrations of man's soul. In the next chapter, this construction describes exactly how God carved, permuted, weighed, and transformed the Wind Path as the first of the three paths to God.

The remaining Doubles specified by Abraham provide us with an expanding numerosity for three different sets of octave Doubles that correspond to the three primordial elements. The three sets of octave Doubles are each separated by orders of magnitude (powers of 10). The "female" octave doubles are 2:4 (Wind Path), 20:40 and 40:80 (Water Path), and finally 200:400 (Fire Path). Within the 231 Gates of Table 7, air mediates between the spiritual waters of fire and water as follows:

- Row 1 is the first of the Three Mothers. It was later called the Kav, the "Breath of God," emanating Ten Utterances of *sealed* tonal material that created the universe.
- Rows 2:3:4 – Female octave double 2:4 is unsealed to harmonize with male number 3, creating the tonal material contained within the image of God that is man's soul during Days 1-4 within Pythagorean tuning. The soul rides along this "Wind Path" as it liberates.
- Row 40 is the second of the Three Mothers, containing tonal material for the flow of time and motion that derives from the primordial element water.
- Rows 20:30:40 and 40:60:80 – Two octaves of doubles 20:40 and 40:80 harmonize with male numbers 30 and 60, respectively, to create tonal material for Days 5 and 6, respectively, within "Just tuning," using the prime number "genetics" of integers 2, 3 and 5, incorporating the number 5 on Day 5. "Creatures that moveth" were created on Day 5, and Adam was created on Day 6.
- Row 300 is the third of Three Mothers. It contains the tonal material for Day 7, creating the fires of heaven and hell which include the purifying fires of redemption to cleanse original sin.
- Rows 200:400 – The octave double 200:400 would normally harmonize with male number 300 to create tonal material within "Archytas tuning" based on "genetic" prime number integers 2, 3, 5 and 7. However, because it is the Day 7 Sabbath construction, row Tav (ת) = 400 is omitted from the 231 Gates table. With no octave double, no new tones can be generated from the prime number 7. The already existing Day 6 tones, however, can be used with the prime number 7 as a multiplier to create a duplicate of the Day 6 scale, but with a higher numerosity. The higher vibration of this Sabbath scale enables man to purge sinful impurities from his vibrational essence.

The KAV is Air; the Breath of God on Day 1 ; A harmonic series of sequential integers begins to get reordered on Day 2.

The image of God later known as Supernal Man generated by Pythagorean Tuning and descends into matter from Days 2 through 4

Differentiating time "flowing like water" as well as defining all "moving creatures" within Just Tuning during Day 5 and Adam on Day 6

The fires of heaven & hell; sin and redemption within a modified Archytas Tuning

Harmonic Progression ⇒

Arithmetic Progression ⇒

	1	2	3	4	5	6	7	8	9	10	20
AIR1	1	2	3	4	5	6	7	8	9	10	20
2	2	4	6	8	10	12	14	16	18	20	40
3	3	6	9	12	15	18	21	24	27	30	60
4	4	8	12	16	20	24	28	32	36	40	80
5	5	10	15	20	25	30	35	40	45	50	100
6	6	12	18	24	30	36	42	48	54	60	120
7	7	14	21	28	35	42	49	56	63	70	140
8	8	16	24	32	40	48	56	64	72	80	160
9	9	18	27	36	45	54	63	72	81	90	180
10	10	20	30	40	50	60	70	80	90	100	200
20	20	40	60	80	100	120	140	160	180	200	400
30	30	60	90	120	150	180	210	240	270	300	600
WATER40	40	80	120	160	200	240	280	320	360	400	800
50	50	100	150	200	250	300	350	400	450	500	1000
60	60	120	180	240	300	360	420	480	540	600	1200
70	70	140	210	280	350	420	490	560	630	700	1400
80	80	160	240	320	400	480	560	640	720	800	1600
90	90	180	270	360	450	540	630	720	810	900	1800
100	100	200	300	400	500	600	700	800	900	1000	2000
200	200	400	600	800	1000	1200	1400	1600	1800	2000	4000
FIRE300	300	600	900	1200	1500	1800	2100	2400	2700	3000	6000

Table 8 – Three Primordial Elements in Four Articulations

Three gates are opened to construct the three paths to God: the Air, Water, and Fire Paths. They are fashioned from the acoustical material that derives from the rows indexed by the *Three Mothers*: row *Alef (א)*, row *Mem (מ)*, and row *Shin (ש)*. We can see all this detail in Table 8.

The Book of Ezekiel within the Hebrew Scriptures provides additional insights into the genetic material of Abraham's great mystical secret. The most graphic biblical description of Abraham's acoustical constructions occurs in the Book of Ezekiel. Ezekiel visions also become the basis for the Book of Revelation in the New Testament. Ezekiel describes his vision of the Divine Presence as a chariot pulled by four creatures, each creature had four wings, four faces (ox, human, eagle and lion), and a wheel (see book cover):

> *I saw one wheel on the ground next to each of the four faced creatures... the appearance and structure of each was as of two wheels cutting through each other... The spirit of the creatures was in the wheels.*[205]

Figure 22 – The Wheels of the Spirit

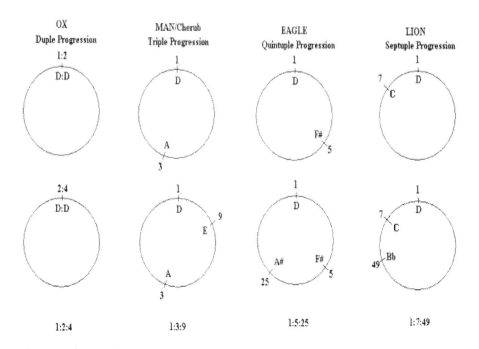

The nature of the wheels suggests that the four "wheels" containing the spirit of God are the four prime number tone circles that we have uncovered and unsealed from the six rings, prime factors 2, 3, 5 and 7. On Day 4 of Creation we will show the first of God's acoustical constructions resemble "two wheels cutting through each other," as described in the previous reference to the Book of Ezekiel. This first path to God, the Air Path (or Wind Path), consists of two wheels that correspond to powers of 2 and powers of 3. These two tone wheels, viewed from the side, pair up and "cut through" each other both mathematically and musically (Figures 23 and 32a). This construction has been identified in the history of music theory as Pythagorean tuning, because up until now, Pythagoras was believed to be the first to use it. Pythagorean tuning, based on powers of 2 and 3, creates what is called the Greek Phrygian (or modern Dorian) mode. The Phrygian mode is the path that brings us closest to God because it defines the image of God that becomes man's soul.

Figure 23 - Ezekiel's Wheelworks

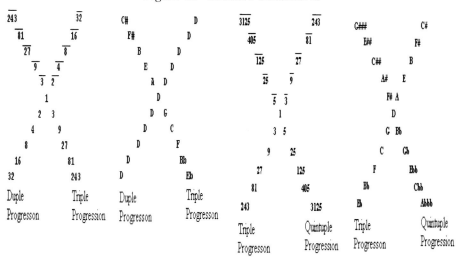

Before we can open up the *Alef* gate and begin to pray along the Wind path that unites our soul with God, we must first open the *Mem* gate and enter the Water Path of our daily prayers. If the essence of man's soul is based on harmonizing powers of 2 and 3, then the compound number 6 can be thought of as a blending of musical tones into the "chord" of man's soul. Man's harmonized soul forms a compound single wheel that is now capable of "cutting through" the next prime number wheel: powers of 5. This musical construction has been known throughout music history as Just tuning. It consists of powers of the prime numbers 2, 3 and 5, resulting in the construction of a diatonic scale on Day 5 that became the essence of all "creatures that moveth," and a chromatic scale on Day 6 that became the vibrational essence and sustenance of man's body as the container of his soul. Our daily prayers along the Water Path will enable us to send God's light throughout all aspects of our mind, body, and soul to balance our mind, and harmonize our body and soul.

The final tuning system and musical scale that God uses to engrave Creation requires us to open the *Shin* gate. In addition to our daily prayers along the Water Path, we must also say our Sabbath prayers along the Fire Path. Abraham tells us that God created the heavens with the primordial element of fire. The Fire Path is Sabbath prayer that will enable us to atone for our sins by purifying our mind, body, and soul. Fittingly, the compound, harmonized wheel, containing the powers of 2, 3 and 5, "cuts through" the Sabbath wheel, which corresponds to powers of 7, in order to construct what I call a modified Archytas tuning.[206] To remain consistent with the Sabbath, the Day 7 scale produced must not contain any new tones. It uses the very same tones created by Just tuning, raised however, to a higher numerosity that brings it into the frequency range of fire. In Figures 15b and 15c we can see that every vibration within the Just tuning chromatic scale of Day 6 has been multiplied by 7 to a higher numerosity, to form the vibrational frequencies of the Fire Path.

In summary, the *Three Mothers*: 1, 40 and 300, "give birth" to Three Fathers: 3, 5, and 7. Man's soul (2 x 3) stays dormant within until man first learns to radiate his body (2 x 3 x 5) with the divine light of the crown (5) through daily prayer. But man was also created with the unique ability to atone for his sins on the Sabbath (2 x 3 x 5 x 7). And although the number 7 does not generate any new tones, it is considered the fourth wheel of Ezekiel because it raises the numerosity of one's daily prayers. It transforms them from a Water Path into a Fire Path that will better enable us to balance the water and fire elements within us, ultimately enabling us to liberate our soul.

The Four Wheels of Ezekiel include: powers of 2 (the ox), 3 (man), 5 (the eagle) and 7 (the lion). These four tone wheels have all the acoustical components necessary to begin constructing our three tuning systems and

---

206 After Plato's friend Archytas. Without this modification, Archytas tuning would result in 18 new tones, and would be inappropriate on the Sabbath.

the musical scales (descendants) created by those tuning systems become the meditation paths that lead us to God.

Each path designates a sophisticated meditation technique that will be explained in detail later. These techniques empower us to master the elements of air, water, and fire that currently mix in an unharmonized fashion within us, but once these elements are harmonized by following Abraham's practice we will learn to bind our mind, body and soul to God. An excerpt from Stanza 1.6 in the Book of Creation states:

> *Ten Sefirot of Nothingness...*
> *And His word in them is "running and returning"*
> *They rush to His saying like a whirlwind*
>   *And before His throne they prostrate themselves.*

The Three Fathers spin their tones within the octave doubles of the Three Mothers, both *"running and returning...They rush to His saying like a whirlwind, And before His throne they prostrate themselves."* When this process is complete we will have constructed all the tones necessary to *permute* the numbers and *weigh* the tonal ratios that enable God to *engrave* and *carve* the multitudes of Creation. The precise musical calculations that fill in the details of Abraham's great mystical secret will be examined in detail as we progress through our explanations of the remaining days of Creation.

Solving the riddle in Stanza 3.2 has given us a glimpse of the meaning of "threeness," and how it applies to balancing the three primordial elements within us, via three paths that will ultimately lead us to God. As we continue to decode Abraham's riddles we will gain a better understanding of the Torah's creation process. We have just scratched the surface of Abraham's secret practice, however, it is important to have an overview of the three primordial elements and how the Wind Path was constructed on Day 4; the Water Path on Days 5 and 6; and how the Fire Path was constructed on Day 7. In the next chapter we will explore how Abraham's writings provide the mathematical framework for the Torah's Creation allegory on Day 4.

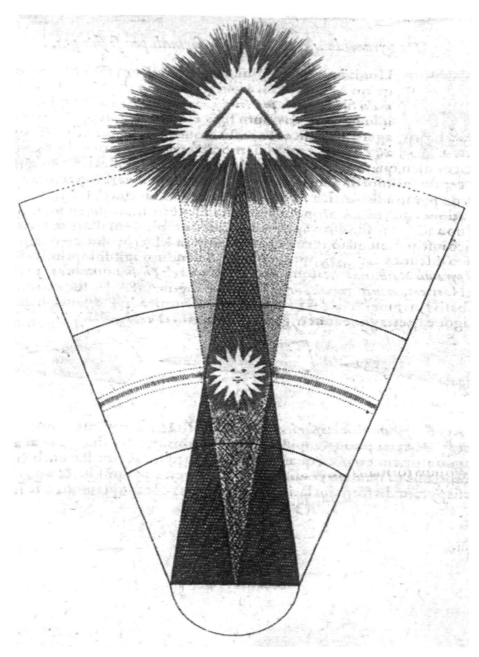

Figure 24 - Threeness in the Universe
(Robert Fludd: utriusque cosmi)

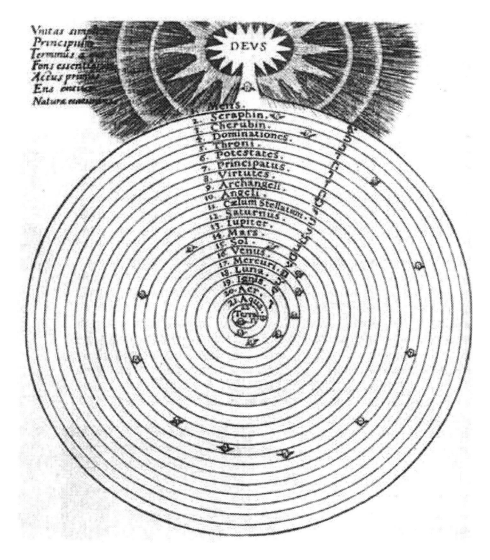

Figure 25 – God fixed the Luminaries in the Firmament
(Robert Fludd: utriusque cosmi)

The Fourth Day of Creation

Sacred Geometry & Astronomy

T he fact that integers could be used to describe something as natural and invisible as sound seemed to the ancient mind to be the hand of God at work. As a result, integers were applied to other unseen phenomena, such as light and time. Time and the calendar manifest as a function of astronomy, one of the four mathematical disciplines of the Quadrivium:

> *God said, "Let there be luminaries in the firmament of the heaven to separate between the day and the night; and they shall serve for signs, and for festivals, and for days and years; and they shall serve as luminaries in the firmament of the heaven to shine upon the earth." And it was so. And God made the two great luminaries, the greater luminary to dominate the day and the lesser luminary to dominate the night; and the stars. And God set them in the firmament of heaven to give light upon the earth, to dominate by day and by night, and to separate between the light and the darkness. And God saw that it was good. And there was evening and there was morning, a fourth day.*[207]

In figure 15c, on Day 4, we can see how God created means to harmonize opposites within two octaves (6:12:24), producing an arithmetic mean within the 12:18:24 rising progression and a harmonic mean within 12:8:6 falling progression. In this manner, God brought forth the *"two great lights,"* creating the "greater luminary" of the sun to rule the day and the lesser luminary of the moon to rule the night. The passage from Genesis "...*and the stars"* appears almost as an afterthought, but their inclusion in the same sentence as the sun and the moon suggests <u>a similar origin</u>, i.e., a duplicate set of arithmetic and harmonic means

207 *Chumush*, Genesis 1:14-19.

to create the vibrational essence of the stars. Day 4 "fixes" luminaries in the firmament and integrally links them to cycles of time with the passage *"...and they shall serve for signs, and for festivals, and for days and years."* For a closer look at the astronomy of the Quadrivium, please refer to the Appendix.

The ancient Quadrivium is a multifaceted lens to view Creation. Abraham's arithmetic must also make sense as music, as geometry, and as astronomy. Geometry tells us that two points determine a line, three points a plane, and four a volume. On Day 4 of Creation, addition of the number 4 creates the most fundamental geometric three-dimensional shape, called a tetrahedron. Just as a triangle is the most elemental two-dimensional shape and the basic building block of all other two-dimensional shapes within ancient geometry, the four triangular sides of a tetrahedron form the most elemental three-dimensional shape and can be considered the basic building block of other three-dimensional shapes. Vertices, sides and edges are the structural determinants of geometry. The tetrahedron has four vertices, four triangular sides, and six edges.

Figure 26 – Tetrahedron

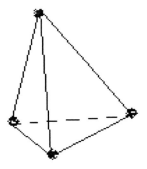

Ancient science put earth at the center of the universe, and it logically became the starting point of Creation. The spiritual essence of everything created on Day 3, including the earth and the seas, was then extended on Day 4 through a greater numerosity, into the firmament of the sky that surrounds and supports it. The triple progression used in Day 3 to create the earth and the seas from the arithmetic and harmonic means echoes into the heavens during Day 4 to create the greater and lesser luminaries: the sun, the moon and the stars. The "threeness" of the triangular divine energy described by "opposites and the mean" extends into matter and then continues to expand into increasingly larger tetrahedrons.

A tetrahedron created by God should not be thought of as a conventional solid that we can touch. It should be thought of in the way that twentieth century architect Buckminster Fuller thought of geometric form: in terms of energy vectors.[208] Fuller formulated his greatest discovery, the geodesic dome, by using the tetrahedron as a building block – he considered it part of "nature's own coordinate system."[209] "What is important to him in the domes is their Pythagorean overtones — the fact that they are tangible, measurable illustrations of laws fundamental to the nature of the universe, of the spread and temper of energy patterns."[210] In creating a geodesic dome one can begin with an icosahedron, a near-spherical surface made of 20 interlocking triangular faces. The vertices of these triangles form a sphere that radiates inward toward the sphere's center, creating 20 interlocking tetrahedrons.

It is the spherical centering of these tetrahedral force vectors that makes the geodesic dome the most stable man-made structure, able to withstand earthquakes, and the only structure that increases in stability with increasing size. Fuller conceived of the geodesic dome as a natural extension of the tetrahedron's geometry, as if he understood the Master-Builder's blueprint for expanding the basic modular unit of three dimensions. In 1985 scientists discovered that the roundest and most symmetrical large molecule then known had the same fundamental symmetry as the geodesic dome and named it the Buckminsterfullerene or "Bucky Ball." This molecule continues to astonish scientists with one amazing property after another. However, before we delve further into three-dimensional geometry, we should take a look at the origins of geometry, and how it first developed within a two-dimensional plane.

Just as counting is said to have evolved from mapping objects to pebbles, geometry is said to have evolved from manipulating small pebbles on the ground to create two-dimensional equilateral arrays. Certain numbers of pebbles could be arranged as triangles, others in squares, pentagons, etc. Here is a brief example of two-dimensional geometry as defined by the Quadrivium:

208 T. Zung, ed., *Buckminster Fuller: Anthology for a New Millennium*, ed. by T. Zung (New York: St. Martin's Press, 2001), 286.
209 Zung, 19.
210 Zung, 40.

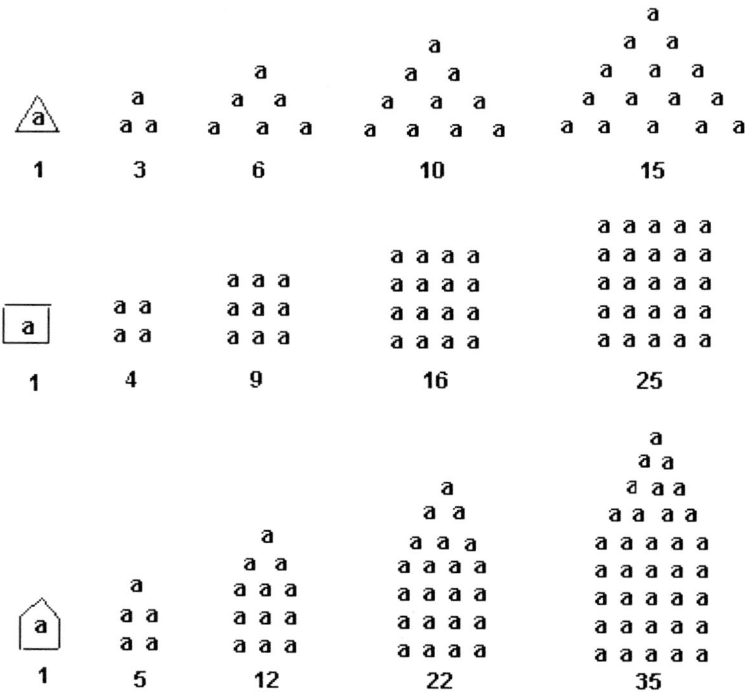

```
                                                              a
                                    a              a   a
                    a           a   a          a   a   a
        a       a   a       a   a   a       a   a   a   a
 /a\    a a     a   a   a   a   a   a   a   a   a   a   a   a
  1      3          6            10              15

                                              a a a a a
                                a a a a        a a a a a
                    a a a       a a a a        a a a a a
        a a         a a a       a a a a        a a a a a
 a      a a         a a a       a a a a        a a a a a
  1      4           9            16              25

                                                   a
                                                  a a
                                        a        a a a
                              a        a a      a a a a
                    a        a a      a a a    a a a a a
           a       a a      a a a    a a a a   a a a a a
 a        a a      a a a    a a a    a a a a   a a a a a
 a        a a      a a a    a a a    a a a a   a a a a a
  1        5         12       22        35
```

Figure 27 – The Geometry of Number[211]

Similarly, three-dimensional space could be arranged as tetrahedrons, pentahedrons, etc. There are only five regular three-dimensional solids, which history has once again attributed to Pythagoras and Plato. They are called the five Platonic solids and include: the tetrahedron, octahedron, cube, dodecahedron, and the icosahedron. Plato associates them with the primordial elements of fire, air, earth, water, and aether, respectively. Based on Abraham's acoustics, however, he would assign the tetrahedron to air, the Octahedron to water, and the icosahedron to fire. The twelve diagonals of the sacred cube, of course, were understood by Abraham to be the "outer light" that contained the expanding "inner light" of God. We will address more about the marriage between acoustics and the geometry of this expansion in a later chapter.

---

211 Nicomachus of Gerasa, *Introduction to Arithmetic,* trans. by M.L.D'Ooge (New York: Macmillan and Company, 1926), Book II, Chapters 8-10, 833-835.

When the two-dimensional triangular array created on Day 3 is extended into matter on Day 4 as a three-dimensional array, it exists along with its inverse, just as every physical entity has its spiritual counterpart. This reflects the rising and falling spiritual waters that derive from the reciprocity of frequency and wavelength.

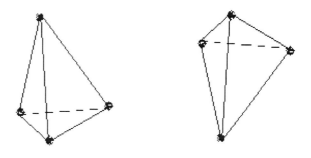

Figure 28a – The Tetrahedron of Day 4

We can then extend this four-pebble tetrahedral structure even further "into matter" by juxtaposing it over the next successive triangular base of six pebbles, to get a ten-pebble tetrahedron.

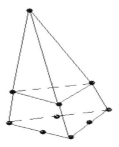

Figure 28b – The Expanding Tetrahedron

The acoustics of this ten-pebble tetrahedron (when taken with its reciprocal) is the image of God that becomes man's soul. Within the Book of Creation, it is the reordered Ten Sefirot of Nothingness, and it is breathed into Adam's nostrils by God on the Sixth Day of Creation. The first three Utterances of the Kav, 1, 2 and 3, which get reordered on

Day 3, correspond to God's number (=1), woman's number (=2), and man's number (=3). The next sequential number of the Kav, the number 4, extends two-dimensional space into three-dimensional space, and continues its decent into matter by absorbing larger triangular bases.

We will soon examine the details of how the first, and most pure of three musical scales born of the *Three Fathers,* is reordered from the Ten Sefirot of Nothingness, to become man's soul. We will also examine how Plato used a slightly different method to arrive at this same musical result in his construction of the World Soul. Although he lived long after the Book of Creation was written, Pythagoras (ca. 570 BCE) has been historically credited for being the father of string theory. However, once the Book of Creation has been demonstrated to be the mathematical framework of all significant allegory within the Hebrew Scriptures, then its author should be properly credited with the origins of monotheistic theology as well as with the origins of string theory. If historians can't be sure that Abraham actually lived, they can be sure that the author of the Book of Creation, whoever it was — and it was a single author — accomplished everything ascribed to Abraham. Therefore, for all intents and purposes, Abraham lived.

Pythagorean Perfection

For Pythagoreans, the limits of God's extension into matter are defined by a point (1), a line (2), a plane (3), and a volume (4). The tuning system used by both Abraham and Pythagoras produces the ten essential vibrations of the soul based on the first four tone generators, i.e., 1+2+3+4=10. These first four tone generators can be marked off on the heavenly monochord. We can refer to figure 29 to illustrate the ratios of string lengths and the musical intervals that derive from the first four integers, 1:2, 1:3, 1:4, 2:3, 3:4. In this diagram we can see how these ratios remain constant as they "extend" into the higher numerosity of the 6:12 octave double on Day 4 of Creation.

If we examine Figure 15c on Day 4 of Creation, we can see how the musical constructions of Day 4 are echoes of Day 3, and include Day 3's 6:12 octave double, but then extend even further into matter within the 12:24 octave double. The ancient Greeks also recognized that 6:12 was the first octave that could contain whole-number integers for both an arithmetic and a harmonic mean. Legend has it that the laws of music were discovered by

Pythagoras, upon hearing the sound of a smith hammering with hammers weighing 6, 8, 9 and 12, forming a diatesseron (perfect fourth) and a diapente (perfect fifth) which harmonize (from the Greek *harmonia*: "fitting together") to form the diapason (octave), regardless of whether 8 or 9 is used as the mean (the harmonic and arithmetic means, respectively). For additional detail about ancient Greek music theory, and the extension into matter from the Greek perspective, please refer to the Appendix. In the passage below, Nichomachus helps us unite arithmetic, music and geometry by pointing out that the number ratios 6:8:9:12 is an example of:

> ...the most perfect proportion, that which is three-dimensional and embraces them all, and which is most useful for all progress in music and in the theory of the nature of the universe. This alone would properly and truly be called harmony rather than the others, since it is not a plane, nor bound together by only one mean term, but with two, so as thus to be extended into three dimensions.[212]

Figure 29 – Day 4 Harmonies

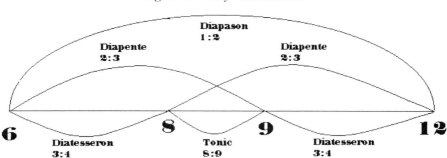

We will examine the acoustical details of how God's light descends into the three-dimensional world for both Abraham and Plato. The focus of both Abraham and Plato was to articulate a theory of Creation based on the mathematical disciplines of the Quadrivium that was consistent with nature, i.e., God's Blueprint for Creation. Both men were also "polarity theorists," who extended tones in a symmetrical fashion around the axis of the Creator in order to construct the vibrational essence of Creation. Plato defines this acoustical construction in his Timaeus, by constructing the "World Soul."

212 Nicomachus, Book II, Chapter 29, 848.

The "Wise Men of Athens"

"In Plato's Timaeus, God begins creation by taking "portions" of primordial space. Plato's Academy "debated the merits of 'taking' his portions in two different ways: (a) exponed in one row (as an arithmetic sequence in scale order), and (b) arranged in the form of a Greek letter lambda, separating the powers of 2 and 3 (leading to a triangular array of integers)."[213] We also know from the Timaeus that these musical ratios were "...bent each around into a circle..." When the Creator constructed the World Soul in Plato's Timaeus, He began by separating powers of 2 and 3 along two legs, to create the shape of the Greek letter lambda. These legs corresponded to the two opposing aspects of the World Soul that needed to be harmonized.

> And he [the Creator] began the division in this way. First he took one portion (1) from the whole, and next a portion (2) double of this; the third (3) half as much again as the second, and three times the first; the fourth (4) double of the second; the fifth (9) three times the third; the sixth (8) eight times the first; and the seventh (27) twenty seventh times the first ...taking the portions of 1, 2, 3, 4, 8, 9 and 27 units...in continued geometric proportion..."[214]

Figure 30a - The Original Portions of the World Soul[215]

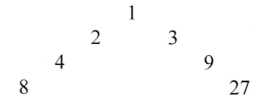

213 Ernest McCLain, *Music & Man,* 343.
214 Ernest McCLain, *Music & Man,* 342; Timaeus 35a-35b
215 McClain, *The Myth of Invariance,* 65; Timaeus 35b-36b.

"Next he went on to fill up both the double and triple intervals" by inserting the arithmetic and harmonic within the original portions.[216] (See *Appendix: Music of the Quadrivium* for a better understanding of mathematical means). Alternatively, one can simply maintain the ratios of the geometric array established between the first three numbers. For example, the left diagonal (/) continues as a geometric array that maintains ratio 1:2; the right diagonal (\) maintains ratio 1:3; while the horizontal (—) maintains ratio 2:3. In a continued geometric array, an element is the geometric mean between adjacent numbers if it forms number pairs of equivalent ratio.[217] The geometric mean between 4 and 9, for example, can be calculated by taking the square root of their product ($\sqrt{4*9} = 6$).

Figure 30b – The Insertion of Means

```
            1
        2       3
      4    6    9
    8   12   18   27
```

Figure 30c - Plato's Chi with Means Inserted[218]

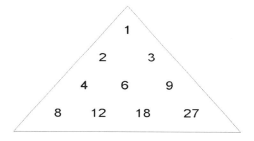

```
1/27  1/18   1/12    1/8          B      E       A          D
   1/9    1/6      1/4              E       A        D
      1/3    1/2                       A         D
         1                                  D
      2      3                           D       G
   4      6     9                     D       G       C
 8     12    18    27             D      G      C        F
```

---

216 McClain, *Music & Man*, 343-344; Timaeus 35a - 35b.
217 See appendix: "The Arithmetic of the Quadrivium" for a more detailed explanation on the various types of mathematical means.
218 McClain, *The Myth of Invariance*, 67.

When taken with its reciprocal the whole fabric splits lengthwise into two halves with the Creator at the center, forming the Greek letter chi (X). As each member of the lambda construction "stands on its essence," this whole fabric splits lengthwise into two reciprocal halves with the "Creator sitting on His base"

The reciprocity of frequency and wavelength in the figure above is consistent with the theme of reciprocity found in Plato's writings, as in his "Dyad of the Great and Small.[219] The seven-note scale produced by this Pythagorean tuning defines Plato's World Soul as the seven vibrations of the Phrygian mode.

Although many scholars still believe that the Book of Creation must derive from the mathematics of Pythagoras. It was Philo of Alexandria, who the Neo-Platonist Church father Clement of Alexandria called "Philo the Pythagorean," who believed that the Jewish teachings were the "summit of philosophy," and he considered Moses the teacher of Pythagoras. As a basis for the approach that Philo used to analyze the allegories of Genesis, he used Plato's description of the "World Soul" in Timaeus, which remained influential throughout Hellenistic times. It is through Dr. McClain's recent work that we understand the acoustical details of the World Soul.

Abraham's Supernal Man

The terms "Supernal Man" and "Adam Kadmon" were both used to reference the configuration of the Ten Sefirot within later kabbalistic tradition. However, until now, the acoustical details of Abraham's reordering of the Ten Sefirot of Nothingness, as well as his methodology for encrypting that configuration have been lost!

Abraham's methodology is very different, but the end result is identical to Plato's acoustical construction within the World Soul.[220] The Book of Creation uses an approach rooted within Hebrew linguistics

---

219 McClain, *Music & Man*, 342.

220 Later Jewish writers, such as Saadia Gaon and Maimonides, can see certain parallels within writings of the ancient Greeks. For example, Maimonides refers to the "wise men of Athens" in his *Guide for the Perplexed*, and specifically mentions the name of Plato's most distinguished pupil, Aristotle.

to derive the same triangular array of ten numbers, taken with their reciprocals, with mathematical means inserted. Abraham, however, calls them the *Three Mothers* and *Seven Doubles*.

This construction is well-cited in later kabbalistic writings, such as the eighteenth-century Chassidic text written by Schneer Zalman of Liadi, founder of the Lubavitch Chassidic sect. Rabbi Zalman's Tanya, gives a recognizable, albeit non-mathematical, account of this construction as one that had been handed down by his kabbalist predecessors. Although the acoustical details had been long lost by the eighteenth-century, the verbal descriptions that Rabbi Zalman inherited clearly reflect Abraham's lambda construction. The Tanya states that "the Sefirot comprise, in general, two extensions – right and left – acting either with forbearance from the aspect of kindness, that is to say, to permit a thing to ascend to G—d, or acting forbiddingly."[221] "According to the Zohar, the two cherubim, which were in the Ark of the Covenant in the Holy of Holies, represent the Sefirot divided into a masculine and feminine array."[222] "All the *Midot* [seven emotions] are either an aspect of *Chesed* (of outpouring and effluence) or of *Gevurah* (of withdrawal and restraint) or an aspect of *Tiferet* (of harmonious blending of the former two aspects)."[223] "Truth [*Tiferet*] is the attribute of Jacob, who is called the 'middle bolt which secures everything from end to end.'"[224]

The Tanya speaks about "three mothers" and "seven multiples."[225] It relates the three mothers to Chochmah, Binah and Da'at — creating the acrostic ChaBaD (another name for the Lubavitch Chassidic sect) which translates to Wisdom, Understanding and Knowledge, respectively. They are called "mothers" because they "give birth to" the seven multiples. However, it is important to recall that the Book of Creation provides us with the original acoustical details and significance of the Three Mothers, which, like most kabbalistic interpretations over the centuries, have been reduced to a shadow of its former meaning and significance.

Use of the word "multiples" is parallel to Plato's lambda construction calling for a "continued geometric array." Maintaining the mathematical ratios that comprise the three mothers implies that the diagonal ratios

221 Zalman, 275.
222 Kaplan, *Sefer Yetzirah*, 36.
223 Zalman, 834.
224 Zalman, 57.
225 Zalman, 9.

(/ and \) of 1:2 and 1:3, as well as the horizontal ratio of 2:3, would be maintained throughout the remaining seven multiples — in a continued geometric array. Mathematical "means" would then harmoniously blend the two opposing legs of the lambda. The Book of Genesis describes God's handiwork on the fourth day as "fixing" the greater and lesser luminaries within the firmament. With the phrase *and the stars,* God's light expands as an extension of musical fifths of ratio 2:3, increasing numerosity but always maintaining the same "genetic" ratio.

To begin Abraham's musical construction, the first gate, *Alef* (א), on Day 1 of Creation, leads us to the first row, which is the *Breath of God,* i.e., the Kav. Since the numeral *Alef* (א =1) corresponds to the transcendent unifying principle of God, it exists within every musical construction. The reordering or "unsealing" of the Kav began on Day 2. After *Alef,* the next sequential gates within the 231 Gates table are the doubles *Bet* (ב =2), *Gimel* (ג =3), and *Dalet* (ד =4).

Figure 31 – Single Digit Doubles and the Day Four Tetrahedron

Doubles
ב = 2
ג = 3
ד = 4

```
              1/4
        1/3   1/2
           1
        2     3
    4
```

We can find the remainder of the necessary tonal material for this lambda within the above subset of the 231 Gates table, as we spell out each successive step of our extension into matter. Since the relationship between any two columns in the 231 Gates table indicates the same geometric ratio, we can extend the 2:3 ratio between man and woman into higher numerosity by reading down the 2 column to 4 and then look immediately to its right to find the number 6 in the 3 column. We also know that 4:6 retains the geometric ratio of 2:3. If we continue to slide further down the 2 column to 6, and look immediately to its right, we see 6:9. This completes the third row of the lambda construction as the geometric progression 4:6:9. We progress down the left leg of the triangle to the next power of 2, the number 8. Maintaining a 2:3 ratio gives us 8:12, then 12:18 and finally 18:27, thus completing the fourth row of the lambda: 8:12:18:27.

Table 9 – Day 4 Subset of the 231 Gates table

AIR 1	2	3	4	5	6	7	8	9
2	4	6	8	10	12	14	16	18
3	6	9	12	15	18	21	24	27
4	8	12	16	20	24	28	32	36
5	10	15	20					
6	12	18	24					
7	14	21	28					
8	16	24	32					
9	18	27	36					

Figure 32a - Reordering the Ten Sefirot of Nothingness

1/27	1/18		1/12		1/8		B		E		A		D
	1/9		1/6		1/4			E		A		D	
		1/3		1/2					A		D		
			1							D			
		2		3					D		G		
	4		6		9			D		G		C	
8		12		18		27	D		G		C		F

Figure 32b – The Ten Sefirot in Three Dimensions

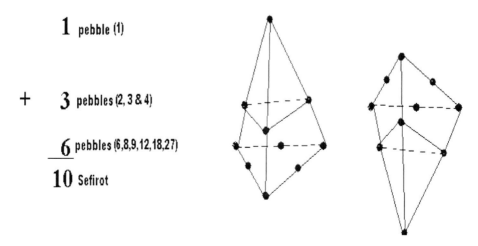

1 pebble (1)

\+   3 pebbles (2, 3 & 4)

6 pebbles (6,8,9,12,18,27)

10 Sefirot

Seven Tones from Ten Sefirot

1.4   Ten Sefirot of Nothingness
ten and not nine
ten and not eleven
Understand with Wisdom
Be wise with Understanding
Examine with them and probe from them
Make [each] thing stand on its essence
And make the Creator sit on His base.

Both Pythagoras and Abraham spent time in Egypt, no doubt learning about Egyptian "unit-fractions." We can see from the 462 Paths table, as well as from Figure 32a, that taking the reciprocal of each ratio can make *each thing stand on its essence.* After taking reciprocals, the denominator of each fraction becomes the number 1, making *"the Creator sit on His base."* The lambda construction, when taken with its reciprocal, creates the Greek letter chi (X) — science's first depiction of divine light. Modern scientists still use the Greek letter lambda to signify a light wave.

The great tenth century sage Saadia Gaon, without understanding ancient string theory, attempted to reconcile Greek and Hebrew interpretations of Creation, and specifically referenced the Greek chi (X) construction.[226] The seven tones generated by this construction can be transposed into a single octave, multiplying or dividing by 2, without changing their tonal value, resulting in a scale practical for use in musical performance — the same scale created by Plato — the Greek Phrygian (modern Dorian) mode. Both Abraham and Plato's methods of construction and encryption of this tuning system can be reduced to what we would today call a musical "circle of fifths" in which each pitch either rises or falls using the geometric progression of ratio 2:3.

Beginning on Day 4 the acoustics of 1, 2, and 3 is ultimately extended into the harmony of man's soul as an image of God. It also serves as the essence of "fixed" luminaries: the sun, moon, and stars, that shed God's light. It is not until Day 5 that the imperfect and movable harmonies of "creatures that moveth" come into existence. And not until Day 6 that Adam's body is constructed to accept the soul defined by God on Day 4.

---

226 Gaon, 51.

As we further examine stanza 1.4, we need to recognize that *Understanding with Wisdom* and *being wise with Understanding* alludes to the mathematical principle of harmonizing divine opposites within the lambda construction. Kabbalistic tradition tells us that the initial occurrence of a thought in its pure, uncluttered form embodies the divine attribute of Wisdom. Pure concept occurs prior to any value judgments and prior to any emotional reaction. Once this initial intuitive thought attempts to resonate with other remaining aspects of our soul, it could get bogged down somewhere in the quagmire of a sinner's emotional reactions; it might also be forgotten or even confused with other thoughts; perhaps it will be colored by preconceptions or misconceptions, etc.

When an intuitive notion is examined from every angle, clarity and a depth of understanding begin to develop. Knowledge (Daat) is acquired by harmonizing the opposites of Wisdom and Understanding.[227] Whereas general knowledge is stored in one's memory for some finite duration of time, the harmonization of Wisdom and Understanding is more profound, and is incorporated into one's soul as eternal knowledge.

The entire process of receiving and processing the initial insights of our soul was first defined by Abraham as the acoustical harmonization of the first three prime integers, 1, 2, and 3, which then reflect into language within philosophic and religious contexts. Stanza 1.4 explains how we must harmonize our Wisdom and Understanding as a basis for relating to the world, and use the resulting Knowledge to ultimately make our way back to God. Once we've achieved the "eternal priesthood," we can "walk with God," and our "three intelligences" (Wisdom, Understanding and Knowledge) can no longer be corrupted by the world in any way.

The sacred practice enables us to harmonize Wisdom and Understanding in a balanced way. In this manner, Enoch and Jesus learned to "walk with God." They completely united with the individual harmonic series that exists within them in order to make their way back to God. It bears repeating, however, that fully realizing one instance of the harmonic series that defines a single soul is not the same as actually becoming the transcendent, omnipresent God; a distinction that belongs only to the universal law that defines the harmonic series itself.

Ten numbers musically generate the seven vibratory aspects of the soul. It is important that we recognize the distinction between ten pure <u>sequential numb</u>ers of the Kav; the ten reordered numbers of Pythagorean

227 Zalman, 829-832.

tuning; and the seven tones that this tuning system generates. When reordering the sequential integers of the Kav into three mothers and seven multiples we leave the realm of pure number. We have simply reordered a specific subset of the Kav into the geometric array defined by Pythagorean tuning. We know that the Ten Sefirot have been unsealed as discrete and separate entities in order to harmonize with one another, moving us from the realm of pure number to the realm of music.

To avoid confusion between the seven tones generated by reordering the Ten Sefirot of Nothingness and the eleven tones generated by the extension of that construction after Adam's sin, we are reminded that the number of Sefirot of Nothingness is *"ten and not nine, ten and not eleven."*[228] We must also take care not to confuse this eleven tone chromatic scale with the twelve vibrational aspects of the body. Stanza 1.4 attempts to ensure that we remain deliberate in our approach to string theory. Only by thoroughly understanding the acoustical details within Abraham's theological context can we be sure to correctly differentiate between six and seven, ten and eleven, eleven and twelve, etc. Without understanding Abraham's use of the Quadrivium it is easy to lose oneself in a sea of numbers. It is precisely for this reason that tradition warns the uninitiated about the dangers of Kabbalah. Abraham's writings provide us with the compass we need to navigate that sea of numbers.

A Comparison of the World Soul and Supernal Man

Without knowing the acoustical details, enough similarities between Greek and Hebrew approaches existed to cause confusion among scholars as to the chronological flow of ideas in the ancient world. Due to a greater familiarity with the work of Plato and Pythagoras, as well as a lack of knowledge about the Book of Creation, many scholars assume that the Book of Creation was written by a Pythagorean or student of the Platonic tradition. However, we will demonstrate that Philo of Alexandria is likely to be correct in his belief that Pythagoras and Plato learned their theology from the Torah, or rather, from the Torah's first patriarch, Abraham.

We will see that the intricate weave of the Bible's allegories around the mathematical framework of the Book of Creation includes even the

228 To add to the confusion, kabbalisitc tradition has added an eleventh Sefirot called *keter* (crown) to the original configuration of Ten Sefirot. We will see, however, that the "crown" takes on a different meaning for Abraham.

earliest Torah allegories, precluding it from having Greek origins. We will study two important examples from the Hebrew Scriptures in great detail: the Genesis allegory, and the Book of Ezekiel. Although Abraham's string theory could not have had Greek origins, there is evidence that it originated as much as 2000 years before Abraham, in ancient Sumer, Mesopotamia, or Egypt. Both Pythagoras and Abraham may have learned their string theory during their sojourns in Egypt, but Abraham would have learned almost 1500 years earlier.

Abraham's central doctrine of "seven circuits around the sacred cube" ties the writing of the Book of Creation directly to the Ka'bah in Mecca. Considering the notion that the cult of the Ka'bah was said to be in existence more than 2000 years before the birth of Mohammed, one could argue that a scientific dating of the Ka'bah might be the best determinant of when Abraham actually lived. Of course, it is doubtful that Muslims would allow this for any number of reasons, not the least of which is the Arab tradition that the Ka'bah is believed to be the original dwelling place of Adam. Another reason it is difficult to date the Book of Creation is that it may have been transmitted orally for centuries before being written down, like the Zohar and the Bahir, which were published in the Middle Ages, but which some believe originated in Talmudic times. The best we may be able to do is conclusively demonstrate that an analysis of the Book of Creation's content provides the mathematical framework for allegory within the Hebrew Scriptures. This would put its date of authorship at sometime before 1000 BCE.

The metaphysics of Eastern religions may also hold some clues to help us better determine the chronology of ancient writings. Traditional Chinese medicine and Chinese Taoism appear to owe a large debt to the Book of Creation. There are very significant parallels, including the specifics of Abraham's three different meditation techniques, as well as the fundamentals of acupuncture. This lends credence to the rabbinical notion that [at least one of] the Eastern religions are an outgrowth of Abraham's "gifts" to the children of his concubines who were sent east. These parallels will be covered in considerably more detail in later chapters.

Figure 33 – Day 5 of Creation

The Fifth Day of Creation

Nature's Imperfection

Within the Book of Genesis, on Day 5 of Creation, God employs the prime numbers 3 and 5 as tone generators. When the tone generator 3 harmonizes with the tone generator 5 there is an unexpected result. If the musical interval of a major third occurring in a quintuple progression is compared with a perfect fifth that occurs in a triple progression, nature suddenly appears to veer off course. According to Western music history, the major third from the quintuple progression was reputed to be discovered as "false" by Pythagoras.[229] In terms of arithmetic, sequences of musical fifths alter the original tone by powers of 3. Sequences of thirds alter the original tone by powers of 5. The following example shows that these progressions don't coincide. The F# in the triple progression is generated by a series of musical fifths,

$$1 - 3 - 9 - 27 - 81$$
$$D - A - E - B - F\#$$

Figure 34a - Triple Progression

while the F# in the quintuple progression is generated by a major third:

$$1 - 5 - 25 - 125$$
$$D - F\# - A\# - C\#$$

Figure 34b - Quintuple Progression

The two F#'s are not "in tune." We can see this more clearly if we transpose the quintuple F# to a higher octave for the purposes of

---

229 Jean Philippe Rameau, *Harmonic Generation*, trans. Deborah Hays (Stanford University: doctoral dissertation 1968), 121.

comparison to get F# = 5 x 2^4 = 80. This will enable us to get a closer look at the differences in tuning between the two F#'s. The F# within the quintuple progression forms a ratio of 80:81 with the F# in the triple progression. A trained musical ear would be able to tell the difference between them. This type of musical imperfection is known as a musical diesis, or comma. The catastrophic discovery of an imperfection within nature had to be dealt with – but how could God or anything made by God be imperfect?

When first learning about this problem Pythagoreans believed it was necessary to avoid it at all costs. Music must stick to the Pythagorean perfection of pure tones produced by the prime factors 2 and 3, which were the tone generators used by Plato to construct the World Soul. The only alternative was to risk damage to one's soul and character and alienation from God. Thanks to Greek influence, the quintuple progression had become equated with sin within the Christian world, thus keeping tone generation restricted to the first four integers of Pythagorean perfection. Offenders were punished in an effort to ensure that polyphony remained within these confines, in order to maintain the *ethos* of the soul and character.

A loosening of the musical reins finally occurred as the interval of the imperfect musical third made its appearance in the English "gymel" as the Renaissance began, while the practice of "fauxbourdon" had carried it to the Continent. In Book II of his chief work *L'Institutioni Harmonie* (1st edition 1558), the music theorist and composer Gioseffo Zarlino illustrates his understanding of the generation of imperfect thirds through the quintuple progressions of "Just" intonation.[230] He was bitterly attacked by the Church for trying to theoretically justify the use of the quintuple progression, even though it had been firmly established in the musical practice of the time. The use of "imperfect" consonances developed into the use of triads, or chords, when two imperfect consonances were stacked together. For example, a major triad is generated by the interval of a major third (4:5), stacked underneath a minor third (5:6), while a minor triad is generated by a minor third (5:6), stacked underneath a major third (4:5). The triad thus became a significant part of the music of the Renaissance and changed the course of Western music.

The Church did not have the advantage of understanding the Book of Creation for the 1000 years that the Church controlled the Western

230 Gustave Reese, *Music in the Renaissance*, rev. ed. (New York: W.W. Norton, 1959), 377.

musical vocabulary. They might not have forbid the use of imperfect consonances if they understood that the Hebrews associated them with the sacred cube and the purification process. Abraham's text developed the quintuple progression as the acoustical centerpiece for the Hebrew metaphysics of sin and redemption, unfortunately, the meaning of the Book of Creation had been long lost.

The unique and elaborate method Abraham developed to isolate the triple progression from the quintuple progression sets the stage for his theology. This acoustical method of isolation became the metaphysical basis for keeping God's creation of man's body distinct from the creation of his soul. The acoustical solution for nature's imperfections assumes that God's light is perfect while containers of divine light are necessarily imperfect. The human body was understood to be an imperfect container of man's perfect inner divinity. The metaphysical concept of a sacred cube was born in order to contain or house divine light. Man's body was crafted by God as a sacred cube to contain divine light just the way a trough contains water.

The sacred cube of the body and the divine light of the soul are two completely separate entities created by two completely different tuning systems. The Pythagorean perfection of the soul was achieved using Pythagorean tuning's prime number tone generators 1 (God's number), 2 (woman's number), and 3 (man's number). The result was a pure seven-tone scale with no musical "commas" or imperfections. These three numbers generated the seven aspects of man's perfect soul as the reordered image of the Ten Sefirot of Nothingness. The second tuning system, Just tuning, used prime-number tone generators; 2, 3 and 5 to create a less-than-perfect product. Generating tones from Just tuning created a sacred cube that would house God's divine light. In this manner, Abraham maintained a separation between the sacred cube's imperfect musical results (a chromatic scale) and the perfect musical results of the soul (the Greek Phrygian/modern Dorian mode). To this day only the octave, fifth and fourth, derived from Pythagorean tuning, are called "perfect" intervals, while imperfect intervals are created through Just tuning.

The Sacred Cube and Its Twelve Elementals

5.1 Twelve Elementals:
Heh (ה), Vav (ו), Zayin (ז),
Chet (ח), Tet (ט), Yud (י),
Lamed (ל), Nun (נ), Samekh (ס),
Eyin (ע), Tzadi (צ), Kuf (ק).
Their foundation is
speech, thought, motion,
sight, hearing, action,
coition, smell, sleep,
anger, taste, laughter.

5.2 Twelve Elementals
HVZ ChTY LNS OtzQ (הוז חטי לנס עצק)
Their foundation is the twelve diagonal boundaries:
The east upper boundary
The east northern boundary
The east lower boundary
The south upper boundary
The south eastern boundary
The south lower boundary
The west upper boundary
The west southern boundary
The west lower boundary
The north upper boundary
The north western boundary
The north lower boundary
They extend continually until eternity of eternities
And it is they that are the boundaries of the Universe

5.3 Twelve Elementals
HVZ ChTY LNS OTzQ (הוז חטי לנס עצק)
Their foundation is [that]
He engraved them, carved them, permuted them,
weighed them, and transformed them,

And with them He formed
    twelve constellations in the Universe
    twelve months in the Year
    and twelve directors in the Soul,
       male and female.

5.6 Twelve directors in the soul
    male and female
the two hands, the two feet,
  the two kidneys,
  the gall bladder, the intestines,
  the liver, the korkeban [stomach],
  the kivah [esophagus], the spleen.

The manner in which the soul's inner vibrations of Ten Sefirot are "housed" within the outer vibrations of the sacred cube's *twelve diagonal boundaries* has been likened to a man wearing a coat. By containing or harnessing the divine sparks of the soul, their containment allows them to be lifted back up to God. It is in this manner that the number 5 can be thought of as the basic tool to contain and lift each of man's divine sparks back up to the Father.

In keeping with its imperfect derivation, a sacred cube is not necessarily a mathematically perfect cube, in which all edges are equal in length, although they certainly can be, but all sacred cubes are considered "harmonic bodies," that exist in a harmonic proportion determined by 6 faces, 8 vertices, and 12 edges.

According to an important Talmudic teaching, Betzalel, who accompanied Moses in the desert after the Exodus from Egypt, "knew how to permute the letters with which heaven and earth were created."[231] "Such esoteric knowledge was required because the Tabernacle was meant to be a microcosm, paralleling the universe, the spiritual domain, and the human body."[232] He was therefore able to build all elements of the Tabernacle in such a manner that it would act as a channel for the spiritual energies of creation. The Tabernacle was the sacred cube called the "Ark of the Covenant," which contained the divine light of the Ten Commandments. Knowing how

231 Kaplan, *Sefer Yetzirah*, 26.
232 Kaplan, *Sefer Yetzirah*, xiv.

to "permute the letters" meant that Betzalel understood the mathematical tables of the 231 Gates and the 462 Paths, and therefore understood the dimensions specified by God necessary to build the Ark of the Covenant into an appropriately sized harmonic cube of 6 faces, 8 vertices, and 12 edges. The spiritual proportions specified by God for the Ark of the Covenant were our familiar musical prime numbers: 2, 3 and 5.

In Exodus 25:10, God gives Betzalel specific instructions on how to build the Ark of the Covenant within the Holy of Holies: *"They shall make an Ark of acadia wood, two and a half cubits its length; a cubit and a half its width; and a cubit and a half its height."* If you create "Egyptian unit fractions" from these dimensions you get 3/2 by 3/2 by 5/2, which should immediately become recognizable from an acoustical standpoint since these are the smallest integer factors of the *Three Mothers*, and exist as a combination of the triple and quintuple progressions within the octave.

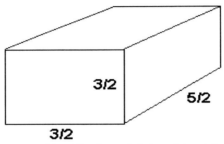

Figure 35 – The Sacred Cube of the Ark

The prime numbers 2 (woman), 3 (man), and 5 (crown) are given as the length, width and height of a scalene cube. It is important to realize that a vessel created by powers of 2, 3 and 5 to contain divine light was itself a vibrational essence and not a physical object. The essence of everything in the physical world that can be seen or touched derives from, and is sustained by, the "outer light" of a sacred cube.

We can see from Stanza 5.2 that the numeral *Heh* (5) is the first of Twelve *Elementals*. The number 5 is the prime-number "genetic" tone generator and is included as one of the *Three Fathers,* 3, 5 and 7. Since God expands outwardly from 1, in the manner of a "Big Bang," God continually radiates His divine energy outward from the center of the sacred cube toward its 12 *boundaries.* These 12 boundaries manifest as the corporeal body's 12 directors. In Stanza 5.6 they are described as: *two hands, two feet, two kidneys, the gall bladder, the intestines, the liver, korkeban, the kivah, the spleen.* Once the soul vivifies the body, the sacred cube that contain the soul's light cannot be completely contained, and light "spills over" continuing on an outward expansion toward its next container, which are the *Twelve Elementals* of action: *speech, thought, motion, sight, hearing, action, coition, smell, sleep, anger, taste, laughter.* Once again, once these vessels become "full," the light spills over to define a series of sacred cubes. In addition to the sacred cube of man's body, divine light spilled over into other sacred cubes, such as: 12 lunar divisions of the solar year that we call months, 12 constellations of the zodiac, etc. Within kabbalistic tradition this "spilling over" of divine light from each successive container came to be known in later kabbalistic writings as the doctrine of *Shevirat Hakelim* (Breaking of the Vessels) and will be explained from a detailed acoustical perspective in a later section.

The acoustical blueprint from which God, the Master-Builder, constructed the human body to house the human soul and contain the divine light has always been a much sought after part of the Blueprint of Creation. The Freemasons believe that mankind once possessed direct knowledge of this blueprint and, like Betzalel, was once able to construct holy places of worship using these architectural proportions to build Solomon's Temple, the Great Pyramids of Egypt, etc. Sacred edifices built from Abraham's harmonic proportions are considered sacred because they are containers of divine light.

Life in the Garden of Eden

God said, "Let the waters bring forth abundantly the moving creature that hath life, and fowl that may fly above the earth in the open firmament of the heaven." And God created the great whales and every living creature that moveth, which the waters brought forth abundantly, after their kind; and every winged fowl after its kind. And God saw that it was good. And God blessed them, saying, "Be fruitful and multiply, and fill the waters in the seas; and let fowl multiply in the earth." And there was evening and there was morning, a fifth day.[233]

233 *Holy Scriptures*, ed. Alexander Harkavy (New York: Hebrew Publications, 1936), Genesis 2:20-23.

The Greeks would call Day 4's creations "fixed tones" and Day 5's creation "moving tones." In other words, the musical intervals of a fifth, 2:3, and fourth, 3:4, are "fixed" tones within the octave, just as the luminaries were fixed in the sky on Day 4. On Day Five, however, the so-called "movable" tones of the scale were created from major and minor thirds of ratios 4:5 and 5:6, respectively. It is therefore appropriate that within Genesis, on Day 5, God *"brought forth abundantly…every living creature that moveth…"* Fish were created from the seas in the lower octave of the Firmament, while birds that *"may fly above the earth"* were created from the higher octave of the Firmament. The Book of Creation contains the original acoustical details for Day 5's *"living creatures that moveth,"* as well as for the creation and flow of time.

God planted a garden in Eden to the East. It was an etheric world of vibrational essence fashioned into innocent "creatures that moveth" along with two important trees to give them shade: the Tree of Knowledge of Good and Evil and the Tree of Life. The two trees correspond to the two tuning systems: Pythagorean tuning and Just tuning, respectively. The first was generated from powers of 2 and 3, while the second was generated from powers of 2, 3 and 5.

In the Tree of Knowledge, the image of God that was built from powers of 2 and 3 is extended through additional powers of 2 and 3 to yield the "forbidden fruit" of good and evil's chromatic tones (the black notes on the piano). These extensions form imperfect thirds with the root (D:F# and D:Bb). The vibrational essence of good and evil therefore derives from the addition of imperfect major and minor thirds, forming imperfect triads within God's perfect octaves, fifths and fourths.

Figure 36 – The Forbidden Fruit

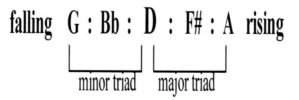

Figure 37 – The Tree Knowledge of Good and Evil

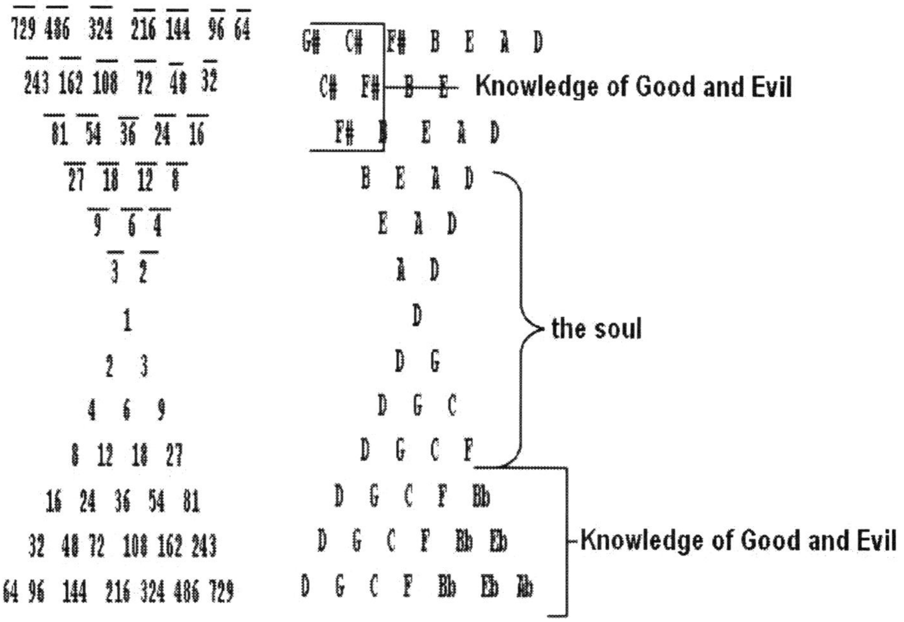

The opposing triangles depicted above became the Creation allegory's Tree of Knowledge of Good and Evil, with upper branches spreading out above, and roots spreading out below. The tones furthest away from God, the Ab and G#, are not the same tones as the Ab and G# on the piano. In a world with no imperfections, as simulated by the piano's equally tempered tuning, they would be the same note. However, nature's integers leave a gap between Ab and G# that was considered the personification of evil, the "diabolus in musica" within the Middle Ages. But how could that be? Pythagorean tuning was supposed to be a pure tuning system with no tonal imperfections. But the perfection of Pythagorean tuning was made possible only by limiting the extension of the triple progression into matter, which is why Adam was safe as long as he followed God's instructions. The structure of the Tree of Knowledge of Good and Evil reveals that God's light descended into matter through additional powers of 2 and 3, into the depths of evil.

This imperfection is known as the "Pythagorean comma" by music theorists, because Pythagoras was believed to be the first to discover it. It is interesting to note that through the centuries the *mark of the beast* has always been understood to be three sixes (666). We can see that this is a misreading of what is actually 3 to the sixth power ($3^6 = 729$).[234]

Figure 38 – Triple Progression

Ab	Eb	Bb	F	C	G	D	A	E	B	F#	C#	G#
729	243	81	27	9	3	1	1/3	1/9	1/27	1/81	1/243	1/729

Figure 39 - The Evils of the "Twelfth Spoke"

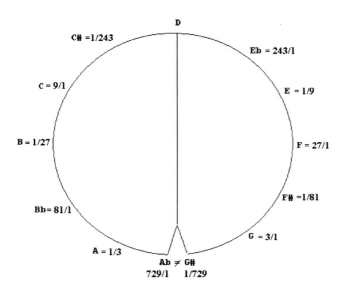

The Tree of Life was placed at the center of the Garden, right next to the Tree of Knowledge of Good and Evil. On Day 5, the Tree of Life would generate sacred cubes containing divine light, and fashion it into *creatures that moveth.* On Day 5 there was only the peace and innocence of creatures, moving beneath the shade of the two trees, in a garden planted by God, surrounded by the birds in the air and the fish in the seas.

The Tree of Life was created from the prime integers 3 and 5. Abraham's explanation for the discrepancies between the triple and quintuple progressions became the basis of his theology. The quintuple progression defining God's imperfect "outer light" contained the pure "inner light" of the triple progression.

---

234 McClain, The Myth of Invariance, 117; We have already learned that the devil's "horns" should be read as "rays" of light, to correct the mistranslation of the root קרן.

The Tree of Life harmonized the goodness of perfection with the evils of imperfection. Learning that there is a way to disentangle man from imperfection became the driving force behind spirituality.

Figure 40 - The Tree of Life

```
15625  9375  5625 3375 2025 1215 729        B###  D###  F##  A##  C##  E#  G#

    3125 1875 1125 675 405 243               G###  B##  D##  F##  A#  C#

       405  375  225  135  81                   E##  G##  B#  D#  F#

         125   75   45   27                        C##  E#  G#  B

            25   15   9                               A#  C#  E

              5   3                                     F#  A

               1                                         D

              3   5                                     G    Bb

            9   15   25                               C   Eb  Gb

         27   45   75  125                         F   Ab  Cb  Ebb

      81  135   225 375 405                      Bb   Db  Fb  Abb  Cbb

   243  405  675 1125 1875 3125               Eb  Gb  Bbb  Dbb  Fbb  Abbb

 729  1215 2025 3375 5625 9375 15625        Ab  Cb  Ebb  Gbb  Bbbb  Dbbb  Fbbb
```

It would solve one of theology's great mysteries to understand how to differentiate "light from light." In other words, how do we differentiate God's inner light from God's outer light; and can we understand these two types of divine light as characteristics of God. Harmonizing the two types of light is part of God's creation process, but extracting divine light from its container is a bit more complicated. Man returns his divine sparks to God upon his death or it can be done through Abraham's lost practice while still living. Abraham teaches us how to extract the divine sparks of our soul by purifying the sacred cube of our body.

The acoustics of this extraction process became the impetus behind the ritual of animal sacrifice and the "Altar of the Burnt Offering." Abraham's acoustics supplied the rational for how the divine light contained within God's imperfect creatures could be extracted as the "fragrance" of a burnt offering on the "four-horned" altar. The acoustical purification process, explained in full acoustical detail within the next section, will provide the transcendental meaning and purpose of the "Altar of the Burnt Offering" within the Holy of Holies.

Altar of the Burnt Offering

1.3   *Ten Sefirot of Nothingness*
         In the number of ten fingers
              five opposite five
         with a single covenant
              precisely in the middle
         in the circumcision of the tongue
         and in the circumcision of the membrum

1.6   *Ten Sefirot of Nothingness*
         Their vision is like an "appearance of lightening"
         Their limit has no end
     And His word in them is "running and returning"
     They rush to His saying like a whirlwind
         And before His throne they prostrate themselves.

To solve the riddles of stanza 1.6 we will assume that Abraham is writing from the musical context implied by *running* and *returning* within a tone circle that *has no end*. Another twist to this riddle is the *appearance of lightening*. The first part of the riddle can be summarized as follows: How can a vision of the Ten Sefirot of Nothingness give an *"appearance of lightening"* and be contained in a *limit with no end*, and how can *His Word* somehow be contained within that appearance of lightening? Perhaps we can find some clues within biblical allegory.

Within the Bible there is a repetitive theme of thunder, lightening and the sound of trumpets at crucial moments. For example, it accompanies God's presence on Mount Sinai when Moses was about to receive the Torah. It accompanies Elijah's time with God on Mount Horeb. It is also present in the New Testament's Book of Revelation, heralding the New Jerusalem's descent from heaven. Similarly, in Hindu allegory, the most powerful God, Indra, hurls thunderbolts off Mount Meru (the Eastern version of Mount Sinai). From this we can surmise that the appearance of lightening in these ancient texts is associated with man's contact with

God on that mountain – it is metaphor for ascending to God through deep meditation amidst the turmoil of the practitioner's physiology; until his physiology becomes calm, and the whisper of God can be heard.

We can also find an important clue from Abraham's ancient surroundings. One of the most prominent aspects of the Babylonian/Mesopotamia religion and tradition is the ziggurat. The ziggurat is a stepped tower, which is also a square-based pyramid. Ziggurats were built to reach nearer the heavens. The size and splendor of a ziggurat would show the city and king's devotion to the particular city god being worshipped.

Figure 41 – The Ziggurat

Both the Tower of Babel and Jacob's ladder are considered ziggurats. Whether we are talking about Moses' ascent to the summit of Mount Sinai or climbing Jacob's ladder or the Tower of Babel, we are talking about getting closer to God by "climbing" across the gradations of vibrational frequencies that lead to God. Against the horizon, the jagged edges of the pyramid take on "*the appearance of lightening*" on the mountain, striking the heavenly vibrations to "burn away" all that is impure.

In the following diagram we will apply what can be called Abraham's "ziggurat method" of filtering the genetic material of the Tree of Life (powers of 3 and 5). From this diagram we can also see how the "four-horned altar" purges unnecessary tonal material, leaving the tonal elements of the Day 5 musical scale. What remains within the four-horned altar after its fiery purge is the sanctified essence of sacrificed creatures; the divine sparks can return to God after the sacrificial death liberates them from the imperfections of their container.

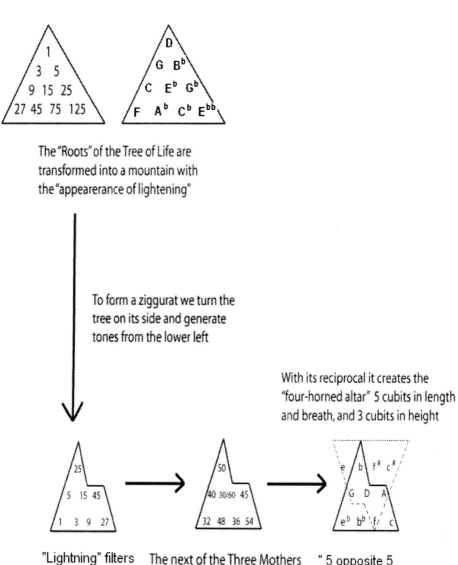

The "Roots" of the Tree of Life are transformed into a mountain with the "appearerance of lightening"

To form a ziggurat we turn the tree on its side and generate tones from the lower left

With its reciprocal it creates the "four-horned altar" 5 cubits in length and breath, and 3 cubits in height

"Lightning" filters smallest integers where $3^q 5^r < 60$

The next of the Three Mothers is 40 which locates the flow of water through octave double 30:60

" 5 opposite 5 with a single covenant precisely in the middle"

Figure 42 – The Ziggurat Method[235]

235 McClain, *The Myth of Invariance*, 141. Adapted from diagrams for Dr. McClain's study of Mesopotamian gods.

The ziggurat method filters out the impure tones generated through Just tuning in order to extract the vibrational essence of all *creatures that moveth*. The pure remnants that remain after filtering and octave reduction i.e., sanctification, is the diatonic scale shown in figure 43. Each octave is once again *engraved* with seven tones of the ascending and descending spiritual waters. However, these are not the same seven tones that define man's soul within the reordered Ten Sefirot of Nothingness. They manifest as the vibratory essence of animals, which include the container's imperfections of major and minor thirds that co-exist with perfect octaves, fifths, and fourths within a diatonic scale:

Figure 43 – Running and Returning Diatonic Scales

30	32	36	40	45	48	54	60	64	72	80	90	96	108	120
D	e	f#	G	A	b	c#	D	e	f#	G	A	b	c#	D
D	c	bb	A	G	f	eb	D	c	bb	A	G	f	eb	D

The ritual of animal sacrifice is just one manifestation of an acoustical sanctification process capable of burning away impurities in order to elevate the divine sparks that remain. We will also examine the sanctification process of man's daily prayers on Days 6 and of man's Sabbath prayers on Day 7. The transcendental purpose of the ziggurat method is to purify the Tree of Life's lambda construction. This acoustics is the encrypted transcendental meaning of sacrifice and salvation that began with God commanding Abraham to sacrifice Isaac, and continued in Christianity with Jesus being crucified on the cross.

We must keep in mind, however, that Adam was not created until Day 6, and he had not yet fallen from grace. Therefore there was not yet a need for redemption, for ritual sacrifice, or perhaps even for prayer. The acoustics of animal sacrifice was considered appropriate to include as part of this chapter because of its juxtaposition to the Day 5 creation of moving creatures. The acoustics of this ritual enables us to isolate the inner light of God's creatures from the outer light of their container, and from the mélange of vibrations within the expanding Tree of Life.

If we were to begin construction on Day 5 of Creation, we would first locate the second Mother (*Mem* מ = 40) in the middle row of the 231 Gates table. The middle gate figures prominently in biblical allegory as the 40 years Israel wandered in the desert; the 40 days of fasting before God spoke to Elijah on Mount Horeb; the 40 days Jesus fasted in the desert before the Temptation, etc. That middle gate opens to the creation of the primordial element of water within the two-octave Heavenly Firmament. The metaphor includes the importance of the Water Path as sustenance to those wandering in the desert for 40 years or fasting for 40 days.

Its first octave is constructed within the 20:40 octave double, "giving birth" to row 30 as the Father, and the second octave is constructed within the 40:80 octave double, "giving birth" to row 60 as the Father. Abraham tells us:

> *And from them* [the Mothers] *are born Fathers,*
> *and from the Fathers, descendants.*

The descendants therefore derive from the two octaves of acoustical material from the Fathers: 30:60 and 60:120. We should keep in mind that the Tree of Life harmonization (called Just tuning) of powers of 2, 3 and 5, maintain these genetic ratios, but are now raised to the numerosity of 30:60:120. The end result is Day 5's Water Path — the very same two-octave diatonic scale depicted in figure 43, that we have already derived from the ziggurat method.

Astronomy and Time

Rows 30:60 of the 231 Gates table contains the range of acoustical material necessary to create time, which flows like the water, in seconds, minutes, hours, weeks, and months. But, Time cannot flow until the fixed luminaries (sun, moon, constellations, etc.) are set in motion. Astronomy is initially defined by setting the fixed configuration of Day 4's sun, moon and stars into motion on Day 5.

If we study the "Time" constructs within Figure 15c, we can see that the 24-hour daily unit is "fixed" on Day 4. It is divided into a daytime and nighttime of 12 hours each, and high and low sea tides of 6 hours each. Once the sun, moon and stars are set in motion, time begins, and its progress is measured by astronomy. The octave double of 30:60 defines (with integer approximations) the number of days in a lunar month; we will see that the solar year is defined on Day 6 as 360 days (plus 5 festival days); the 12 monthly signs of the zodiac indicate the motion of the Sun against the stars over a solar year. Nothing new was created by God on Day 7. However, since the concept of 7 days in a week has no astronomical basis, it appears to have been established by the Book of Creation and then adopted by the Bible and civilization in general. Seven days of the week is therefore structured according to the soul and Abraham's sacred practice.

One final element of time defined by Day 5's musical scale is the lifespan of man. We may recall that the upper bound of the 30:60:120 construction was built by God as 120 "houses" from 5 "stones" – in arithmetic terms, 5 factorial (5!) = 120. "In Solomon's Temple there were 120 'priests who were trumpeters.'"[236] We also find that 120 is the number of years in a man's lifespan as referenced in the following Torah passages;

- Man since he is but flesh; his days shall be a hundred and twenty years[237]
- Moses was one hundred and twenty years old when he died.[238]

Later Kabbalistic Works

An important reference to an alternate acoustical tradition that grows out of the Book of Creation's acoustics, is found within a later kabbalistic source: the *Bahir*.[239] The 72-letter name of God is "unexpectedly combined with the conclusion of the Book of Creation, as if there were a link between the two traditions. The seventy-two magical names are also [said to be] sealed with the name YHWH, much as the six directions of heaven in the Book of Creation are sealed with the name of YHW."[240] The acoustics for the 72-letter name of God *runs* and *returns* with the Day 5 construction for lunar months as follows:

Figure 44 – The 72 Names of God[241]

30	32	36	40	45	48	54	60
144	135	120	108	96	90	80	72
D	e	f#	G	A	b	c#	D
D	c	b♭	A	G	f	e♭	D

236 McClain, *Myth of Invariance*, 125.
237 Genesis 6:3
238 Deuteronomy 34:7
239 Kaplan, *Bahir*, 34-44.
240 Gershom Scholem, *The Origins of Kabbalah*, ed. R.J. Zwi Werblowsky, trans. Allan Arkush (Princeton, NJ: Princeton University Press, 1962, 1987), 100.
241 McClain, *The Myth of Invariance*, 124-127.

A so-called, "new" Kabbalah, began with Isaac Luria, the "Ari" (the Holy Lion: 1534-1572).[242] The Tanya also mentions the importance of R. Luria's contribution: "The doctrine of *Tzimzum* refers to a refraction and concealment of the radiating emanation from the G-dhead, in a number of stages and in a progressive development of degrees, until finite and physical substances become possible. This intricate theory is first treated in detail by R. Isaac Luria."[243] "This is [also known as] the concept of the *Hishtalshelut* (downward gradation) of the worlds and their descent, degree by degree, through a multitude of 'garments'[244] "...by means of cause and effect..."[245] "With Luria these ideas are bound up [not so coincidentally] with his preoccupation with letter combinations as a medium for meditation."[246] It should be clear that the foundation of Luria's doctrine is actually the Book of Creation's acoustics and meditation practice.

A Lurianic concept that derives from Tzimzum is *Shevirat Hakelim* (Breaking of the Vessels), which describes how God's light (*orot*) cannot be contained by its 'garments,' known as *kelim* (vessels). McClain quotes both the Tanya and Scripture, which describe Shevirat Hakelim as encoded both symbolically and acoustically in the word *hovered* (מרחפת).[247] It appears only twice in the Old Testament. In both cases the *spirit of God hovered*. In Genesis 1:2 *The Breath of God hovered upon the face of the waters;* in Deuteronomy 32:11-12:

> *As an eagle stirrith up her nest,*
> *Hovereth over her young,*
> *Spreadeth abroad her wings, taketh them,*
> *Bearth them on her pinions*
> *The Lord alone did lead him [Israel]*
> *And there was no strange god with Him.*

Genesis 36.31 also speaks of eight Kings of Edom who reigned "*before a King reigned over the Children of Israel.*" The *Tanya* references this in its explanation of how Luria's doctrine is embedded in the word hovered. "The

---

242 Scholem, *Kabbalah*, 74.
243 Zalman, 819.
244 Zalman, 163.
245 Zalman, 23.
246 Scholem, *Kabbalah*, 74.
247 McClain, *The Myth of Invariance*, 124-125.

word מרחפת [hovered] divides into two parts, separating the prefix and suffix from the root רחפ, yielding מ"ת and רפ"ח ("died," and the number 288), referring to the death of the kings [eight kings of Edom] and the division of the residue of Divine Light into 288 sparks."[248] After the eight kings "reigned" they "died" causing the 288 divine sparks to fall from the Supernal Realm and extend further into matter. "...these 288 sparks were subdivided into an even greater number of smaller sparks..."[249] Once the King (Yahweh), reigned over Israel, the children of Israel would be empowered to raise their divine sparks back to God.

Within the doctrine of Tzimzum, mankind can raise the divine sparks back up to God by beginning at the bottom of this scale and "reciting" the 72 names of god like a mantra. The scale built from *the subdivision [of 288 sparks] into an even greater number of smaller sparks*, is exactly reciprocal to the Day 5 scale. The Ari was proposing that man's prayer could ascend and descend these reciprocal scales. The Ari's doctrine derives directly from the Book of Creation's Day 5 acoustics.

Figure 45 – Tzimzum and Day 5 as Reciprocals[250]

30	32	36	40	45	48	54	60	64	72	80	90	96	108	120
288	270	240	216	192	180	160	144	135	120	108	96	90	80	72

D	e	f#	G	A	b	c#	D	e	f#	G	A	b	c#	D
D	c	b♭	A	G	f	e♭	D	c	b♭	A	G	f	e♭	D

Acoustically, 288 can serve as an index for a two-octave diatonic scale within Just tuning, yielding 22 chromatic tones when taken with its reciprocal. Luria's "new" Kabbalah derives from the acoustics of Day 5, the scope of which Abraham limited to movement and imperfect containers, such as time, the calendar, "creatures that moveth," and the ritual of animal sacrifice. It is therefore not as powerful as Abraham's Day 6 and 7 theology of man purifying the container of his body in order to liberate the divine sparks of his soul.

---

248 Zalman, 557, 870 fn. 15.
249 Zalman, 868.
250 McClain, *The Myth of Invariance*, 124-127.

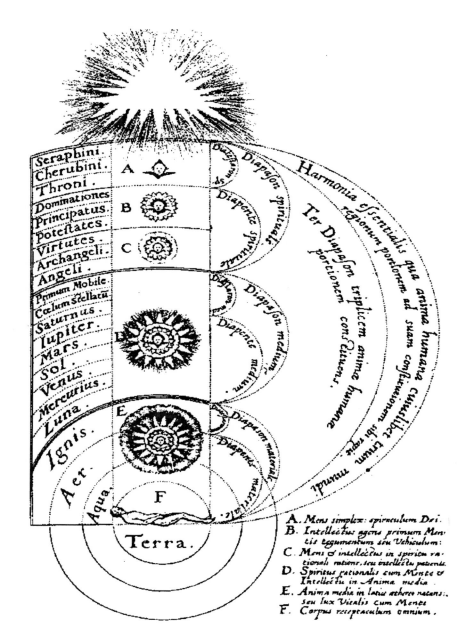

Figure 46 – The Six Tone Circles of Creation
(Robeert Fludd: Man and the World Octave)

The Sixth Day of Creation

Revealing the Lost Word of God

On Day 6 we see a new type of being created, man. On Day 6, God created Adam's body without sin. Due to his purity and unique status as God's most sophisticated creation, Adam was given the task of tending to the two trees that held the secrets of existence. Adam had not yet sinned, and so, had not yet acquired knowledge of good and evil. But we must keep in mind that musical imperfections are built into every container of divine light. The structural fragility of the quintuple progression left Adam vulnerable to sin. Ultimately, he would not be able to contain God's light within the upper realms of heaven. Without the ability to discern good from evil, he disobeyed God, and gave in to temptation. Since his body was no longer able to contain the divine light, he fell from grace. As the vibrations of Adam's soul acquired the impurities of knowledge, he lost his innocence and sacrificed eternal life. He would now have to endure an endless cycle of birth, pain, suffering, and death, until his soul could somehow be redeemed. Adam and his descendents would be in exile, with little hope of salvation. Noah would save the species, but it would be up to Abraham to save men's souls and teach mankind the way back to Paradise. Abraham's instructions to mankind were encrypted in the Word of God.

Thomas Jefferson, John Adams, and Benjamin Franklin created the Great Seal of the United States, found on the back of the dollar bill. The Great Seal uses esoteric symbols to depict what the Founding Fathers believed to be an encryption of God's architectural blueprint of creation within the Holy Tetragrammaton (יהוה = *YHVH*) — known as Jehovah or *Yahweh*, the holiest name of God. Since the inception of Freemasonry, the quest of every Freemason has been to uncover the divine blueprint that is encrypted within the Word, *Yahweh*. Since the time of Solomon's Temple, the Jewish High Priests, as well as the general Jewish population, must say Adonai (אדני) instead of the unspeakable Name.[251] This practice must continue until the true vocalization and transcendental meaning of the ineffable Name is understood in the "world to come."

It will be shown that the Freemasons are correct in their belief that a kabbalistic book exists definitively explaining the transcendental meaning and pronunciation of the Lost Word. What Freemasons never knew is that the book in question is the Book of Creation. The Koran states that Abraham's book may "lead mankind from darkness to the light."[252] One must decide for oneself whether the information presented in this chapter is the true meaning and pronunciation of the Word.

The non-Canonized III Enoch, the "Hebrew Book of Enoch," contains a long discourse on the ascension of the "Celestial Chariot" by Rabbi Ishmael, the last High Priest before the destruction of the first Temple. Understanding this Celestial Chariot (as depicted on this book's cover) requires a detailed understanding of Abraham's entire mathematical system as encrypted in the Lost Word. Only then will we be in a position to discuss the implications of Abraham's teaching.

We can begin this discussion by addressing the six sides of Abraham's sacred cube, which indicate the six spatial directions of God's expanding energy toward the sacred cube's 12 diagonal boundaries. It is Abraham's mathematical metaphor for modern science's "Big Bang":

1.13 He chose three letters
from among the Elementals
[in the mystery of the three Mothers
Alef Mem Shin (אמש)]
And He set them in His great Name
and with them, He sealed six extremities.
Five: He sealed above and faced upward
and sealed it with YHV (יהו).
Six: He sealed below and faced downward
and sealed it with HYV (היו).
Seven: He sealed "east" and faced straight ahead
and sealed it with VYH (ויה).
Eight: He sealed "west" and faced backward

251 It must be said that even God's name Adonai (אדני) is not to be uttered in vain. The point to be made here is that when praying and reading יהוה one pronounces Adonai.
252 Koran 14:1.

and sealed it with VHY (והי).
Nine: He sealed "south" and faced to the right
and sealed it with YVH (יוה).
Ten: He sealed "north" and faced to the left
and sealed it with HVY (הוי).

In the excerpt below (see Stanza 2.5, page 30), the Book of Creation verifies the Freemason belief that one Name emanates all of Creation:

> *... It comes out that all that is formed*
> *And all that is spoken*
> *emanates from one Name.*

In Stanza 1.13, Abraham tells us how to extract an important acoustical subset from God's Great Name. *"He chose three letters from among the Elementals ... He set them in His great Name,"* YHVH (יהוה). *The* three Elementals in His Great Name are *YHV* (יהי). We may recall the Freemason's description of this Holy Trinity of letters:

> For by י they understand the origin of all things.
> By ה they mean the Son, by whom all things were made.
> By ו which is a conjunction copulative, they understand the
> Holy Ghost, who is the love which binds them together, and
> proceeds from them. [253]

From Stanza 1.13 of the Book of Creation we can see that Abraham configures a subset of three Elementals contained in God's Name, which appears to corroborate the importance of a Holy Trinity of divine letters as explained by the Freemasons. We can summarize Stanza 1.13 as follows:

Table 10 - Emanation of the Holy Trinity

Up   YHV
Down   HYV
East   VYH
West   VHY
South   YVH
North   HVY

---

253 Macoy, 554

Complicating our attempts to make acoustical sense out of this is the existence of multiple versions of the Book of Creation. According to Aryeh Kaplan there are four important versions:[254]

1. The Short version
2. The Long version
3. The Saadia version
4. The Gra version

The most significant variation between different versions of the Book of Creation can be found in the permutations of the three letters in God's Great Name. Kaplan chooses to translate and interpret the Gra version. Kaplan chose the Gra version because it was considered the most authentic by the kabbalists.[255] For this particular stanza, however, the version used by most of the commentators is the Short version,[256] which proceeds as follows:

Table 11 - The Short Version:

Up	YHV
Down	YVH
East	HYV
West	HVY
South	VYH
North	VHY

Kabbalists have determined that in the Short version the letter in the first column of His Great Name determines the axis of direction. The assignment for column one is therefore:[257]

Table 12– The Short Version

Column: 1 2 3		Column 1
Y |H|V	=	up-down
H |Y|V	=	east-west
V |Y|H	=	north-south

254 Kaplan, *Sefer Yetzirah,* xxv.
255 Kaplan, *Sefer Yetzirah,* xxv.
256 Kaplan, *Sefer Yetzirah,* 83.
257 Kaplan, *Sefer Yetzirah,* 83.

If we adopt this approach, then once the direction of the axis is determined, the next two letters can be interpreted in a straightforward acoustical manner:

Table 13– The Short Version

	Col. 1	Cols. 2 & 3
Y-HV =	Up	5:6
Y-VH =	Down	6:5
H-YV =	East	10:6
H-VY =	West	6:10
V-YH =	South	10:5
V-HY =	North	5:10

If we assume that these specific musical ratios are significantly linked, in some way, to these specific directions, we should be able to come up with the appropriate diagram. However, great and learned rabbis have been arbitrarily permuting this Holy Trinity of letters for centuries with no apparent success. Our one advantage is the firmly held belief that acoustics provides the only meaningful and correct solution.

We can begin our acoustical interpretation by "decoding" the first letter of the "unspeakable name," *Yud* (׳) as the Hebrew numeral 10. The Freemason's explanation, "For by ׳ they understand the origin of all things," is corroborated by Kaplan's account of kabbalists who state that *Yud* (׳) designates Wisdom, and that "all Ten Sefirot are included in the simple nature of Wisdom."[258] The words "included in" should immediately bring to mind God's "rainbow principle" of unity that structures the diversity of Creation. The first letter of His Great Name is therefore a harmonic series, the mathematical structure of the rainbow as the foundation of Creation.On Day 1, before Time existed, God's first extension into matter was not the number 2, it was all Ten Sefirot of Nothingness as a single entity, replicating to the boundaries of the universe. Today's scientists call it the Big Bang, but for the scientist Abraham it was the gentle whisper of unity that he called God.

It is Abraham who is also the first to tell us that there are two major steps to the Creation process. The Big Bang was the first step. It was the Breath of God. In the second major step, a subset of six tone circles within the Ten Sefirot of Nothingness were "uncovered" to reveal prime number tone generators, which were then "unsealed" in order to harmonize with one another. This second step is called *Tikun* (reordering).

258 Kaplan, *Sefer Yetzirah,* 15.

For Abraham, God and the rainbow were a transcendent unity. Once the reordering of God's light began, the laws of nature and the mathematical disciplines of the Quadrivium made God accessible. Once the divine light of God was uncovered and unsealed, then the One became the numeral 1, and could be extended into the numeral 2. Modern scientists might say that time began with the Big Bang, but Abraham would say that time began at the moment the tone circle of the Heavenly Firmament (1:2) was created *with no beginning and no end.* Once this reordering process began, the *Yud* in His Holy Name was transformed into the Heavenly Firmament that is the womb of Creation; the octave double that would be the musical container of all that was to follow. To accomplish this, God divided the waters from the waters on Day 2.

Day 3 brought the creation of the earth, the seas, vegetation, and an understanding of threeness. The first of the Three Mothers was the primordial element air, i.e., the Breath of God, God's Ten Sefirot. The most sacred path, the Wind Path, was fashioned during Days 2 - 4 from the winds that derive from the Breath of God. It would become the soul of man.

The global law of the Ten Sefirot is transcendent and inaccessible to man, but a subset of four tone circles were incovered and unsealed to harmonize Creation. The Book of Ezekiel identifies these four tone circles as: 2, 3, 5, and 7 (figure 22). These four tone circles can be thought of as four primary colors, four primary sounds, and four primordial elements. The number 4 can also be thought of as a functional subset of the Creation process that derives from the Decalogue. The number 4 therefore became a proxy for the *Yud's* 10. Ten Sefirot embodied the divine light of step one, while four Sefirot embodied the harmonization process of step two. Aryeh Kaplan offers the following explanation for the Hebrew numerals contained in the Word, *Yahweh:*

> The primary ordering of these letters is Yud, Heh Vav. According to the book *Raziel* this is because Yud includes the first four letters (1+2+3+4=10). After 4 comes 5, the numerical value of Heh, and then 6, the numerical value of Vav. [259]

Similarly, for Pythagoreans, the number 4 represents the limits of God's extension into matter, a point (1), a line (2), a plane (3), and a volume (4), therefore the tetrad became the foundation of Greek music

259 Kaplan, *Sefer Yetzirah*, 81; Sefer Raziel 12a (31).

theory. Although a single point (1), a line (2), a plane (3) and a volume (4) are all embedded in three-dimensional space, it was common practice to use only volume (4) when describing space as a sort of shorthand that "includes" the separate dimensions. As in the Hebrew explanation, the number of dimensions, colors, and elements of Creation can be thought of as shorthand for embedding all ten aspects of Creation within the number 4. Once we decode the numeral 10 as encrypted by the numeral 4, the rest of the acoustics falls neatly into place.

Later kabbalistic writings provide us with another clue on how to proceed. The *Tanya* tells us that the letters of the Holy Tetragrammaton can be represented by the figure of a bird that corresponds to the archangel Metatron, God's highest ranking angel. "In Tikun 45 it is written that the figure of a bird represents Metatron. His head is the letter *yod* [י = 10], and the body is the letter *vav* [ו = 6], and the two wings are the two letters *hai* [ה = 5]."[260] This provides us with a spatial orientation, since Metatron travels "up" and "down" as the messenger between God and man, while his wings can also take him in the four horizontal directions of the compass. We can safely assume that Metatron is not a bat that spends its time hanging upside down, and we will assume that Metatron's head (*Yud*: י = 10 = 4) is *above,* with his body (*Vav*: ו = 6) *below* his head, and with two wings (*Heh* ה = 5) at his side.

Metatron represents the image of God that is man's soul (seven reciprocal circuits are made by opposing snakes around the axis of the sacred cube). But since the sacred cube of man's body cannot fully contain God's expanding light, the light continues to expand to the twelve boundaries of the universe, i.e., the twelve diagonals of the macrocosm's sacred cube. Later, in ancient Greece, Hermes was the messenger between God and man, who carried the caduceus depicted here.

Figure 47 – Yahweh Depicted as Metatron

260 Zalman, 203.

The bird-like configuration of God's holiest name also provides an acoustical basis for the cross as a symbol of Christianity.

Figure 48 - The "bird-like" configuration of Metatron

יהו = 456

The "Holy Trinity" of the Lost Word: "Three That Stand Alone"

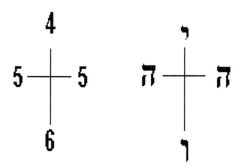

The Essence of Creation Arrayed as Metatron

Since God's light fills each sacred cube and expands outward, we can think of Metatron at the center of our sacred cube, as if Metatron's head, wings and body were poised to expand into all six directions. If we are *sealing above,* Metatron's head (*Yud*) would be on top of his body (*Vav*), therefore we see the ratio of 4/6. Finally, 5/4, 4/5, 5/6 and 6/5 describes the horizontal movement of Metatron's wings and motion through the four horizontal directions: side to side, forward and back. Abraham only described the acoustics of Metatron, he never used the name Metatron. It may be related to the Greek *metron* (measure, rule), and the notion that Metatron not only carried God's name, but also measured Him.

Yahweh, as Metatron, includes the "inner light" expanding from the center of the sacred cube, but also includes the "outer light" of the sacred cube itself. "In discussing the twelve diagonals, the Bahir says, 'On the inside of them is the tree.'"[261] In Stanza 1.5, "The singular Master God faithful King dominates over them all from His holy dwelling...."

261 Kaplan, *Sefer Yetzitrah*, 206; Kaplan, *Bahir*, 95.

The mobility provided by the wings of Metatron extend the divine light outward in the six directions of space.

Once we understand that the *Yahweh* takes on the form of this "highest ranking angel," then we are able to spatially orient him within the sacred cube as the axis of the sacred cube, where the world and the transcendent meet.[262]

Figure 49 – The Expansion of Yahweh's Divine Light

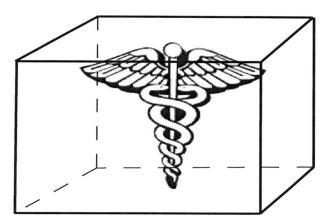

These facts combine to create a new set of permutations for the three elementals of God's Great Name. It will acoustically configure him as described above, permuting the three divine letters within stanza 1.13 as follows;

> ***1.13*** *He chose three letters*
> *from among the Elementals*
> *[in the mystery of the three Mothers*
> *Alef Mem Shin (שמא)]*
> *And He set them in His great Name*
> *and with them, He sealed six extremities.*
> *Five: He sealed above and faced upward*
> *and sealed it with **HYV**.*
> *Six: He sealed below and faced downward*
> *and sealed it with **HVY**.*
> *Seven: He sealed "east" and faced right*
> *and sealed it with **VHY**.*
> *Eight: He sealed "west" and faced left*

*and sealed it with **VYH**.*
Nine He sealed "south" and faced to the back
*and sealed it with **YVH**.*
Ten: He sealed "north" and faced straight ahead
*and sealed it with **YHV**.*

To complete this interpretation we will borrow the method used by the Short and Saadia versions in which the first letter corresponds to the axis. The last two letters correspond to acoustical ratios. The new configuration would read as follows;

Table 14– A New Interpretation

H – YV	=	*Up -*	4/6
H – VY	=	*Down -*	6/4
V – H Y	=	*East-*	5/4
V – YH	=	*West -*	4/5
Y – VH	=	*South -*	6/5
Y – HV	=	*North -*	5/6

Within the acoustical context of the Heavenly Firmament tone circle, facing up would take on the meaning of a tone ascending, traveling in a clockwise direction from the circle's apex, while facing downward would correspond to a tone descending from the same point in a counterclockwise direction. We can plot this configuration across the Heavenly Firmament tone circle or as the six expanding directions of the sacred cube's light.

The musical ratios of Metatron within the sacred cube make spatial sense as ratios that rise and fall, advance and retreat, move right and left, and expand outward from its center in six directions as determined by the six faces of the sacred cube and contained by the sacred cube's 12 diagonal boundaries. We can also view the three-dimensional figure of Metatron as a two-dimensional hexagon extending God's Light in the six directions. No matter how it is depicted, however, we must keep in mind that God's expansion of divine light will translate acoustically into a progressively higher numerosity, but one that always maintains genetic ratios.

Figure 50 – The Heavenly Firmament Tone Circle

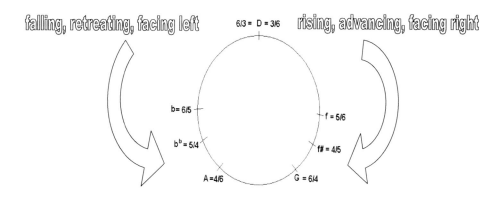

Figure 51 – The Six Directions of the Sacred Cube

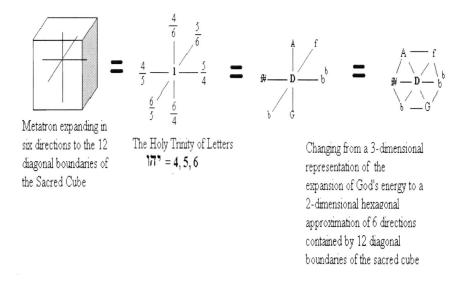

Metatron expanding in six directions to the 12 diagonal boundaries of the Sacred Cube

The Holy Trinity of Letters
והי‎ = 4, 5, 6

Changing from a 3-dimensional representation of the expansion of God's energy to a 2-dimensional hexagonal approximation of 6 directions contained by 12 diagonal boundaries of the sacred cube

Figure 52 – Deriving the Four-Horned Altar and the Star of David[263]

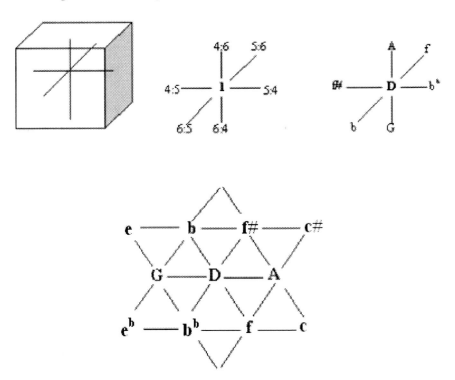

On Day 5 of Creation we may recall that the first step of the ziggurat construction flipped the Tree of Life on its side to become a mountain with the *appearance of lightening*. In other words, the hexagon uses the same ratios as the lambda construction, but now the tones are generated from the center of His holy dwelling rather than from the lambda's vertex.[264] The result is that the hexagon of tones generated by Metatron's expansion are the same tones that result from the ziggurat filtering method producing the four-horned altar. In addition, the Star of David (also known as the Shield of Solomon) can be viewed as two-dimensional opposing lambdas

263 Ernest G. McClain, "Musical Marriages in Plato's Republic," *Journal of Music Theory* (18, no. 2 (1974)), 258.
264 To switch between the two different constructions just twirl the hexagon so the triple progression runs up and down for the Metatron construction, and side to side for the ziggurat construction.

or as three-dimensional opposing tetrahedrons. Their intersection creates the four-horned altar, as seen in Figure 52.

We have just learned Abraham's mathematical encryption of the Blueprint of Creation within the Word of God, *Yahweh*. After Creation was complete, Adam's sin led mankind on a great quest for special knowledge that could return him to Paradise. Understanding the transcendental meaning of the Blueprint of Creation as Abraham encrypted it in the Word, *Yahweh*, has been a big part of that quest, but perhaps even more sacred than understanding the Creation process would be to learn the true pronunciation of the Unspeakable Name.

The long awaited true "pronunciation" of *Yahweh* is not a verbal pronunciation as one might logically expect. It is an articulation of the mind, making "seven circuits around the sacred cube." The details of this sacred practice are discussed in Part 4, explaining exactly how man must "walk" the three paths to God. It explains how to enter the state of deep meditation that will purify the body and ultimately liberate the soul. Once the methods are perfected a *tzadek* will be able to ascend and descend the seven heavens at will. Abraham's sacred practice will free all the souls of Israel from their exile — their true exile within the corporeal body and not their superficial geographic exile — and this would fulfill all the prophecies of Scripture.

We are all children of God who must learn Abraham's practice of irradiating the mind, body, and soul with divine light. The High Priests of Solomon's Temple transfigured their soul using this ancient practice so they could pass behind the veil to the other side of the curtain of palms and pomegranates — it is the veil between life and death. Abraham teaches us that man does not have to die to "give up the ghost." Abraham's practice results in what the New Testament calls a "true baptism of the spirit." He teaches us that every man can and must become a Messiah, i.e., an "anointed one," by learning to "pronounce" God's Great Name correctly.

Increasing the Numerosity of Abraham's Geometry

Uncovering and unsealing the genetic tone circles of the Kav begins to reorder the light of Yahweh so that prime numbers 2, 3 and 5 can be used in the acoustical construction of the primordial elements, the building blocks that God used to fashion Creation. During the expansion of divine light, He increased numerosity while keeping the same genetic ratios. "Binding a crown" is metaphor for harmonizing the imperfect consonances of the quintuple progression with the perfect consonances of a triple progression. This particular harmonization process has been called Just tuning within the history of Western music theory.

Figure 53 - Yahweh and the Genetic Material of Creation[265]

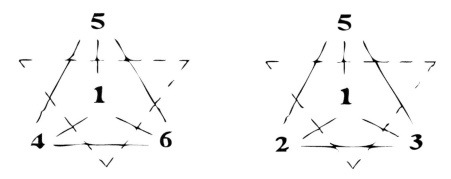

God contained and shaped "inner light" into objects and beings by binding the crown of His Great Name (*Heh* ה = 5) to that inner light, enveloping it in an "outer light" that functioned like an acoustical envelope.[266] The Talmud tells us that this expansion continued until it reached the infinite and eternal boundaries of the 12 diagonals of the sacred cube, which are the 12 pillars upon which the universe rests.[267]

We can see from the extended tetrahedron in figure 54, that the "outer light" of the quintuple progression (the "divine influx") could be said to contain both the triple progression (male aspect) and the duple progression (female aspect) of the "inner light," fulfilling the function of the Sacred Cube. *Yahweh*, or *Yah* (יהוה = 4, 5, 6, 5), extends the "Holy Trinity" of His Great Name (יהו = 4, 5, 6) into progressively larger tetrahedrons. Each new triangular base becomes the vibrational essence of more and different beings and things. This corresponds to the Freemason quote *"For by ׳ they understand the origin of all things."*

265 McClain, The Myth of Invariance, 44.
266 Zalman, 21. Discussion of "inner" versus "outer" light.
267 Kaplan, *Sefer Yetzirah*, 206 (citing Chagigah 12b)

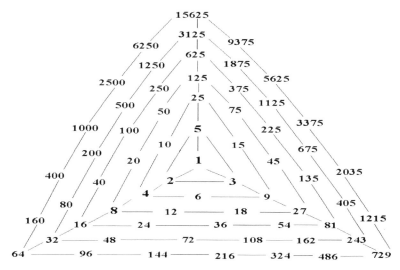

Figure 54 – Increasing Numerosity of the Tree of Life Tetrahedron

The square-based pyramid depicted in figure 55 embodies His Great Name יהוה (= 4, 5, 6, 5), just as the triangular-based pyramid (tetrahedron) described in figure 54 embodies the "Holy Trinity" of the three Elementals within His Great Name (יהו = 4, 5, 6, which, when uncovered, yield prime factors 2, 3 and 5) .

In Figure 55, the divine sparks of the soul (the Holy Ghost) *Vav=* 6 = (2 x 3) are acoustically "contained" and raised up "on the wings of Metatron" — the divine influx of the crown (*Heh*=5). This divine influx occurs as a result of man meeting "God on the mountain" through prayerful meditation, until he has learned to liberate the soul (the Shechinah) so that it hovers overhead. It ascends and descends through the seven heavens "on the wings of Metatron," as a messenger that can ascend and descend to and from God. This liberated Shechinah resonates with, and stands before, the transcendent Ten Sefirot of Nothingness that is called En Sof or Kav (the harmonic series).

Within the square-based pyramid of Figure 55, the compound number 6, describing man's soul, can be reduced to its prime factors 2 and 3, while the compound number 4 can be factored into a two-octave Heavenly Firmament (2 x 2 = 4). The head of Metatron is the *Yud* = י = 4; the two "wings of Metatron" are the two *Heh*'s = ה = 5; the body of Metatron is the *Vav* = ו = (2 x 3) = 6. The configuration of Metatron as the square-based pyramid in this diagram can then be expanded into a pentagonally-based pyramid (Figure 56a) or into a two-dimensional hexagon (Figure 56b) by simply factoring the compound numbers 4 and 6.

Figure 55 - The "Bird-like" Metatron and its Acoustics

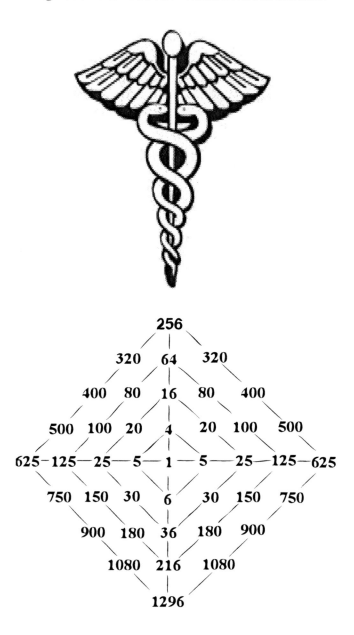

Figure 56a - Yahweh as a Pentagonally-based pyramid

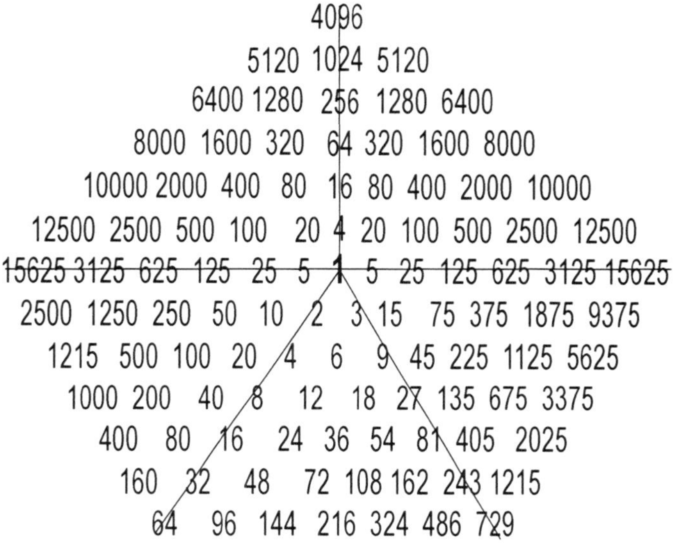

4096
5120 1024 5120
6400 1280 256 1280 6400
8000 1600 320 64 320 1600 8000
10000 2000 400 80 16 80 400 2000 10000
12500 2500 500 100 20 4 20 100 500 2500 12500
15625 3125 625 125 25 5 1 5 25 125 625 3125 15625
2500 1250 250 50 10 2 3 15 75 375 1875 9375
1215 500 100 20 4 6 9 45 225 1125 5625
1000 200 40 8 12 18 27 135 675 3375
400 80 16 24 36 54 81 405 2025
160 32 48 72 108 162 243 1215
64 96 144 216 324 486 729

Figure 56b - Yahweh as a Two-Dimensional Hexagon

Heavenly
Firmament
Just Tuning
Just Tuning
Wings of Metatron
God
Wings of Metatron
Just Tuning
Just Tuning
the soul
Pythagorean Tuning

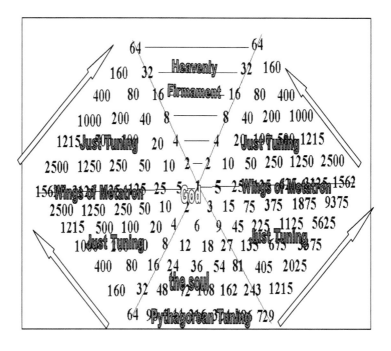

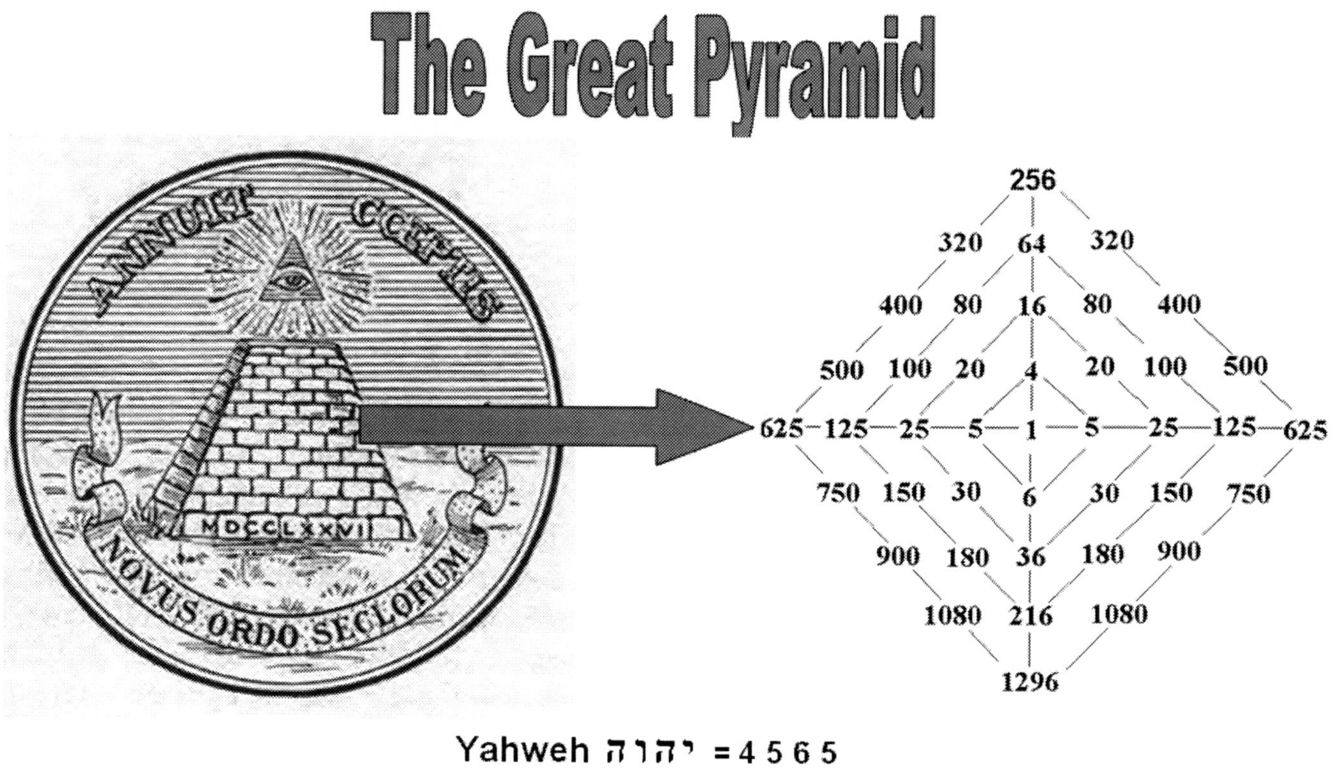

The Great Pyramid

Yahweh יהוה = 4 5 6 5

Figure 57 – The Greeat Pyramids of Egypt (An Octahedron with its reciprocal)

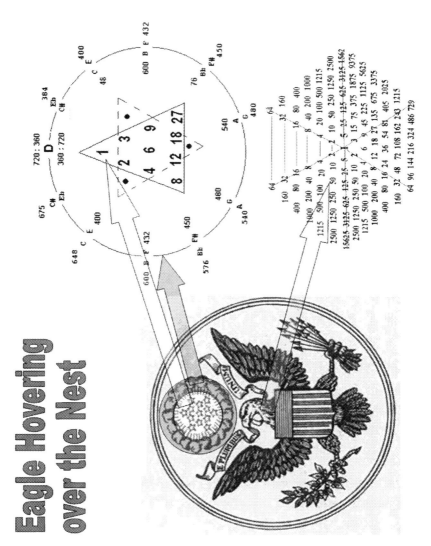

Figure 58 – The Eagle Hovering Over Its Nest

The Great Seal of the United States encrypts the acoustics for the Great Pyramids of Egypt, topped off by the "all-seeing eye" — an allusion to the gift of prophecy that results from liberating the soul (Figure 57). Metatron was symbolized by an eagle in the Great Seal (Figure 58). God was equated with an eagle "hovering" over its nest (Deuteronomy 32:11). The dollar bill depicts 13 stars in the nest, configured as a Star of David, representing the 13 colonies. The tone circle of the nest (Figures 58 and 73b) depicts how the eagle nurtures and purifies the fledgling souls within the nest until they learn to take flight.

Two-dimensional shapes like triangles, squares, pentagons, hexagons, etc., are called polygons. A polyhedron is a three-dimensional solid with polygon faces joined at their edges. A line segment where two faces meet is called an edge. A point where three or more faces meet is called a vertex. There are only five regular polyhedrons known as the Platonic solids: tetrahedrons, cubes, octahedrons, dodecahedrons, and icosahedrons. They are called regular because they are edge-uniform, vertex-uniform and face-uniform. In other words, they are equilateral and equiangular.

The interior angle of an equilateral triangle is 60° and therefore the interior angles of polygons meeting at a vertex of a regular polyhedron would have to add up to less than 360°. On a regular polyhedron, only 3, 4, or 5 triangles can meet at a vertex, since 6 angles or more would add up to 360° or more.

o 3 triangles meeting at each vertex would form a Tetrahedron.
o 4 triangles meeting at each vertex would form an Octahedron.
o 5 triangles meeting at each vertex would form an Icosahedron
o 3 squares meeting at each vertex would form a cube.
o 3 pentagons meeting at each vertex would form a Dodecahedron.

If it can be assumed that the Big Bang occurred in a spherical direction, then Abraham's expansion of light in six directions presents us with the problem of explaining how spherical harmonics can be geometrically derived from the "One," within the framework of the Quadrivium's sacred geometry. Since the force vectors of God's light expands from a single point from within the sacred cube, one can speculate that increases in numerosity and geometric complexity might ultimately realize all five regular polyhedra. God would have first inscribed a regular tetrahedron (air). The midpoints of the 6 edges of this tetrahedron happen to be the vertices of a regular octahedron (water). Then, a point on each of the 12 edges of the octahedron can be chosen according to the golden mean, $(a+b)/a = a/b$, so that its 12 division points become the vertices of a regular icosahedron (fire). Our pentagonally-based pyramid can be shown to be the structural framework of an icosahedron; and we have already discussed how a geodesic sphere can be circumscribed around the vertices of an icosahedron. The centers of the 20 faces of this icosahedron finally become the vertices of a 12 sided, pentagonally faced, dodecahedron.

Figure 59a
Tetrahedron within Cube

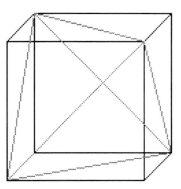

Figure 59b
Icosahedron within Octahedron

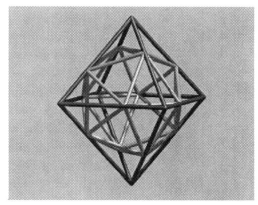

Figure 59c -
Dodecahedron within Icosahedron

Figure 59d -
Expansion of Yahweh's Light

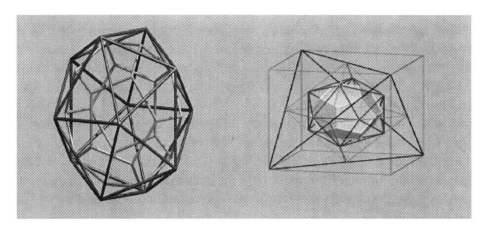

Binding Man's 22 Aspects to God

6.5 *Three: Each one stands alone*
one acts as advocate
one acts as accuser
and one decides between them.
Seven: Three opposite three
and one is the rule deciding between them.
Twelve: Twelve stand in war:
Three love,
three hate,
three give life
and three kill
Three love: the heart and the ears.
Three hate: the liver, the gall, and the tongue.
Three give life: the two nostrils and the spleen.
Three kill: the two orifices and the mouth.
And God faithful King rules over them all
from His holy habitation until eternity of eternities.
One on three, three on seven, seven on twelve,
And all are bound, one to another.

On Days 4, 5, 6, and 7, God "binds" or harmonizes the genetic material of the Three Mothers (three pair of octave "Doubles," i.e., powers of 2) and Three Fathers (powers of 3, 5 and 7) to "procreate" the primordial elements of air, water and fire, which were then used by God to engrave Creation. "Binding a crown" is mathematical metaphor for the manner in which God expanded His light. Just as liquid assumes the shape of any container to which it is poured, God radiates an "outer light," defined by the Hebrew numeral *Heh* (ה) = 5, that shapes His expanding "inner light" into the objects and creatures of existence.

God's creation of sacred cubes, with their 12 aspects, molds divine light's 10 aspects into an array of energy vectors and geometric shapes, which were then set in motion. When the Ten *sealed* Utterances of the Kav (the harmonic series) expanded into the divine light matrix on Day 1, they were unsealed on Day 2 and were reordered and harmonized within geometry's expanding numerosity. All animate and inanimate objects were shaped by their harmonic containers and then set in motion. The creation of man on Day 6, however, involved a special subset of this expanding acoustics. The creation of man manifests the 22 Foundation Letters: Three Mothers, Seven Doubles, and Twelve Elementals, as: 3 aspects of the mind; 7 aspects of the soul; and 12 aspects of the body.

On Day 6, God's infinite light, emanating from the *Yud* (י), was unsealed and irradiated the *Vav* (ו) with the "divine influx" of a *Heh* (ה), harmonizing the three elements, air, water and fire, into the vibrational essence of Adam's being. Just as God used these three elements to create the essence of man, man can learn how to access and control these elements by mastering the paths to God: the Wind Path, the Water Path, and the Fire Path.

The Breath of God (air) harmonizes the ascending fires with the descending flow of waters. These three primordial elements do not include the downward tug of the element earth. God created man's physical body from the dense element earth, as Adam's outermost garment. It enclosed the inner light of his soul and the outer light of what might be called a subtle, or etheric body — a spiritual reflection, shaped like the physical body.

From Abraham's perspective Adam's soul would initially have dwelled within the lofty vibrations of the Garden of Eden, even while his physical body inhabited earth. One might think of the Garden of Eden as "Heaven on earth." When Adam sinned and fell from Grace, his soul would be sustained by the lower vibrations that sustains modern man. We will see in the next chapter that Abraham defines Hell as a substantive dwelling place for the soul that is separate and distinct from both Heaven and earth. From Abraham's perspective, "Hell on earth" would describe a soul tormented by the "fires of Hell" who still lives in his physical body. Keep in mind that it is always the balanced "threeness" of the three primordial elements that permeate the mind, etheric body, and soul. These elements provide the underlying structure of man's initial creation and subsequent return to God. We will now examine what it means to "bind a crown" to one's being.

> *And God faithful King rules over them all*
> *from His holy habitation*
> *until eternity of eternities.*
> *One on three, three on seven, seven on twelve,*
> *And all are bound, one to another.*

Binding a Crown to the Three Mothers

3:7 He made the letter Alef (א) king over Breath
   And He bound a crown to it
   And He combined them one with another
 And with them He formed
   Air in the Universe
   The temperate in the Year
   And the chest in the Soul:
 The male with AMSh (אמש)
 And the female with AShM (אשמ).

3.8 He made Mem (מ) king over water
   And He bound a crown to it
   And He combined one with another
 And with them He formed
   Earth in the Universe
   Cold in the Year
   And the belly in the Soul:
 The male with MASh (מאש)
 And the female with MshA (משא)

3.9 He made Shin (ש) king over fire
   And He bound a crown to it
   And He combined one with another
 And with them He formed
   Heaven in the Universe
   Hot in the Year
   And the head in the Soul:
 The male with ShAM (שאמ)
 And the female with ShMA (שמא)

The Three Mothers are the primordial elements of air, water, and fire used by God to create the Soul, Time and the Universe. Within the soul, Abraham describes how God concentrated air in the chest, water in the belly, and fire in the head. The chest fulfills air's main function, to harmonize the opposites of the head's fire, and the belly's water. Each of these primordial elements engenders its own unique harmonization process, its own tuning system, and its own musical path to God. The three tuning systems and integer components that define them are:

- Air (Wind) - powers of 2, 3 harmonized by Pythagorean tuning
- Water - powers of 2, 3, 5 harmonized by Just tuning
- Fire - powers of 2,3,5,7 harmonized by Archytas tuning

On Day 5, *Yahweh* continues to engrave Creation by binding a crown (*Heh*=5) to the Three Mothers. Kaplan tells us that "[Yah] engraved it,… can also be read in the imperative, 'Engrave it.'[268] Therefore God's creative act of binding a crown (*Heh*=5) to the Three Mothers can also be read in the imperative as instructions telling man to "Engrave." This is metaphor for inducing a "divine influx" through Abraham's deep meditation practice. Just as God binds a crown, man also binds a crown, inducing the divine influx to judiciously harmonize the mind's opposing aspects. The *three that stand alone* can be found in the gematria of God's Great Name: *YHV* (יהו = 4, 5, 6). As we have already seen in detail, this "Holy Trinity" of divine letters is the foundation of Creation:

Figure 60 – Binding a Crown to the Mind

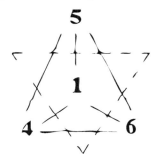

Three:
Each one stands alone
one acts as advocate
one acts as accuser
and one decides between them

---

268 Kaplan, *Sefer Yetzirah*, 90.

The "mind of God" manifests in three aspects: the opposites of *advocate* and *accuser* harmonized by *"one [who] decides between them."* The *one who decides between them* corresponds to the judgment of both God and man, since the image of God is the inner light of man. Abraham's theology makes sense within the context of Kaplan's interpretation of the imperative, since man can judge like God judges — by harmonizing the mind's opposites with the divine influx of the crown (*Heh* = 5).

Binding a Crown to the Seven Doubles[269]

***4.14** He made the letter Tav (ת) king over Grace*
  And He bound a crown to it
  And He combined one with another
  And with them He formed
   Jupiter in the Universe
   The Sabbath in the Year
   The mouth in the Soul,
    male and female.

In the chapter on Day 3, there is an extensive discussion about Doubles, i.e., octave doubles. Abraham lists three pairs of octave doubles, and each pair delineates octave tone circles of the appropriate numerosity to contain either the Wind Path, the Water Path, or the Fire Path. By binding a crown to the Seven Doubles, Abraham was harmonizing these octave containers (powers of 2) with the crown (powers of 5). In other words, by invoking the divine influx (*Heh* = 5) through meditation, one is being instructed to irradiate the three different types of tone circles (octave doubles) that live within us: The Wind circle, the Water circle, and the Fire circle.

When *Yud* (4) and *Vav* (6) are considered in terms of wavelength, they create rising perfect fifths (4/6) and falling perfect fifths (6/4). On Day 4, the soul is created from the "genetic" prime factors of 2 and 3 within Pythagorean tuning. We have seen how the first of Three Fathers, the numeral 3, procreates with the first of Three Mothers, octave double 2:4, to generate descendents: a seven-note Phrygian (modern Dorian) mode.

The resulting seven aspects of the soul are arrayed as *"Three opposite three and one is the rule deciding between them."* Once the *three that stand*

269 Only one of seven stanzas are quoted; for complete text refer to *Sefer Yetzirah: The Book of Creation*. translated by Aryeh Kaplan.

alone have been balanced within the mind, Abraham instructs us on how meditation's divine influx will harmonize the two opposing groups of three that reside within the soul's seven aspects: each of the opposing groups of three will be harmoniously balanced within themselves, and with each other.

Seven:
Three opposite three
and one is the rule deciding between them.

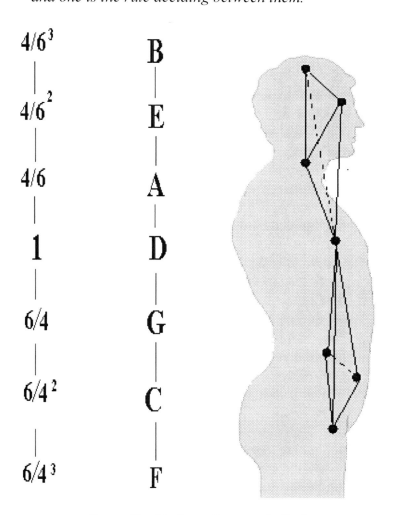

$4/6^3$

$4/6^2$

$4/6$

1

$6/4$

$6/4^2$

$6/4^3$

B

E

A

D

G

C

F

Figure 61 – Binding a Crown to the Soul

Binding a Crown to the Twelve Elementals[270]

5.7 He made the letter Heh (ה) king over speech
    and He bound a crown to it
    And He combined one with another
And with them He formed
    Aries in the Universe
    Nissan in the Year
    And the right foot in the Soul
        male and female.

He made the letter Vav (ו) king over thought
    And He bound a crown to it
    And He combined one with another
And with them He formed
    Taurus in the Universe
    Iyar in the Year
    And the right kidney in the Soul
        male and female

He made the letter Zayin (ז) king over motion
    And He bound a crown to it
    And He combined one with another
And with them He formed
    Gemini in the Universe
    Sivan in the Year
    And the left foot in the Soul
        male and female.

The twelve diagonals of the sacred cube of man's body is just one manifestation of Yahweh's expanding light. We will describe God's creation of Adam as an example of that expansion. It is important to remember that we are not describing Adam's physical body, but rather the vibrational essence of his etheric body that clothed his soul in Eden. To create Adam on Day 6, God first binds the crown (*Heh* ה = 5) to the harmonized light

270 Only three of twelve stanzas are quoted; for complete text refer to *Sefer Yetzirah*, trans. by Aryeh Kaplan.

of Adam's soul — powers of 2 (Bet ב) and 3 (Gimel ג). After God created the sacred cube of Adam's etheric and physical bodys, *He blew into his nostrils the soul of life.*[271]

In terms of wavelengths, within Figure 62, powers of 5/6 create rising minor thirds while powers of 6/5 create falling minor thirds; powers of 4/5 create rising major thirds and powers of 5/4 create falling major thirds. This occurs with powers of 2, 3 and 5 according to Just tuning.

The three that stand alone were harmonized within the mind; the two groups of three within the seven aspects of the soul were harmonized; and the four groups of three that reside within the twelve opposing aspects of the ethereal body were harmonized. At the center of all 22 combined aspects, *"God faithful King rules over them all From His holy habitation until eternity of eternities."*

> *Twelve stand in war:*
> > *Three love,*
> > *three hate,*
> > > *three give life*
> > > *and three kill*
> *Three love: the heart and the ears.*
> *Three hate: the liver, the gall, and the tongue.*
> *Three give life: the two nostrils and the spleen.*
> *Three kill: the two orifices and the mouth.*

Figure 62 – Binding a Crown to the Body

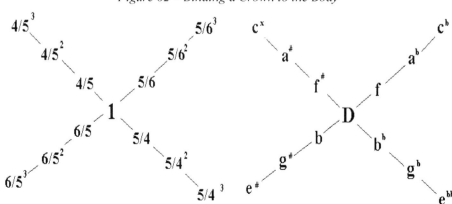

---

271 Genesis 2:7

Figure 63a, b & c – Three on Seven on Twelve

One on three = the mind   Three on seven = the soul

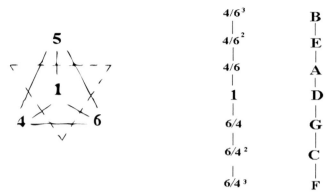

Seven on twelve = body

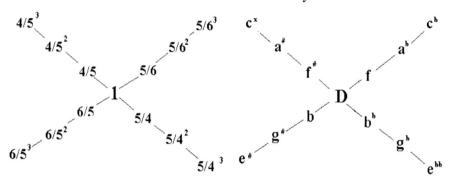

One on three, Three on seven, Seven on twelve, And all are bound, one to another[272]

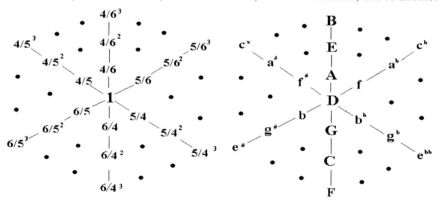

---

272 McClain, *The Myth of Invariance*, 77.

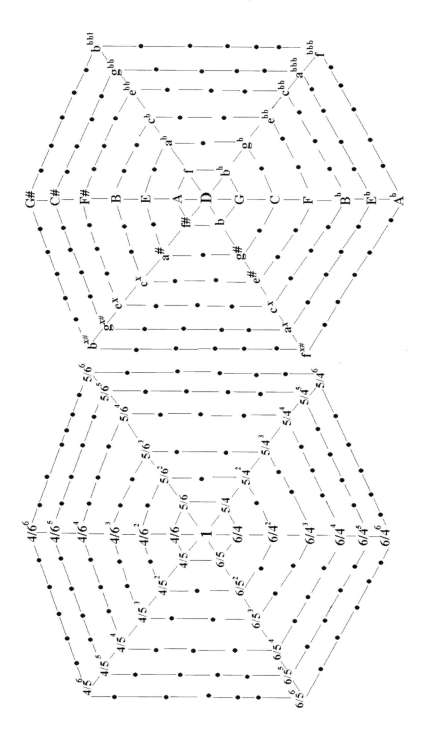

Figure 64 – God's Sacred Cubes Expanding Toward the Twelve Boundaries of the Universe (cubes viewed in 3/4 perspective)

Extending Light through Five Realms

2.3 *Twenty-two Foundation Letters*
     He engraved them with voice
     He carved them with breath
     He set them in the mouth
  In five places
     Alef Chet Heh Eyin (אחהע) in the throat *(Gutturals)*
     Gimel Yud Kaf Kuf (גיכק) in the palate   *(Palatals)*
     Dalet Tet Lamed Nun Tav (דטלנת)
        in the tongue   *(Linguals)*
     Zayin Samekh Shin Resh Tzadi (זסשרץ)
        in the teeth   *(Dentals)*
     Bet Vav Mem Peh (בומף) in the lips.   *(Labials)*

The outward expansion of divine light, which was described within kabbalistic tradition as the "downward gradation of the divine sparks," came to be known as *Shevirat Hakelim* (Breaking of the Vessels). It was alternatively called *Tzimtzum* or *Hishatalshelut.* The Tanya describes the Ten Utterances of God as far too powerful to be the life-force for any living creature:

> They [creatures] can receive their life-force only when it descends and is progressively diminished, degree by degree, by means of substitutions and transpositions of the letters and by Gematriot, their numerical values, until the life-force can be condensed and enclothed and there can be brought forth from it a particular creature.[273]

At this point we should realize that the degree-by-degree descent corresponds to the ratios of frequency and wavelength within the harmonic series defining the divine light which descends into matter. The degree-by-degree descent of light that issued forth from the transcendent "One" created four "worlds" or realms.

---

273 Zalman, 289.

…the radiation and efflux of vivification, issuing forth from the breath of His blessed mouth, divides into four different levels. These are the four worlds of *Atzilut, Beriah, Yetzirah* and *Asiyah.*[274]

The Tanakh describes Ezekiel seeing the Divine Presence as he sat on His Throne of Glory. Kabbalistic tradition underscores the transcendence of God by stating that Ezekiel could not see God's face in the transcendent realm of *Atzilut*, but could only see His reflections into the reordered light of *Beriah*. What Jewish tradition could not know, without the benefit of Abraham's teaching, was that Ezekiel saw his own image sitting in the Chariot-Throne of Glory within Beriah. The Divine Presence (the Shechinah), seen by Ezekiel, was his own soul being liberated, and "swept away in a whirlwind," just as the prophet Elijah was swept away in the same chariot (see Figure 91).

After the world of *Beriah*, God created the vibrational essence of the Garden and all living creatures within the etheric world of *Yetzirah*. It is only after Adam's sin that man "fell from Grace." Without the Grace of eternal life, he had to endure the sufferings of life and death within the physical world of *Asiyah*. From this point forward Adam's soul was in "exile," embedded within the animalistic appetites of the physical body within the world of Asiyah.

Abraham's division of the Hebrew alphabet into five phonetic families is a manifestation of five acoustical articulations that create four worlds. These articulations are shown in Table 15, which highlight the various subsets of the 462 Paths table. Abraham did not mention the worlds by their later kabbalistic names, but he understood that the divine light matrix was differentiated by five acoustical articulations creating five different foundations for being and existence.

The transcendent God corresponds to the undifferentiated Monad, represented by the Hebrew letter *Alef*. The Ten Utterances of God were first articulated by the "gutturals" or "breath of God." On Day 1 of Creation, before any reordering took place, these Ten Sefirot of Nothingness were sealed as a single rainbow entity and corresponds to the transcendent God in Atzilut. Atzilut, the realm of the harmonic series, exists as global law and was never accessible to man — not even to the greatest of prophets.

---

274 Zalman, 541

Harmonic Progression →

Arithmetic Progression →

The KAV is Air; the Breath of God on Day 1 ; A harmonic series of sequential integers begins to get reordered on Day 2.

The image of God later known as Supernal Man generated by Pythagorean Tuning and descends into matter from Days 2 through 4

Differentiating time "flowing like water" as well as defining all "moving creatures" within Just Tuning during Day 5 and Adam on Day 6

The fires of heaven & hell; sin and redemption within a modified Archytas Tuning

Arithmetic \ Harmonic	1	2	3	4	5	6	7	8	9	10	20
AIR 1	1	2	3	4	5	6	7	8	9	10	20
2	2	4	6	8	10	12	14	16	18	20	40
3	3	6	9	12	15	18	21	24	27	30	60
4	4	8	12	16	20	24	28	32	36	40	80
5	5	10	15	20	25	30	35	40	45	50	100
6	6	12	18	24	30	36	42	48	54	60	120
7	7	14	21	28	35	42	49	56	63	70	140
8	8	16	24	32	40	48	56	64	72	80	160
9	9	18	27	36	45	54	63	72	81	90	180
10	10	20	30	40	50	60	70	80	90	100	200
20	20	40	60	80	100	120	140	160	180	200	400
30	30	60	90	120	150	180	210	240	270	300	600
WATER 40	40	80	120	160	200	240	280	320	360	400	800
50	50	100	150	200	250	300	350	400	450	500	1000
60	60	120	180	240	300	360	420	480	540	600	1200
70	70	140	210	280	350	420	490	560	630	700	1400
80	80	160	240	320	400	480	560	640	720	800	1600
90	90	180	270	360	450	540	630	720	810	900	1800
100	100	200	300	400	500	600	700	800	900	1000	2000
200	200	400	600	800	1000	1200	1400	1600	1800	2000	4000
FIRE 300	300	600	900	1200	1500	1800	2100	2400	2700	3000	6000

Table 15 – Abraham's Five Stages of Light: Day 1, Days 2-4, Day 5, Day 6, and Day 7

The second acoustical articulation took place in the world of Beriah. It corresponds to the first "cooling" or "contraction" of divine light after God's Big Bang expansion into the harmonic series matrix of Day 1. It is characterized by a reordering (Tikun), or *unsealing* of the "Breath of God" into a subset of harmonies that will create the primordial element of air. During Days 2 to 4, the most pure subset of God's light is used to create the vibrational essence of the soul's "Winds" within Pythagorean tuning. Beriah is the realm of Supernal Man, where every man's disembodied eternal soul was created and is rooted. Man meditates religiously to ultimately "walk with God" by resonating with the soul's root vibration in Beriah, the highest level attainable by man.

The world of Yetzirah, containing the Garden of Eden, was created from the next two articulations of divine light on Days 5 and 6 within Just tuning. Within Yetzirah, the primordial element of water was created from the diatonic scale of Day 5 (creatures that moveth), as well as from the chromatic scale (creation of Adam's body) on Day 6. On Day 6, Adam was created in God's grace, before original sin and therefore before he was exiled from Eden. God created Adam as a pure and innocent creature from the mélange of pure and impure that characterized the Tree of Life. The second Mother, row *Mem* (מ) of the 231 Gates table, opens to provide the tonal material for the two-octave chromatic Water Path.

In the final acoustical articulation, God created heaven and hell from the element of fire. The third Mother, *Shin* (ש), leads us to the final row of the 231 Gates table; the gates of both Heaven and Hell open into the Fire Path continuum of vibration that functions as the soul's crucible for sin and redemption. Man can only return to heaven by partaking of the Tree of Life — the Torah — the essence of which is embodied by Abraham's sacred practice.

The Altar of Sanctification

The imperfection of Just Tuning that occurs between the triple and quintuple progressions also occurs as a result of Day 6's increase in numerosity. Only a limited subset of the triple and quintuple progressions within the Tree of Life can be sanctified. Including the sanctification process as part of this chapter, however, presumes that Adam has already sinned, and and that mankind needs to redeem itself (the topic of sin and redemption is dealt with more fully on Day 7). A preview was included in this section because the sanctification process is an important acoustical operation that is performed along Day 6 musical paths.

Just as we applied the ziggurat method to sanctify animal sacrifice we must apply it to the concept of human sacrifuce. For Jews, God stopped Abraham from killing Isaac; for Muslims, God stopped Abraham from sacrificing Ishmael; for Christianity, Christ is considered the sacrificial lamb. Abraham's method of sanctification did not really require human sacrifice. The author of the Book of Creation would have understood that the "truth" and significance of these biblical parables/historical events, even the one's bearing the name of Abraham, was to provide the theology and practice of salvation — by purifying one's inner vibration through the sacred practice of seven circuits around the sacred cube.

However, seven generations after Abraham, Israel was in exile within Egypt, and had lost all knowledge of the transcendental meaning and pronunciation of *Yahweh*. This is the first time that knowledge of the blueprint and the practice were lost. God needed to reveal the Word of God to Israel once more. Moses received the Ten Commandments on Mount Sinai, engraved by God's Ten Utterences. According to Jewish tradition, the Written Law received by Moses includes divine revelations for the Five Books of Moses, i.e., the Torah, along with its 613 commandments. The purification process that we are concerned with in this section is actualized by the 365 prohibitive commandments, the vibrational essence of which is depicted in Figures 65 and 66.

The Sanctification process requires Abraham's practice from the perspective of performing the prohibitive commandments with *kavanah* (meditative intent as prescribed by Abraham's three meditation methods), and for non-Jews, includes performing the seven Noahide Laws, in which non-Jews may omit performance of the 365 commandments, but must still fulfill Abraham's practice of seven circuits around the sacred cube. Abraham's practice should therefore be understood as the basis of daily prayers for all three faiths. Tradition tells us that Moses also received the Oral Law on Mount Sinai, which would have included this acoustics, as well as a detailed knowledge of Abraham's practice, which would then have been handed down to the High Priests.

The purification process of the four-horned altar will "burn away" all impurities to create the Day 6 scale, just as it did for the Day 5 scale. In

Exodus 27:1 we read that the dimensions of this altar would be 5 cubits squared by 3 cubits in height. The horns were to be made from the altar itself, not made separately and then attached. The impure tones within the Tree of Life would be "burned away" by binding a crown to the 12 aspects of the sacred cube. The 11-tone chromatic scale that remained corresponds to the purified vibrational essence of man's body.

The process of acoustical "circumcision" selects subsets of "descendants" who will keep God's Covenant. After Adam's sin, circumcision symbolized this purification process, sealing God's Covenant with Abraham by "cutting away" impurities within the Tree of Life. In Figure 66, Abraham's Covenant with God imposed circumcision on Abraham to rid him of impurities. Non-Jews must realize that circumcision is among the 613 commandments, and they may choose not to be physically circumcised, but would still need to fulfill Abraham's Covenant of seven circuits, as the renewed Covenant of the seven Noahide Laws. The acoustics of the purification scale is followed by the steps necessary to manifest it:

Figure 65 – Ascending and Descending over Reciprocal 11-Tone Paths[275]

360	384	400	432	450	480	540	576	600	648	675	720
720	675	648	600	576	540	480	450	432	400	384	360
D	eb	e	f	f#	G	A	bb	b	c	c#	D

This perfect inverse symmetry is unique in music theory.
"…life force flows to the stone … running or returning… waxing or waning… either in direct or reverse order …"

1. Begin with the lambda acoustics for the Tree Life.
2. The ziggurat method with "*an appearance of lightening on the mountain*" flips the tree on its side generating tones from the lower left, while the "lightening" begins to filter out impure tones.
3. Multiplication by powers of 2 transposes all remaining tones to the 360:720 octave double.
4. Tones of the altar were chosen as a subset of:
   "*five opposite five with a single covenant precisely in the middle in the circumcision of the tongue and in the circumcision of the membrum.*"

---

275 McClain, *The Myth of Invariance*, 33.

Figure 66 – The Creation of Adam as the Scale of the Covenant

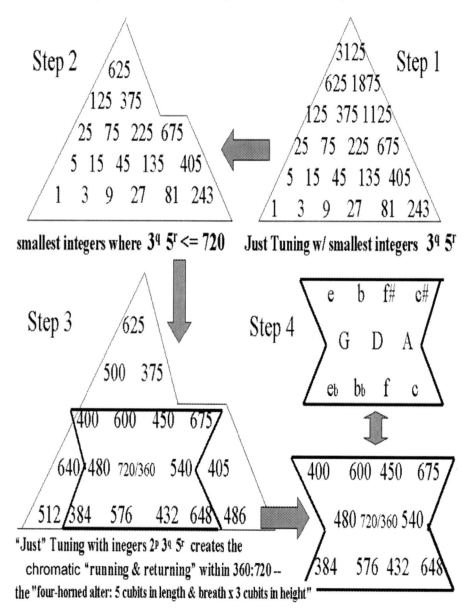

The Descendants of Adam

The name of Adam (אדם) can be interpreted as 1440. The numbers would have to be understood as placeholders rather than addends.[276] Therefore the numeral *Alef* (א) would correspond to 1000, *Dalet* ד = 4, and *Mem* מ = 40. The gematria of Adam's name (1-4-40) is depicted in the acoustics of Figure 67a.

The acoustics of Adam is therefore an expansion of the Book of Creation's acoustics for Day 6. The divine sparks that comprise the soul of Adam were the musical seeds for his descendants. Adam's sparks descend from the octave double 1440:720 to the lower octave double 720:360. "The soul of Adam was composed of all the worlds and was destined to uplift and reintegrate all the sparks of holiness..."[277] After Adam's fall from grace, man's vibrational life occurs within the octave double 360:720. Beginning with Abraham, however, man can learn to ascend toward God and might even return to the higher set of vibrations that defined Adam's vibrational life in Eden. "The monochord number 1,440 leads us to the very beautiful notion of Adam as containing the 'seeds' of all future generations."[278] The Zohar states: "When God showed Adam all future generations, he saw them in the Garden of Eden in the form in which they were destined to assume in the world."[279]

Figure 67a – Adam Before His Fall from Grace

720	768	800	864	900	960	1080	1152	1200	1296	1350	1440
1440	1350	1296	1200	1152	1080	960	900	864	800	768	720
D	eb	e	f	f#	G	A	bb	b	c	c#	D

Figure 67b – The Generations of Adam[280]

D	eb	e	f	f#	G	A	bb	b	c	c#	D	eb	e	f	f#	G	A	bb	b	c	c#	D
360	384	400	432	450	480	540	576	600	648	675	720	760	800	864	900	960	1080	1152	1200	1296	1350	1440

---

276 As in the English-speaking world, Arabic numerals are generally used in today's Israel. However, using the aleph as a placeholder for numbers between 1000 and 1999 is common practice when counting in Hebrew.
277 Scholem, *Kabbalah*, 162.
278 McClain, *Myth of Invariance*, 126.
279 Zohar, 91b.
280 McClain, *The Myth of Invariance*, 126.

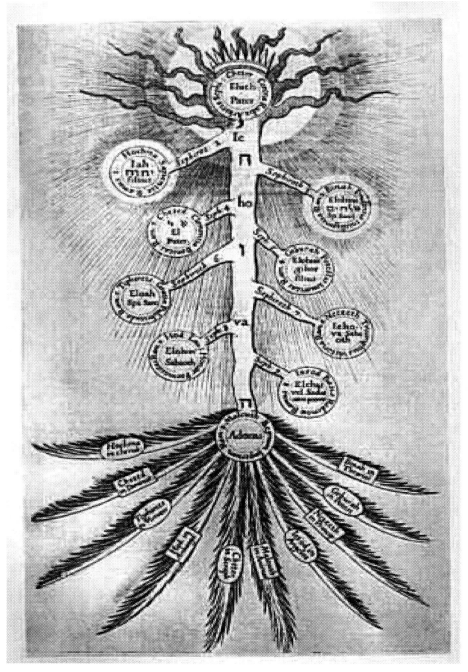

Figure 68 – Robert Fludd: The Sephirothic Tree of Life

The Seventh Day of Creation

The Moral Imperative of the Bible

The Book of Creation defines Time, the Soul, and the Universe within the ten directions of God's expanding light. In the last chapter, we saw the acoustical detail for how *Yahweh*'s light expanded in the six directions of space, until it reached the 12 boundaries of the Universe. In addition to space, stanza 1.5 defines two directions of Time: *a depth of beginning*, and *a depth of ending,* defining the mandala of time and the calendar; and finally, two directions of the Soul, which are *a depth of good* and *a depth of evil.* Eight of these directions define what scientists now call the space-time continuum, while the remaining two are related to the concepts of free will and morality as a function of one's choices between good and evil.

The presumption is that Abraham's core practice naturally makes us moral human beings. But, Abraham's work never reached the masses. It took the Torah, then the Tanakh, the New Testament, and the Koran, to bring biblical morality to the masses. We are finally in a position to understand that humanity's moral compass was based on the mathematical framework prescribed by Abraham.

> 1.5 *Ten Sefirot of Nothingness:*
> *There measure is ten*
> *which have no end*
> *A depth of beginning*
> *A depth of end*
> *A depth of good*
> *A depth of evil*
> *A depth of above*
> *A depth of below*
> *A depth of east*

> *A depth of west*
> *A depth of north*
> *A depth of south*
> *The singular Master*
> *God faithful King*
> *dominates over them all*
> *from His holy dwelling*
> *until eternity of eternities.*

Scripture contains a suite of allegories that were carefully crafted to extend Abraham's acoustical constructs for the purpose of providing mankind with a reason for being. Original sin imposed the moral imperative of redemption from sin, and acoustically encoded it within the Creation allegory of two trees in the Garden of Eden: the Tree of Knowledge of Good and Evil and the Tree of Life. The Zohar states:

> The Tree of Life, according to a tradition, extends over five hundred years journey, and all the waters of Creation issue from its foot. This tree was in the middle of the garden, and it collected all the waters of Creation, which afterwards flowed from it in different directions.[281]

A state of perfection ensued in the Garden of Eden before any bite was taken from the fruit of the Tree of Knowledge. After Adam's sin, *"The Lord God said, 'Behold, the man is become as one of us, to know good and evil: and now, lest he put forth his hand and take also of the tree of life, and eat, and live forever:' Therefore the Lord God sent him forth from the Garden of Eden."*[282] Adam and Eve were exiled from the Garden. Clearly, he did not partake of the Tree of Life, and therefore he did not become like God and the angels, who had eternal life. Adam's fall from Grace corresponds to an acoustical fall into impurity. Once Adam tasted the fruit of the Tree of Knowledge of Good and Evil, his soul fell through additional powers of 2 and 3, into the lower vibrations of the physical world, with all the pain, suffering, and struggle to transcend one's lower nature.

---

281 Zohar, 35a
282 Genesis, 3:22-23.

Figure 69a – Adam's Fall from Yetzirah into Asiyah

Ab	Eb	Bb	F	C	G	D	A	E	B	F#	C#	G#
729	243	81	27	9	3	1	1/3	1/9	1/27	1/81	1/243	1/729

Figure 69b – The Tree of Knowledge of Good and Evil

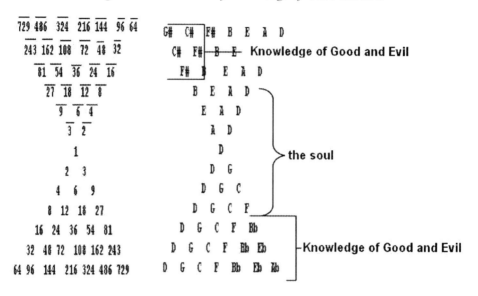

Figure 69c – Adam's Fall "Bent Around into a Tone Circle"

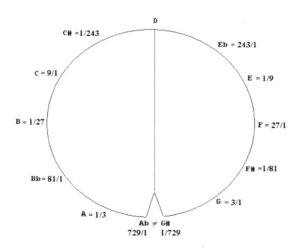

On Day 7 of Creation, the element of fire was used to raise the numerosity of Day 6's vibrations into the fires of Heaven and Hell by using a modified form of Archytas tuning (modified because it cannot generate any new tones on the Sabbath). Although Adam was created in God's Grace, his earthly appetites distracted him from God and he sinned. As a result, God exiled Adam from Eden, and his physical body now obscured God's light. The final realm of Asiyah is the physical realm fashioned from the primordial element of earth. The element of earth functions as a very dense outer garment to contain the vibrations of both the inner light of the soul and the outer light of the etheric body. It is man's mission to eliminate all obscurations of divine light by focusing on the internal motion of inner and outer light, enabling the soul to ascend and descend the ziggurat of Jacob's ladder and return to God's Grace.

The harmonies that make up the Water Path and Fire Path are the vibrational essence of man's daily prayers. They cause the divine light to descend like water or rise like fire through the twelve aspects of the body, eliminating any obscurations, making us healthy and whole, and bringing us closer to God. Man can also raise the numerosity of "inner fire" in his daily prayers to enter the gates of Heaven through Sabbath prayer; but, he is always free to raise his numerosity by doing and personifying evil to enter the gates of Hell. In either case, man's actions position the soul's vibration somewhere along the vibrational continuum of Heaven and Hell (Figure 81). When the mind is balanced through prayer, so is the judgement and free will to choose appropriately between good and evil, giving man the restraint to refrain from evil, and the kindness to do good works. Once the mind, body and soul are in balance, the Wind Path allows man to liberate his soul from its captivity within the body.

Man has the ability to ascend and descend across the 22 Foundation Letters in order to purify the body in Asiyah, to liberate the soul into Yetzirah, and even to "walk with God" by resonating with the reordered Ten Sefirot of Nothingness in Beriah. The harmonic series defining God, however, remains transcendent as universal law within Atzilut. If a man "boils down" his own existence, through Abraham's practice, to arrive at his soul's essential harmonic series, it is not the same as saying that he can boil down his existence to encompass everything and everyone else's harmonic series. The omnipresent God is the global law called the harmonic series.

Imperfections of the Flesh

1.3   Ten Sefirot of Nothingness
> *In the number of ten fingers five opposite five*
> *with a single covenant precisely in the middle*
> *in the circumcision of the tongue*
> *and in the circumcision of the membrum*

Sin is associated with the farthest point from God, bisecting the octave tone circle somewhere between the A and the G, *precisely in the middle* of the octave, and it is therefore consistent with the location of the tongue and sexual organ.[283] Thus one's thoughts, speech and impulses are vulnerable to the temptations of the flesh. If each power of 2 brings us full circle to God at the apex of the tone circle, then "doing evil," within Pythagorean tuning ($2^p\,3^q$), would establish the farthest musical distance on the tone circle from God, the ratio 729:512 or ($729 = 3^6$: $2^9 = 512$), which would bisect the tone circle to locate a twelfth spoke somewhere within the "Pythagorean comma" (Ab ≠ G#).

We have seen that bisecting the octave tone circle exactly in half within Pythagorean tuning produces the Pythagorean comma; a musical "flaw" created by an inability to precisely locate the square root of two ($\sqrt{2}$), an irrational number. By the term irrational number we don't mean "without reason" but rather "without numerical ratio." This problem is related to the proportional relationship between the side of a square and its diagonal. It is not straightforward.

Figure 70 – Imperfections of Nature due to Original Sin

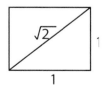

Legend has it that when Pythagoreans learned of this they swore an oath never to reveal it to the world because it seemed to indicate the imperfection of God and nature. We are told that around 520 BC, a

---

283 Kaplan, *Sefer Yetzirah*, 37.

Pythagorean named Hippasus revealed this great secret and was therefore drowned. Because we are able to go beyond simple integers in today's numbering system we can approximate the number better than the ancient geometers as 1:1.414..., an infinite decimal.

Mankind was forced to ponder the possibility that God's Creation was imperfect. Biblical allegories, however, argue against that, stating that it was Adam's free will that chose evil, precipitating his fall from perfection. Adam's soul may have been vibrationally perfect, but his containment of divine light was not. Adam disobeyed God resulting in his fall from Grace. The Tree of Life mixed triple and quintuple progressions, and the vulnerability of Adam's outer light manifested in him to create animal appetites within a dense physical body. Once Adam was exiled from the Garden there was no longer ample opportunity to simply *put forth his hand and take also of the tree of life, and eat, and live forever.* In the physical world, there were now significant steps to be taken in order to return to Eden, none of which Adam knew or understood. Mankind still struggles with understanding exactly what it means to partake of the tree of life. The three faiths have each evolved their own ideas about this allegory, and how to return to paradise.

Abraham's mathematics appears to have come out of an ancient tradition that had its beginnings in Sumer, Mesopotamia, and Egypt. Those beginnings were the fledgling steps of a science that attempted to explain the mechanisms of the mind, body and soul. The Book of Creation, however, appears to be the oldest extant work to expound a method of isolating music's triple progression from its quintuple progression. This, of course, set the stage for Abraham's monotheistic theology and the subsequent allegories of Scripture.

Within the Jewish tradition, the Shechinah is said to hover over the head of every righteous man performing the Torah's commandments. It is compared to the flame of a lamp, which clings to the wick, while the wick is likened to a man's body. Scholem states that "every commandment [of the Torah] has its mystical aspect whose observance creates a bond between the world of man and the world of the *Sefirot*."[284] The Ten Sefirot that comprise the souls of Adam, Eve, and all of Israel, are in exile from the purity of the Garden. Abraham shows us exactly what it means to partake of the "Tree of Life" and return to the Garden.

---

284 Scholem, *Kabbalah*, 176.

God's Covenant with Abraham

Within the context of the Torah, Abraham inherited original sin and the knowledge of Good and Evil that goes with it. But, unlike Adam, Abraham had developed the moral judgment to distinguish between good and evil. God had waited ten generations, since His Covenant with Noah, to find such a man. He then reestablished His Covenant with Abraham.

Until Abraham's ninety-ninth year he was called Abram, with no *Heh* = ה = 5 in his name. The name Abram אברם = 243 = 3^5 serves as the upper limit for an important subset of the Tree of the Knowledge of Good and Evil; a subset that does not include the extra power of 3 associated with the essence of evil, 3^6 = 729. That one additional power of 3 is the difference between knowing good and evil and actually doing and personifying evil.

Figure 71 – The Soul That Knows Good and Evil

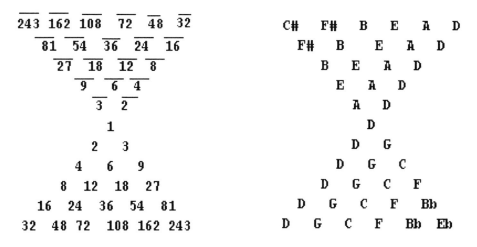

Abraham's method of acoustical isolation kept the creation of man's soul distinct from the creation of his body. To accomplish this he used two separate tuning systems, Pythagorean tuning and Just tuning. They are encoded within biblical allegory as the Tree of Knowledge of Good and Evil and the Tree of Life, respectively.

Subset of Tree of Knowledge Embodied by Abram	Subset of Tree of Life Embodied by Binding a נ = 5 to Abram's name

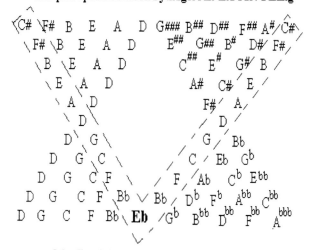

243	162	108	72	48	32	3125	1875	1125	675	405	243
81	54	36	24	16		405	375	225	135	81	
17	18	12	8			125	75	45	27		
9	6	4				25	15	9			
3	2					5	3				
1						1					
2	3					3	5				
4	6	9				9	15	25			
8	12	18	27			27	45	75	125		
16	24	36	54	81		81	135	225	375	405	
32	48	72	108	162	**243**	405	675	1125	1875	3125	

Abram <==> Abraham
The pivot point between Pythagorean and Just Tuning

The essence of the Torah is a tonal subset of the Tree of Life, which serves as an exact
"antidote" for the totality of knowledge within the Tree of Knowledge of Good and Evil

Figure 72 – Two Trees in the Garden

The 11 chromatic tones that derive from powers of 3 within the Tree of Knowledge have an upper limit of 243, while the same 11 chromatic tones can be found within the Tree of Life, since one of its legs also derives from powers of 3 with an upper limit of 243. The tones of the Tree of Knowledge are uniquely determined by a triple progression, since a duple progression (powers of 2) does not generate any new tones, only octave duplication of existing tones. The tones of the Tree of Life, however, are determined by both a triple and a quintuple progression. Since both trees contain a triple progression it is said that one tree is embedded in the other. The transition from Abram → Abraham indicates that his soul's "knowledge of good and evil" was mitigated by his meditation teaching which incorporated the Tree of Life's quintuple progression.

In the Tree of Life, i.e., Just tuning, the extra *Heh* = ה = 5 appears to "hover overhead" as the first power of 5 within the Just tuning diagram above. Abraham teaches man to bind that crown (*Heh* = ה = 5) to the Three Mothers, the Seven Doubles, and the Twelve Elementals. God Himself did this when he first created the three paths: the Wind Path, the Water Path, and the Fire Path. Binding the crown is the "divine influx" which man can initiate through deep meditation in order to extract the various paths of Wisdom from the Tree of Life.

After "engraving" the three paths with the divine influx of the crown, Abram was able to harmonize and purify his mind, soul and body, and, before long, he was deemed righteous by God. With the added *Heh* incorporated into his being, his name changed from Abram to Abraham (אברהם = 248),[285] and God said to Abraham, the tzadek:

> *Walk before Me and be perfect…you and your offspring after you throughout their generations…shall circumcise the flesh of your foreskin, and that shall be the sign of the covenant between Me and you…An uncircumcised male the flesh of whose foreskin shall not be circumcised – that soul shall be cut off from its people…[and] you shall be a father of a multitude of nations; your name shall no longer be called Abram, but your name shall be Abraham…*
> *--Genesis 16-17*

---

285 Genesis 17:5; Zalman, 247.

Once a crown (*Heh* = ‫ה‬ = 5) was added to Abram's name (243 +5 =248) it was spelled Abraham, and from that point forward "*a King* [God's *Shechinah*] *will reign over the children of Israel.*" In other words, God's Covenant with Abraham would be passed on to his descendents as their birthright, and all of Israel would one day be able to liberate their Shechinah (soul). To accomplish this, Abraham's practice will bind a crown to the Three Mothers, Seven Doubles, and Twelve Elementals, giving man a measure of control over the divine light of the primordial elements within us. Raising the divine light of the soul up to God (like a flame), can be accomplished by performing the 243 positive commandments, while performance of the 360 commandments will extract and contain God's light. This will substantiate the quality of *Chesed* (effluence, kindness or mercy), as well as the quality of *Gevurah* (strength and restraint), within one's character.

The patriarch's transformation from Abram → Abraham is defined by his soul's acoustical transition from 243 to 248, and from Pythagorean tuning to Just tuning. Abraham's name is the patriarch of numbers, since 243 functions as the acoustical lynch pin between man and God. The musical scale created on Day 6 is the essence of 360 prohibitive commandments (plus the crown (*Heh* = 5), to yield a total of 365 prohibitive commandments.[286] The two hovering crowns within the equations 243 + 5 = 248 and 360 + 5 = 365 need to be understood as the two wings of Metatron within the Holy Tetragrammaton's bird-like configuration. Abraham's practice will enable the soul to be contained and raised up on the two "Wings of Metatron."

Genesis pays considerable attention to this important transition between tuning systems. For example, in a different allegory echoing the familiar theme of sibling rivalry, Jacob receives the birthright from Isaac, instead of his firstborn brother Esau, who "remained in his wickedness from beginning to end, and never repented." Genesis 36.19 tells us that Esau is Edom, and the Kings of Edom were Esau's descendants. Genesis 36.31 speaks of the reign of the "8 Kings of Edom" (also described in Kings I), "...*before a King reigned over the Children of Israel.*" The reign of the eight Kings of Edom and their subsequent death also came to symbolize the transition from the seven tones (plus octave duplication of the eighth tone) generated by Pythagorean tuning to the eleven tones generated by Just tuning when "*a King will reign over the children of Israel.*"

286 360 is also the number of days in the solar year plus five festival days, for a total of 365 days.

As man meditates he radiates the essence of each commandment, providing them with "Wings." When this process is complete, the mind and body have been harmonized, and the soul can be liberated. Man's soul, time, and the universe were created from 32 paths of Wisdom. Man can retrace those paths and return to God by meditating along the 22 paths of Wisdom. The soul can be liberated as a golem, and ultimately, after all sin is purged through Sabbath prayer, the golem can be transformed into a Shechinah. A Shechinah will resonate with the reordered Ten Sefirot of Supernal Man in Beriah — 10 paths of Wisdom in Beriah: the reflected light of the transcendent Ten Sefirot of Nothingness in Atzilut.

Each person's Shechinah can be considered an individualized and perfect image of the universal and transcendent harmonic series that exists in Atzilut. Common sense, modern science and Abraham, tell us that no man or prophet can actually become God, i.e., the most global of all physical laws — the harmonic series — the rainbow principle.

The Twelfth Spoke

Abraham (gematria = 248) is said to epitomize *Chesed,*[287] and Enoch, the sixth generation after Adam, is said to epitomize *Gevurah* (he lived 365 years). Biblical scholars generally agree that when the Old Testament was canonized the most important writings among the Apocrypha and Pseudopigraphia were the Books of Enoch.[288] According to III Enoch: Chapter IV, God took Enoch to become Metatron, His highest-ranking angel.[289] In Genesis 5:23-24, the description of Enoch's time on earth is unique. It does not say that he lived and died, it states, *"All the days of Enoch were three hundred and sixty-five years. And Enoch walked with God; then he was no more, for God had taken him."*

Thus we have the "Torah and its Song": the vibrational essence of all 613 commandments of the Torah (248 + 365). The ascending 11-note Chesed scale helps raise the soul up to God, and the descending 11-note Gevurah scale restrains the temptations of the body's sacred cube. The gravitational "tugging" on the soul by the element earth occurs because earth obscures the divine light and prevents it from rising up. The body's physical appetites also keep the soul earthbound due to the

287 Zalman, 459.
288 Porter, 6.
289 III Enoch, Chapter IV; Halevi, 3

twelfth "spoke" of the sacred cube's vulnerability to temptation and sin. In order to partake of the Tree of Life and liberate one's soul from its vibratory prison, man must exercise perfect restraint (Gevurah) when dealing with his animalistic appetites and aversions, and a perfect giving nature (Chesed) to raise up the soul and transcend the 12 boundaries of the body's sacred cube.

Hebrew word for "circumcision" is *milah,* which also means "word." The meaning of this can be found in the biblical phrase "The spirit of God spoke in me, and His word (*milah*) is upon my tongue."[290] The "circumcision of the tongue" refers to the ability to have God "speak through us." When we are spiritually united with God we can understand and explain His divine mysteries, and the divine attributes of Wisdom and Understanding manifest in words that roll off our tongue. During the Priestly Blessing, when the High Priest raised his hands, he must raise them precisely to the level of the mouth as he made the blessing. The raised hand position was used to focus spiritual energy,[291] because the ten fingers bring forth the power of the Ten Sefirot. In the East, different hand positions during meditation are called *mudras,* which resemble antennae that send and receive energy.

"Circumcision of the membrum" represents the channeling of sexual energy to help one to the highest mystical states.[292] In the East, tantric sex (Sanskrit: woven together) also incorporates sexual energy into the "path to enlightenment." Within certain sects of Buddhism, Taoism and Hinduism, at a certain point in a monk or yogi's training, an equally trained consort can be taken as a means to stimulate one's nervous system to the necessary levels during meditation. After learning what is required to control one's inner energy during meditation, the monk or yogi may no longer need the consort. The bliss of deep meditation is said to be incomparably more blissful than orgasm.[293]

The renowned Jewish meditator and kabbalist Abraham Abulafia was noted for a meditation practice called "Ecstatic Kabbalah" due to the rapture of his meditation.[294] Although it is not known to incorporate a sexual practice, one's rechanneled sexual energy provides the ecstatic

---

290 Kaplan, *Sefer Yetzirah,* 35; Zalman, 291; II Samuel 23:2.
291 Kaplan, *Sefer Yetzirah,* 35-36.
292 Kaplan, *Sefer Yetzirah,* 37.
293 Lama Thubtan Yeshe, *The Bliss of Inner Fire* (Boston: Wisdom Publications, 1998), 149; Daniel Cozort, *Highest Yoga Tantra* (Ithaca, NY: Snow Lion, 1986), 71.
294 Moshe Idel, *Studies in Ecstatic Kabbalah* (Albany: SUNY Press, 1988).

element. The Taoist practice of "alchemy" involves certain meditation and breathing techniques that enable the practitioner to convert his semen into "chi" (Hebrew: "orot" = light), thus enhancing spiritual development. For Eastern religions the operative spiritual principle of celibacy is non-ejaculation. Ejaculation is discouraged within Taoism, for example, because it diminishes the meditation experience.

It is logical that sexuality plays a significant role within the nervous system, and one must therefore come to terms with it within a spiritual context. The phallic symbol of the evil serpent tempting Eve to partake of the "forbidden fruit," followed by Eve's temptation of Adam, has clear sexual connotations. The West has therefore come to identify sex with sin. Man's sexual appetites distract him from God, giving rise to a tradition of celibacy among clerics. In the East, sexual intimacy has become integrated into the path toward enlightenment. While Eastern and Western approaches to restricting ejaculation are very different, their goals converge in an attempt to channel sexual energy into spiritual enlightenment.

The divine sparks of man's soul are in exile within the sacred cube of the body, subject to a variety of irrational appetites that tempt us, such as gluttony, lust, and greed. To become one with God, one must detach oneself from the physical senses, appetites, and materialistic desires of sin by "circumcising" that twelfth vibration from our body's sacred cube, and raising the root vibration of our soul on the Sabbath. The real problem lies in precisely identifying the sinful behavior within us. The acoustical analog for this can be found in the large gap between the fixed tones of A and G. This range of frequencies might be thought of as the "devil's workshop," not only because it is the farthest from God on the tone circle, but also because we cannot pin down the exact location of the twelfth spoke, since there is no integer to define $\sqrt{2}$. As a result, this range of frequencies is thought to be the root vibration for a range of behaviours that must be restrained.

The 22 Paths of the Shechinah

A tzadek's kavanah (meditative intent) enables him to ascend and descend the ziggurat of Jacob's ladder at will, to harmonize and balance the opposing energies contained in the musical tones and scales of man's mind, body and soul. A tzadek has developed the strength of character to refrain from the evil inclinations of the "twelfth spoke" within the body.

Omitting this twelfth tone and meditating on only the eleven notes of the chromatic Gevurah scale purifies the human body's sacred cube. A tzadek has incorporated this restraint into his character, and his actions make the body translucent enough to allow the divine light of the soul to rise up the spinal column and leave the body. A tzadek must balance restraint with the effluence and kindness that manifests from meditation on the eleven-note chromatic Chesed scale. When the energies are balanced, and their numerosities raised from Sabbath prayer, the seven aspects of his soul will naturally rise like a flame toward God. Once man learns to stay balanced he can transfigure or liberate his soul, it will begin to resonate within the seven heavens created by the reordered Ten Sefirot in Beriah, which, in turn, derives from the transcendent God in Atzilut.

The Shechinah hovered over the sacred cube of the Holy of Holies, holding the Ark of the Covenant, directly between the "22 spans" separating the wings of the two Cherubim that adorned the Ark. The "Cloud of the Divine Presence," that hovered above the Ark, consisted of the two eleven-note musical scales totaling 22 tones, musically generated when a tzadek has learned to pray as meditation in a way that will bind a crown (5) to each aspect of his soul (powers of 2 and 3).

All prophecy originated from this location over the Ark. It is called the wellspring of prophecy. Prayer ascends to God along 22 paths of the Shechinah while prophecy and blessings descend from God along the same 22 paths. The acoustical diagram of the Shechinah manifests within Islam as the seven circumambulations around the Ka'bah. It is therefore interesting to note that the Ka'bah in Mecca was said to have 360 idols, arranged around it in a circle. One of Mohammed's first acts was to "cleanse" the Ka'bah of its pagan idols.[295] There is speculation that it represented the days of the year.[296] Without an understanding of the Book of Creation's Lost Word there was no way for Mohammed to know that the 360 objects removed from around the Ka'bah, were put there by Abraham, and were related to other sacred cubes, such as the tabernacle that existed in Jerusalem. Isaiah 35:20 states, *"a tabernacle that shall not be taken down; not one of the stakes thereof shall ever be removed, neither shall any of the cords thereof be broken."* If Mohammed had realized that the 360 stakes around the Ka'bah were part of Abraham's teaching, he would not have felt the need to "cleanse" it.

295 Renard, 86.
296 Armstrong, *Islam: A Short History,* 11.

Figure 73a – The Divine Presence that Hovered over the Ark
"Exponed in a Row"

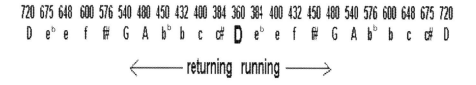

Figure 73b – The Divine Presence that Hovered over the Ark

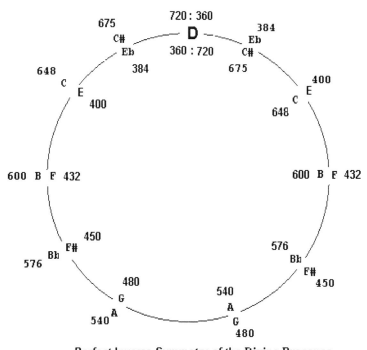

Perfect Inverse Symmetry of the Divine Presence

The 11 notes of the Ark of the Covenant that ascend and descend across 22 "spans"

The Fires of Heaven & Hell

3.4 *Three Mothers, AMSh (אמש),*
   in the universe are air, water, fire.
   Heaven was created from fire
   Earth was created from water
   And air from Breath decides between them.

4.15 *Seven Doubles: BGD KPRT (בגד כפרת)*
   With them were engraved
      Seven Universes, seven firmaments,
      Seven lands, seven seas,
      Seven rivers, seven deserts,
      Seven days, seven weeks,
      Seven years, seven sabbaticals,
      Seven jubilees,
         and the Holy Palace.
   Therefore, He made sevens beloved
      under all the heavens.

Day 7 transposes our Day 6 musical scale to a higher numerosity with multiplication by 7 to create the fires of heaven and hell. In order to remain consistent with the meaning of the Sabbath as the day of rest, use of the number 7 cannot generate any new tones. On the Sabbath we learn to control the last of the Three Mothers (ש), the element of fire, where the expression the "gates of Hell" and the "gates of Heaven" acquire meaning. The letter *Shin* (ש) exists in the last row of the 231 Gates table and opens to the path of the lower octave's 11-note chromatic scale defining the essence of Hell, followed by the higher vibrations of the upper octave's 11-note scale defining Heaven.

As we attempt to locate the twelfth spoke in our Just tuned tone mandala between the notes G# and Ab, we will see how the increased numerosity of the Sabbath scale facilitates closer approximations to $\sqrt{2}$, allowing us to better locate the subtle and elusive twelfth spoke, which identifies the "devil within us." Within Just tuning, music theorists call this imperfection a diesis rather than a comma.

We will learn to raise our "inner fire" with an enhanced Sabbath meditation that increases our ability for introspection and self-observation, so that we enter a deepened state of consciousness that distills our thoughts and places our angers and attachments in clear relief. Clearly identifying what causes our distractions from God makes it easier to "refrain from evil." Clarifying the forces within us that comprise the twelfth spoke of the tone circle may even make it possible for us to constructively transform those inner forces and utilize them "in the path" toward God.

The acoustical mechanics is straightforward enough. We transform the Day 6 scale into the Day 7 scale by simply multiplying all Day 6 tones by the number 7. When we transpose to a higher numerosity in this way, we may ask ourselves why the notes of the Day 6 scale never seem to change. It is as if the notes were multiplied by powers of 2, and not powers of 7.

This happens because Abraham's tone circles are never fixed to an absolute frequency, like today's standard of concert A = 440 cps. There are no fixed frequencies in nature, everything is relative! "The One" is a unification principle that can begin at 440 cps, just as easily as it can begin at 1 cps. Only the integer ratios remain constant, and are only meaningful in relation to one another. When multiplying or dividing a string by 7, we would normally be adding new tones of ratio 6:7 and 7:8, however, because of the Sabbath we are not using the number 7 as a tone generating ratio. We are simply multiplying the existing ratios of the Day 6 scale by 7, which slides the entire scale to a higher numerosity within the continuum of frequency and wavelength without interpolating new tones into the octave.

Figure 74 – The Sabbath Scale

D	eb	e	f	f#	G	Ab	G#	A	bb	b	c	c#	D
360	384	400	432	450	480	500	512	540	576	600	648	675	720
x7	x7	x7	x7	x7	x7	x7	x7	x7	x7	x7	x7	x7	x7
2520	2688	2800	3024	3150	3360	3500	3584	3780	4032	4200	4536	4725	5040
D	eb	e	f	f#	G	G#	Ab	A	bb	b	c	c#	D

Stanza 3.4 tells us "Heaven was created from fire." Abraham confirms the scale's upper numeric limit by telling us that 7 "stones" are used to build 5040 "houses" = 7! (7 factorial). The number 7 fulfills its role as the day of atonement and forgiveness within the week. It continues in this role when it defines the seventh year as a Sabbatical Year, or "Year of Remission," devoted to the cessation of agriculture, and holding in the period of seven years a place analogous to that of the Sabbath in the week (Book of Creation: Stanza 4.15).

Thanks to Abraham, civilization marks each week's time in terms of his ancient practice of "seven circuits around the sacred cube." As a simulation of God's seven day creation process, man's daily meditation of seven circles around the sacred cube must be done seven times on the Sabbath. This makes the Sabbath unique. The Sabbath prayer is man's day of rest because, unlike the rest of the week, we are not in the market place. Increasing the intensity of our practice puts us into a deep meditation that takes us home to rest in the bosom of God. By raising our inner numerosity, man's consciousness and ability for introspection is increased. As a result we can better identify that twelfth spoke, and better atone for it. We are also put in closer proximity to God with each multiple of seven that we perform the seven circuits.

Not only do we mark the passing weeks by Abraham's practice, but also the passing years of our lives. The Torah states; "You shall number seven Sabbaticals, seven times seven years…making forty-nine years…And to sanctify the fiftieth year, and proclaim liberty throughout the land…it shall be a jubilee to you" (Leviticus 25:8,10). Meditating along the Fire Path implies that we raising the numerosity of our inner fire in order to resonate with the fires of redemption. This will further purify our already liberated golem into a Shechinah, in what is called the Jubilee, the "remission of our soul" to God. Legislation concerning the year of Jubilee is found in Leviticus, xxv, 8-54, and xxvii, 16-24:

- rest of the soil;
- reversion of landed property to its original owner, who had been driven by poverty to sell it;
- the freeing or manual remission of those Israelites who, through poverty or otherwise, had become the slaves of their brethren.

Figure 75 – The Ziggurat and Sanctified Sabbath Scale[297]

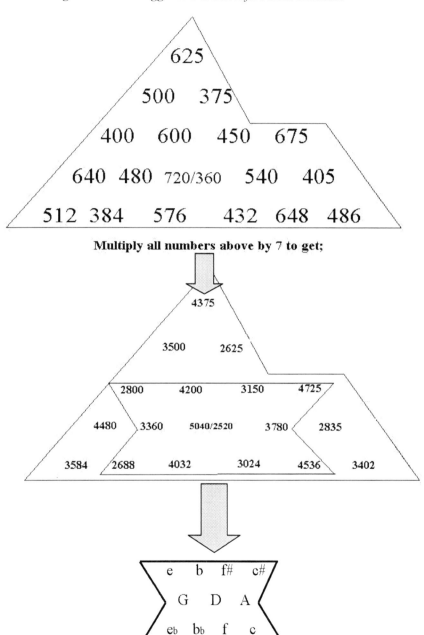

297 McClain, *The Pythagorean Plato*, 102.

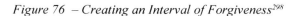

Figure 76 – Creating an Interval of Forgiveness[298]

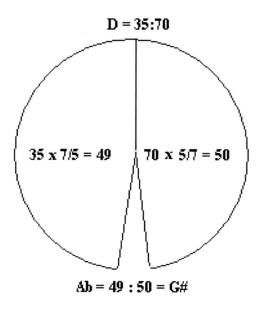

Figure 77 – The Jubilee Year

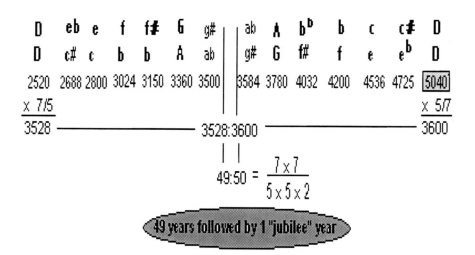

298 McClain, *The Myth of Invariance*, 97.

The Sabbath occurs every 7 days; the Sabbatical occurs every 7 years; and 7 Sabbaticals result in a 50th Jubilee year. "The Jubilee Year, which defines forgiveness of debt, is 49:50, which occurs within the 35:70 octave to yield the reciprocal multipliers of 7/5 and 5/7. After multiplication by the reciprocal sanctifying ratios of 7/5 and 5/7, the resulting diesis of 3528:3600 is reducible to 49:50. The Jubilee Year functionally behaves like a calendar's leap year, forgiving a man's debts and sins. On a spiritual level, Abraham's teaching of Sabbath prayer is necessary to attain the final forgiveness and the complete freedom from the exile of sin necessary for the remission of one's soul back to God. We must also read the entire Book of Exodus from this same perspective. Moses freeing the Israelites from exile and slavery in Egypt has its deepest kabbalistic meaning in the liberation of the soul from its exile within the body.

The Teli, the Cycle & the Heart

6.1 *There are the Three Mothers AMSh (שמא),*
And from them emanated the Three Fathers,
and they are air, water and fire,
and from the Fathers, descendants.
Three Fathers and their descendants,
And seven planets and their hosts,
And twelve diagonal boundaries
A proof of this
true witnesses in the Universe, Year and Soul
and a rule of twelve
and seven and three:
He set them in the Teli, the Cycle, and the Heart.

6.3 *The Teli in the Universe is like a king on his throne.*
The Cycle in the Year is like a king in the province.
The Heart in the Soul is like a king in war.

In the prophecies of the Book of Revelation, a great dragon pursued the woman who will bring forth Christ to the world, in order to devour the child, but the woman was given "*two wings of the great eagle that she might fly into the wilderness unto her place, where she is nourished for a time and times and a half time, away from the serpent.*"[299] The ensuing battle between the archangel Michael and his angels against the dragon and his angels resulted in *"that great dragon being cast down [to earth], the ancient serpent, he who is called the devil and Satan, who leads astray the whole world."* McClain explains the woman's time of nourishment by relating a "time" to the 360-day solar calendar, plus "times" meaning 2 x 360, plus "half a time" of 180, for a total of 1260 days.[300] The New Testament itself confirms McClain's arithmetic in Revelation 12:6, *"...where she has a place nourished by God, that there they may nourish her a thousand two hundred and sixty days."* This arithmetic helps confirm the vibrational essence of Hell by defining the octave double 1260:2520. McClain explains that the serpent has a central role across many cultures:

> In Tantric Buddhism ...there is a myth of Kundalini, translated 'Serpent Power' and meaning 'coiled' which may preserve the same cabala for 1,260...Kundalini normally lies asleep in the form of a serpent in three and a half coils ... at the base of the spinal column...There is the precedent for supposing that a 'coil' may represent the unit of a year of 360 'days' in which case 3½ would allude secretly to 1,260.[301]

This is the amount of time that the serpent in Revelation was given to tempt man to do evil. The beast was given a mouth and the authority to speak "great things and blasphemies" for 42 months in order to gather the forces of evil together for the final battle with good. McClain also points out that 42 months on the lunar calendar is the same 1260 days of the beast since 42 x 30 = 1260 days.[302] The final battle between good and evil is to take place on the battlefield of Armaggedon, which is a transliteration from the Hebrew Har-Megiddo, meaning "mountain of Megiddo." In other words, the "final battle" encrypts the final purification meditation.

The great "Beast of the Sea" had seven heads and ten horns, *"And all the earth followed the beast in wonder. And they worshipped the dragon because he gave authority to the beast."* The forces of evil will wear the

---

299 Revelation 13:14-15.
300 McClain, *Myth of Invariance*, 118.
301 McClain, *Myth of Invariance*, 122-123.
302 McClain, *Myth of Invariance*, 118.

"mark of the beast" on their right hand or foreheads. We may recall that the "mark of the beast," usually depicted by three 6's (666), is a misreading of what is actually 3 to the sixth power ($3^6 = 729$). In the triple progression below, as well as in the Day 6 and Day 7 construction, we can see that the beast was cast down into the "great abyss" which lies between Ab and G#. The incongruity between Ab and G# was considered the personification of evil, the "Diabolus in musica" associated with original sin.

Figure 78 - Triple Progression

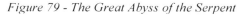

Ab	Eb	Bb	F	C	G	D	A	E	B	F#	C#	G#
729	243	81	27	9	3	1	1/3	1/9	1/27	1/81	1/243	1/729

Figure 79 - The Great Abyss of the Serpent

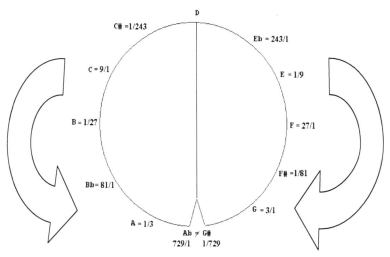

We may recall our previous discussion about the rays of divine light shining from Moses' head as he descended from Mount Sinai. The word "horns," as used in Revelation's 13:1 description of the beast of the sea *having seven heads and ten horns,* is a mistranslation of the Hebrew root קרן, which may be read as either "horn" or "ray," as in "ray of light." As with all *creatures that moveth* (including the great serpent), the Day 5 diatonic scale has 7 tones (7 heads) and was derived from reordering the Ten Utterances of God, i.e., ten rays of divine light (ten horns).

Many kabbalistic authorities identify the Teli mentioned within Stanza 6.1 as the pole serpent or coiled serpent. From Isaiah 27:1 we read about what would become Revelation's "beast of the sea":

> *On that day with His great harsh sword, God will visit and overcome the Leviathan, the Pole Serpent, the Coiled Serpent, and He will kill the dragon of the sea.*

Slaying the Leviathan is metaphor for man overcoming the evils of the twelfth spoke. From the Zohar (Chapter 1 of *Sifra Detzniyutha*) we read, "The engraving of all engravings appears as a long serpent, and extends this way and that. The tail is in the head..."

Figure 80 – The Teli

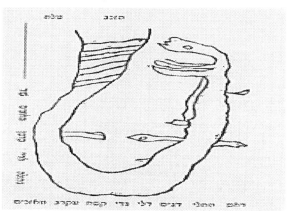

Revelation 12:4 describes the dragon, "*And his tail was dragging along the third part of the stars of heaven...*" Kabbalists associate the Teli with the pole serpent and the constellation of Draco [the dragon]. [303] Today, the heavens appear to rotate in a circular motion around the north star, but due to a slight wobble in the motion of the earth's axis[304] during the time of Abraham, a star in the tail of the constellation Draco, named Thuban, functioned as the north star, around which all the other stars rotated. Draco traveled in a complete circle around the heavens as the only constellation with stars in every house of the zodiac.

---

303 Kaplan, *Sefer Yetzirah*, 232-235.
304 Astronomers refer to this wobble as precession. You can see an example whenever you spin a top – the top rotates about the axis while the axis "wobbles."

In figure 81, the ancient serpent uncoils 3½ times from out of the "great abyss" to span across the 1260:2520 octave double that defines Hell. In Revelation the beast is given 42 months (1260 days or 3½ years) to slither across the acoustics of Hell to recruit evildoers, gathering the forces of evil for the last great battle at Armaggedon.

Following that same logic it would take the twin serpents of the soul's caduceus, seven years (or seven solar circuits) to cross the Fire Path, ascending and descending across the octave double that defines the 11 sanctified aspects of the sacred cube, 2560:5040. A perfect reciprocity for all 11 chromatic tones appears only in the upper octave of 2520:5040 which defines Heaven (note the missing numerical ratio in figure 81 for the C# and Eb in the lower octave). The lower octave defining Hell is depicted in the Hebrew Scriptures as a great beast who swims around the depths of the sea (the Leviathan), to ultimately be overcome by God; or, in the New Testament, as the beast who is defeated in the final battle at Armaggedon, and thrown into the great abyss (square root of two). The perfect reciprocity of Heaven creates "twin serpents" that can travel clockwise or counterclockwise around the axis where the "world and transcendent meet." The "final battle" corresponds to the final meditation process, in which the golem is purified into a Shechinah within the Jubilee gap of 49:50.

It is important to realize that Revelation is a mathematical allegory attempting to define the Fire Path used in Abraham's practice. The 3½ years of the beast that is Satan, defining Hell itself, is simply a parable meant to explain the lower octave acoustics describing the tumult of the meditation process that will lead us from sin. The great battle that ensues between good and evil is only waged on the battlefield within us. Abraham intended the Christian Armaggedon and Muslim Jihad to be waged only as an inner struggle, otherwise they become distractions from God. The true Ka'bah is within us! The third temple is within us!

Even when the body has been purified and harmonized through one's daily prayers, one must use Sabbath prayers to completely atone for sins. This will help ensure that any root vibrations of the soul from the octave double 1260:2520 are transposed to the octave double 2520:5040. The "waters" of daily prayer will liberate the golem into Yetzirah, and the "fires" of Sabbath prayer will purify it into a Shechinah within Beriah.

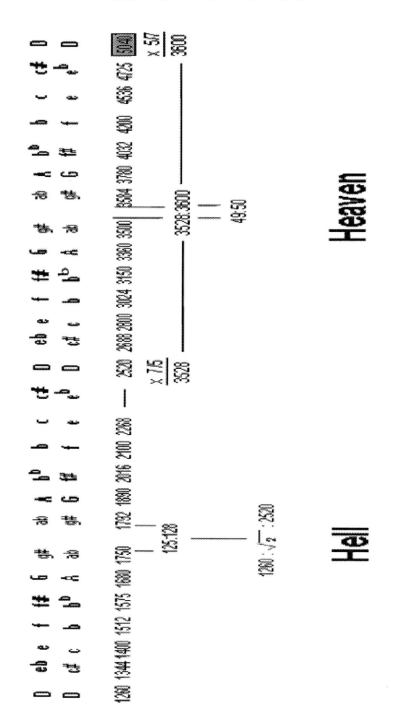

Figure 81 – Heaven & Hell

The twin serpents of the caduceus correspond to the mind's ability to harmonize the opposing energies of the soul, and lead them up the spine in a balanced way until the "third eye" opens, and the meditator is given the gift of prophecy. The seven circumambulations around the axis of the sacred cube is where the world and the transcendent meet.[305] The Zohar describes "*the circle and the square within*"[306] as follows:

> *Those who penetrate into the space of the circle-square, treading on the spot where the central point is situated…That point is called Ani (I) (Lev. 19:30), and upon it rests the unknown, the Most High, the unrevealed One which is YHVH (the Lord)…*[307]

Abraham's "small circle" meditation vibrates in harmony with the "great circle" around the heavens. The Teli is described as eating its tail. It situates the acoustical tone mandala of 22 letters comprising the Shechinah as manifest in the macrocosm of the Universe; the microcosm of our own Soul; and also defines the cycle of Time. These are the lost acoustical details for what the Middle Ages commonly called the Music of the Spheres.

Stanza 6.3 states: "*The Teli in the Universe is like a king on his throne,*" accounting for how God sets the seven tones as "*the seven planets and their hosts*" in the Teli, as well as the *seven universes, seven firmaments, seven lands, seven seas, seven rivers, seven deserts.* Within the acoustics of the Lost Word, the seven derives from God's expansion of divine light in six directions with the Holy Palace precisely in the middle.

When God sets the seven tones in the Cycle (Time), He accounts for the *seven days, seven weeks, seven years, seven sabbaticals, seven jubilees.* In later kabbalistic and Christian writings the seven aspects of the soul are either described as seven emotions, or as man's free will to judge between seven deadly sins and seven cardinal virtues. In the Book of Creation, when God sets them in the Soul, He accounts for the seven pairs of opposites:

- *Wisdom/Folly*
- *Wealth/Poverty*
- *Seed/Desolation*

---

305 Sells, 14.
306 Zohar, 5b.
307 Zohar, 6a.

- *Life/Death*
- *Dominance/Subjugation*
- *Peace/War*
- *Grace/Ugliness.*

In the Teli, the 12 diagonal boundaries of the sacred cube accounts for the 12 constellations of the zodiac. In the Cycle it accounts for the 12 lunar months within a solar year; in the Heart it accounts for the 12 directors in the soul (12 organ meridians), including : two kidneys, spleen, liver, etc., as well as 12 qualities: sight, hearing, smell, speech, taste, coition, action, motion, anger, laughter, thought, and sleep.

In summation, accomplishing complete freedom from sin requires the purifying fires of introspection and repentance on the Sabbath in order to carefully identify how and where we sin. The fires of Heavenly redemption can then counteract the sinful fires of Hell.

Hiding Imperfection

"Equal temperament," the tuning system widely in use today is not really a tuning system. It is more appropriately called a temperament because we temper, or alter, nature's musical intervals rather than tune them to nature's integers. To equally temper the piano, each octave is theoretically divided into 12 equal parts, and each semitone would have to approximate the twelfth root of 2 or: ($\sqrt[12]{2}$). The art of tuning a piano is to learn how much to mistune nature's intervals. Even with today's sophistication we have the same musical problem that confronted the ancients. Equal temperament is considered the most efficient way to hide the "imperfections" of nature, by spreading any commas or diesis evenly across the octave until they become imperceptible.

Plato was an exponent of equal temperament, as was Zarlino during the Renaissance. In allegory, Plato equated tones with the fine citizens of Athens, in which each citizen did not demand exactly what he was owed, but remained flexible, that is to say, "temperate" in nature.[308] Abraham would have held to the position that using equal temperament would be tantamount to denying one's sin, rather than facing it and seeking redemption and perfection in the "world to come."

308 McClain, *The Pythagorean Plato*, 5.

Science is well on its way to empirically corroborating that Abraham's theory of everything, which he called God, is fundamentally correct, because it bases Creation on the harmonic series as the essence of everything. Since music may be the most powerful determinant of the character of a man's soul, perhaps it is time to reassess whether our current musical tuning system, equal temperament, has run its course. All of the chaos and confusion in today's world suggest the need to focus on the inner stillness of the chord of nature, the harmonic series, to guide the evolution of our musical vocabulary, and our lives. This will help us return the essence of our soul to God and nature.

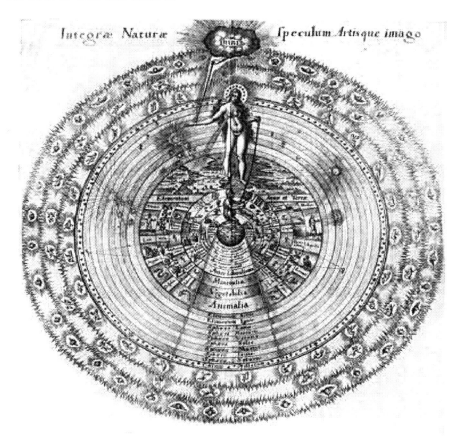

Figure 82 – The Tone Circles of Creation
(Robert Fludd: Utriusque cosmi II)

PART IV. ABRAHAM'S MEDITATION TEACHING

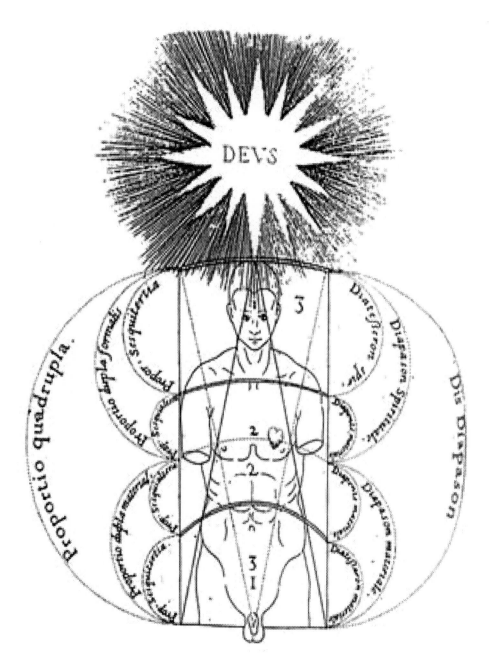

Figure 83 – Returning Man to Paradise
(Robert Fludd: Utriusque cosmi II)

The Sacred Practice

Meditation as Prayer

Since "meditation is, for all practical purposes, no longer practiced in Jewish circles, the meaning of the vocabulary associated with it has been forgotten."[309] The one word that is consistently used by commentators, philosophers, and kabbalists as a term for meditation is *hitbodedut* (self-isolation).[310] This term is understood as the highest of all practices, being the method used by the prophets to attain their revelation.[311] It was Melchizedek who blessed Abraham within Genesis, saying: "Blessed be Abram of God, the Most High."[312] Melchizedek was in the lineage of the secret practice of High Priests, and Abram's contact with him can be interpreted as his initiation into that practice – the only practice capable of going "behind the veil."

As pointed out in Part 1, the Torah usually makes reference to Abraham's practice in terms of a prophet meeting God within a "Storm on the Mountain." The storm is usually characterized by earthquakes, wind, fire, smoke, lightening, thunder, rain, hail, dense clouds, the sound of trumpets, etc. The Book of Creation's description of Abraham's practice in Stanzas 1.9 through 1.12 similarly uses the primordial elements of fire, wind, water, and clay (earth).

1.9   *Ten Sefirot of Nothingness:*
   One is the Breath of the Living God
      Blessed and benedicted is the name
         of the Life of the Worlds
      The voice of breath and speech
      And this is the Holy Breath.

309 Kaplan, *Meditation and the Bible*, i-ii.
310 Kaplan, *Meditation and Kabbalah*, 15.
311 Kaplan, *Meditation and Kabbalah*, 16.
312 Genesis 14:18-19.

1.10 *Two: Breath from Breath*
   With it He engraved and carved
      22 Foundation letters
         Three Mothers
         Seven Doubles
         and Twelve Elementals
   And one Breath is from them.

1.11 *Three: Water from Breath*
   With it He engraved and carved
      [22 letters from]
         chaos and void
         mire and clay
   He engraved them like a sort of garden
   He carved them like a sort of wall
   He covered them like a sort of ceiling.
      [And He poured snow over them
         and it became dust
         as it is written
      For to snow He said, 'Become earth'"

1.12 *Four: Fire from Water*
   With it He engraved and carved
      the Throne of Glory
      Serafim, Ophanim, and holy Chayot
      and Ministering angels
   From these three he founded His dwelling
      as it is written:
      "He makes His angels of breaths,
         His ministers of flaming fire"

1.14 *These are the Ten Sefirot of Nothingness:*
   The Breath of the Living God
   Breath from Breath
   Water from Breath
   Fire from Breath
   Up down east west north south.

Rabbi Kaplan references kabbalistic tradition, citing examples of various visualization techniques that use the Book of Creation as their starting point. For example, based on Stanza 1.11, in which "the initiate contemplates the ground, visualizing it as murky, black mud, he must then "engrave" the 22 letters "like a garden," forming each one in his mind. Then he must stand each one up, making a circle of letters, surrounding him "like a wall," in which he is instructed to imagine 231 lines connecting the 22 letters, and "deck them like a ceiling" over his head. Another visualization derived from the Book of Creation is described as follows:

> First visualize this blackness beneath your feet. Your feet may than appear to dissolve, a phenomenon that is also mentioned in other mystical texts. Slowly make this blackness creep over you, surrounding you completely like a wall. Finally let it cover and surround you like a ceiling of inky black mire. At this point you will have no visual sensation whatever, neither physical nor mental. All through this process, you are constantly aware of the feeling of water, cool and absolutely calm. It is the dark, wet feeling of the womb, where you are totally isolated from all sensation.[313]

Knowledge of Eastern meditation enables us to determine that what is being discussed by Kaplan as visualization techniques inspired by the Book of Creation may derive from actual visions experienced during meditation. The Hebrew perspective of these visions is referenced in the Book of Creation as *"engraving and carving [of the 22 letters] from chaos and void, mire and clay."* Kaplan finds similar descriptions in the Torah:

> In Hebrew, mire is Refesh, and clay is Tyt. The only place in the Bible where the two are mentioned together is in the verse, "The wicked are like the troubled sea. It cannot rest, and waters cast up mire and clay" (Isaiah 57:20). In describing the original state of creation, the Torah states, "The earth was chaos and void, and darkness on the face of the deep (tehom)" (Genesis

313 Kaplan, *Sefer Yetzirah*, 91.

1:2). According to the commentaries, the word Tehom denotes the mud and clay at the bottom of the sea.[314]

The Hebrew experience reflects the turbulence of water, mire, and clay that is cast up around us as God began engraving from the primordial soup. Compare this to the Tibetan meditative visions that speak of a "mirage of water seen in the desert heat," followed by "rising plumes of smoke," the flickering of fireflies, followed by the billowing of what Tibetans describe as "butterlamps."[315] Comparing the subjective meditation experiences of different cultures is like comparing descriptions of a piece of music. Common physiological responses, however, do conjure up images that are strikingly similar. The darkness and chaos of great earthquakes, raging waters, lightening and thunder, fire and brimstone, hail and snow represent the turbulence of Creation's primordial forces within us all. Everyone must learn to meditate in order to "climb the mountain," to tame the primordial forces within, and ultimately to transcend all worldly turmoil, if one is to unite with God.

Thirty-Two Mystical Paths of Wisdom

1.1 With 32 mystical paths of Wisdom
engraved Yah
 the Lord of Hosts
 the God of Israel
  the Living God
 King of the universe
  El Shaddai
 Merciful and Gracious
 High and Exalted
 Dwelling in eternity
 Whose name is Holy –
  He is lofty and holy ---
 And create His universe

---

314 Kaplan, *Sefer Yetzirah*, 75.
315 Butterlamps are a popular part of Tibetan culture. Tibetan monks lighting butterlamps on a dark night brings hope to the people. Their soft glow describes one of the four "visions" during Tibetan meditation.

> *with three books (Sepharim),*
>   *with text (Sepher)*
>   *with number (Sephar)*
>   *and with communication (Sippur).*

1.8   *The Ten Sefirot of Nothingness*
         Bridle your mouth from speaking
             and your heart from thinking
And if your heart runs
   return to the place.
      It is therefore written,
         "The Chayot running and returning" (Ezekiel 1:14).
      Regarding this a covenant was made.

The 32 mystical paths of Wisdom have been explained by kabbalistic tradition as "32 states of consciousness."[316] These progressive states of consciousness would be attained by all who have learned how to bind themselves to God. Abraham's teaching provides the tools necessary to realize the Secret of the 22 Letters so that man can liberate his golem (soul) into Yetzirah (Paradise) and ultimately resonate with its root vibration of 10 reordered Sefirot in Beriah (Shechinah). The Shechinah stands before the Ten Sefirot of Nothngness in Atzilut — the transcendent and omnipresent One.

Within man's evolving consciousness, Abraham's definition of free will includes the concepts of good and evil, but the complex morality this implies is not emphasized until the allegorical writings of the Torah. Instead, Abraham focuses on defining man's judgment as the harmonization of two opposing tendencies within the mind. He goes on to describe how man's entire being is similarly organized as a harmonization of these two opposing forces. Like a divine physician, Abraham prescribes three different meditation techniques that will judiciously balance the opposing primordial forces within us until we have entered a "balanced" state of being that will facilitate the liberation of the soul from the prison of our body.

Kabbalistic tradition warns, however, that those attempting to reach the highest vibrational levels necessary to liberate the soul should bind their soul with an oath so that it returns to their body.[317] Traveling to and returning from the heavens is described by Abraham's phrase "*The Chayot*

316 Kaplan, *Sefer Yetzirah*, 297.
317 Kaplan, *Sefer Yetzirah*, 68.

running and returning, " which can be understood in the acoustical context of the Covenant's ascending and descending musical scales. The Chayot are the "living angels" witnessed in Ezekiel's vision of heaven – the rising and falling vibrations of the "living God" that carry our consciousness within the vibration itself.

Abraham's first meditation principle is *"Bridle your mouth from speaking and your heart from thinking."* How speaking and thinking would distract us from meditation is obvious, however, one may wonder how the heart can think. The number 32 (*Lamed Bet,* לב) translates to the word *Lev,* or "heart," which plays a central role in the Hebrew language and culture, as well as in the human body. The Hebrew letters *Bet* and *Lamed* acquire a spiritual significance. "32 Paths form the 'heart of Creation,' which is understood as the essence of the Torah. The first letter of the Torah is the *Bet* (ב) of *Bereshit* (בראשית) - 'in the beginning.' The last letter of Torah is the *Lamed* (ל) of *Yisrael* (ישראל) – 'Israel.'"[318] The heart therefore embodies all 32 Paths, i.e., the 3 aspects of the mind, the 7 aspects of the soul, the 12 aspects of the body, and the 10 transcendent aspects of God. This corresponds to the Buddhist belief that a being's entire life force withdraws into a harmonized "drop" of essence within the heart during death (in preparation for rebirth), as well as during the deepest phases of meditation.

The לב also has a grammatical connection to the 32 Paths. Kaplan points out that the three letters of the holiest name of God – the Tetragrammaton: *Yud* (י), *Heh* (ה), and *Vav* (ו) – serve as suffixes for personal pronouns: *Yud* (י) means "me," *Heh* (ה) means "her," and *Vav* (ו) means "him." In the entire alphabet there are only two letters to which these suffixes can be joined in this manner, and these are *Lamed* (ל) and *Bet* (ב).[319] Thus one might say that the divine essence *runs* and *returns* to mankind grammatically, as follows:

Table 16 - Lamed (ל) and Bet (ב) as the "Heart" of Mankind

לי - to me	בי - in me
לה - to her	בה - in her
לו - to him	בו - in him

The primary rule of meditation is to quiet one's thoughts and speech, so the heart can be free to *run* and *return* to God along the 32 Paths. A heart

---

318 Kaplan, *Sefer Yetzirah,* 9.
319 Kaplan, *Sefer Yetzirah,* 10..

that is busy thinking worldly thoughts creates a distraction that derails the meditation process. Meditation should become a way of life that requires dispelling all aversions and attachments that initiate conceptual thought. Even the slightest distraction would be considered a vestige of ego that must ultimately be eliminated to master Abraham's techniques. Binding to God requires the soul to transcend on subtle energies that would be "short-circuited" by conceptual thought.

Kaplan equates the 32 paths of Wisdom with the 31 nerves that emanate from the spinal cord, while the highest and thirty-second of these paths corresponds to the entire complex of 12 cranial nerves.[320]

The Twelve Directors of the Soul

5.6 *Twelve directors in the soul*
male and female
the two hands, the two feet,
the two kidneys,
the gall bladder, the intestines,
the liver, the korkeban,
the kivah, the spleen.

In this passage we can also see that the Book of Creation speaks about twelve directors of the soul and ties them to one's internal organs, in a manner that is more than just reminiscent of Chinese traditional medicine's acupuncture theory, revolving around 12 organ meridians. Within Chinese traditional medicine there are 12 organ meridians which can be "needled," using acupuncture to either stimulate or sedate the appropriate meridian in a way that will "tune" the meridians to a proper balance. The 12 diagonals of the sacred cube are the organ meridians of the body that provide life-force (Hebrew: *orot,* Chinese: *chi*) to the 12 Directors of the Soul (12 body organs). The entry points to these "diagonals" are situated around Abraham's tone circle. They correspond to the location of acupuncture theory's "small circle" of 12 Chinese acupuncture points. The small circle serves as a resevoir to feed life-force to the body's internal organs via the autonomic nervous system.

As we explore similarities between Taoism and Abraham's teachings we will continue to find that there is more than coincidence at play. Clear parallels between Taoist philosophy, medicine and cosmology and Abraham's

320 Kaplan, *Sefer Yetzirah,* 8-9.

metaphysics strongly support the Talmudic teaching that "Abraham taught occult "mysteries" to the children of his concubines[321] and he sent them away ... to the lands of the east" (Genesis 25:6).

Chinese traditional medicine derives from the *Yellow Emperor's Classic of Medicine*, also known as the *Neijing*. Another important early Taoist work is the *I Ching*.[322] Both works are based on a "doctrine of opposites and the mean," which manifests in the opposites of "yin" and "yang" around the Taoist "pivot point." Yin is understood as the flow of one's inner energy (life force), or "chi," in a downward direction, and is likened to the flow of water; yang rises upward like fire; and wind balances or harmonizes these two opposites. The *I Ching* is noted for its comprehensiveness in addressing the manifestations of yin and yang in every conceivable situation and time of life. Through meditation, man naturally develops the judgment to harmonize all manifestations of yin and yang within, and through meditation becomes "One with the Tao" to bring him into harmony with the world around him.

The *Neijing* describes 365 acupuncture points on the body [323] sharing an obvious correspondence with the solar year. Similarly, the kabbalistic tradition speaks of 365 veins or "sinews"[324] that become purified by the 365 prohibitive commandments of the Torah. The Chinese system's 12 meridians within the microcosm also correspond to the 12 months of the year and 12 times of the day within the macrocosm. These parallels all contribute to the case for "gifts that traveled East."

Chinese traditional medicine recognizes 12 organ meridians and 8 "extraordinary" or "psychic" vessels within the human body. The three most important psychic vessels (or channels) utilize chi to judiciously balance the opposing aspects of yin and yang within them. The Chinese call them the conception vessel, the governing vessel, and the thrusting vessel (carrying balanced energy). The conception and governing vessels are semi-circles that form a circular reservoir which continually feeds chi to the 12 organ meridians, thus sustaining the 12 organs and keeping them healthy. Even without the small circle meditation, chi flows through each of the 12 organ meridians every 2 hours, thereby completing a "great circle" every 24 hours.

---

321 Tanakh, Genesis 25:6; Sanhedrin, 91b; Zohar 1:99b, 1:133b, 1:233a.
322 Richard Wilhelm and Cary F. Baynes, trans., *The I Ching* (Princeton, NJ: Princeton University Press, 1950, 1977).
323 Maoshing Ni, trans., *Yellow Emperor's Classic of Medicine* (Boston: Shambala, 1995) 203.
324 Zalman, 585-586.

Figure 84 – The Great Circle: 24-Hour Energy Flow thru 12 Organ Meridians

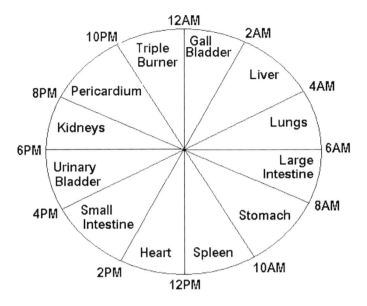

Figure 85a, b & c – The Small Circle: Abraham's Three Meditation Techniques

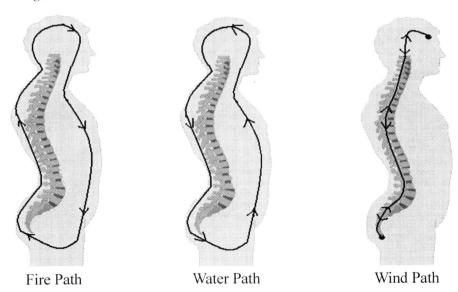

Fire Path   Water Path   Wind Path

Figure 86 – The 12 Directors of the Soul

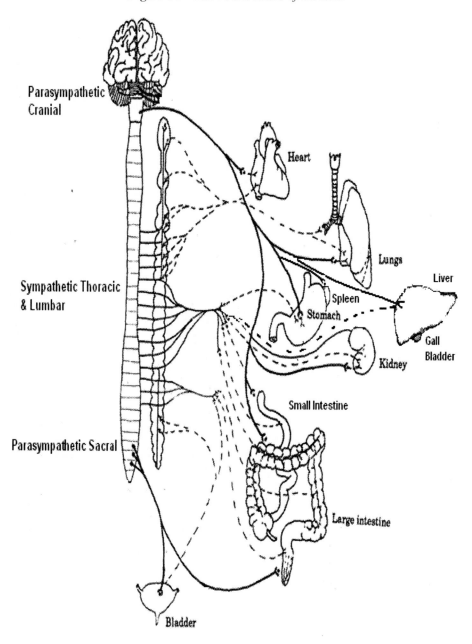

Three Mothers

6.2 *Three Mothers: AMSh (אמש)*
Air, water, and fire.
Fire is above, water is below,
and air of Breath is the rule
that decides between them.
And a sign of this thing
is that fire supports water.
Mem hums, Shin hisses,
and Alef is the breath of air
that decides between them.

Creation's primordial forces are the *Three Mothers*: Air, Water and Fire. The first Mother, *Alef* = א, the "Breath of God," manifests in the subtle "winds" of the soul. With the second Mother, *Mem* = מ, God's light flows downward into matter like water requiring the vibrational essence of all the "sacred cube" containers of God's light, such as the human body. The third Mother, *Shin* = ש, defines the fires of sin and redemption for mankind, i.e., the vibrational essence of Heaven and Hell. The metaphorical "flames" of Hell will torment a man's soul, while the sanctifying flames of Heaven will rid us of sin and tonal impurities. These three Gates "open" to reveal three musical paths: the vibrational essence of the three primordial elements that God used to "engrave" Creation. But man can also use these three musical paths defining Creation to find our way back to God.

Abraham's three meditation techniques correspond to Taoism's "small circle" meditations, as practiced by Chinese Taoist monks and martial artists. The Water Path, Fire Path, and Wind Path adjust and redistribute the elements of water, fire, and air within us to harmoniously balance our being. In Stanzas 1.10 – 1.12 we have Abraham's name and description for these three meditation techniques: *Breath from Breath, Water from Breath, and Fire from Water.* These three techniques are depicted in Figure 85a, b, and c as three separate circuits, which are the 3 main energy paths or channels. The components of these energy channels can then be broken down into 7 aspects of the soul and 12 aspects of the body.

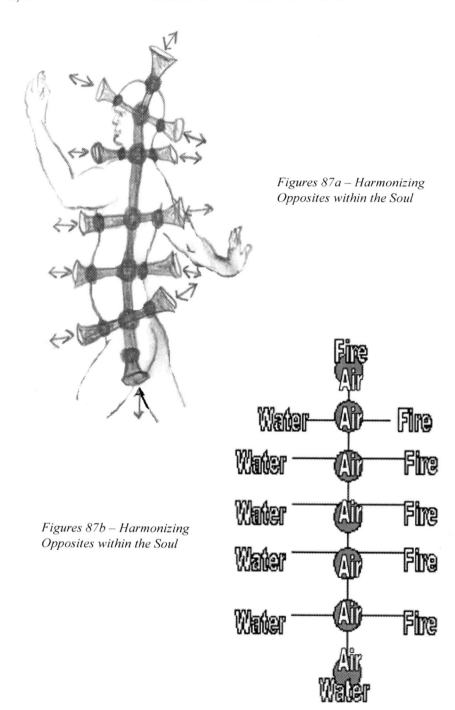

Figures 87a – Harmonizing Opposites within the Soul

Figures 87b – Harmonizing Opposites within the Soul

Figure 88 – The Acoustics of 3 "Mothers," 7 "Circuits" and 12 "Directors"

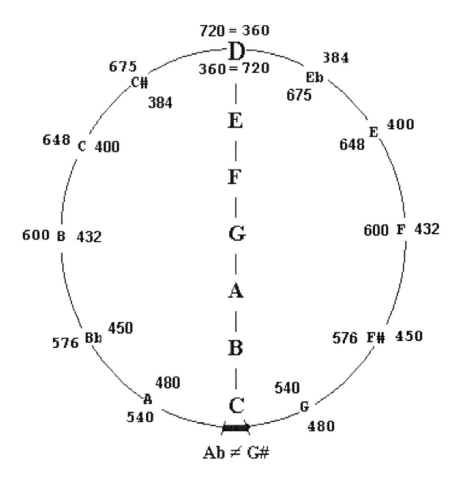

Three Channels of the Mind
Seven Aspects of the Soul
Twelve Aspects of the Body

The Wind Path

__1.10__ Two: Breath from Breath
With it He engraved and carved
22 Foundation letters
Three Mothers
Seven Doubles
and Twelve Elementals
And one Breath is from them.

The three Gates can be found along the *y* axis of the 231 Gates table (*AMSh* = אמש). The first gate opens to the "Ten Utterances" of Day 1 of Creation. The Ten Utterances get "reordered" in Days 2 through 4 to generate the "Wind Path." This is the musical path that defines man's central channel within the body, where the "Breath of God" can be thought of as inhaling our soul, and exhaling it back into our bodies. The Breath of God also manifests as the air of human respiration to "fan the flames" of our metabolism. One controls this element using the Wind Path.

The respiratory system, obviously necessary to sustain life, plays a critical role in various physiological functions. Within the context of the Book of Creation, man's breath is said to derive from the Breath of God. This becomes evident in Stanza 1.10. The word *ruach* translates to three words: breath, spirit, and wind. In this context the word ruach can be read as either *Breath from Breath, Wind from Breath,* or *Spirit from Breath.* These three valid perspectives manifest as man's breath from God's Breath; reordering the Breath of God into the primordial element of Air or Wind; as well as reordering the Breath of God into man's spirit or soul.

Within Taoism the Wind Path is the central mediating, or harmonizing, element of air that will blend and balance the opposing yang energy of heaven's fires with the yin energies of earth and water. Within the Book of Creation, the Wind Path corresponds to judgment with respect to balancing the elemental opposites of fire and water within the body, mind and soul. Breathing technique, one of the most important tools in a meditator's arsenal, is typically the first thing taught to those beginning a meditation practice. We can see from the following passage that meditation enables the mind to override the autonomic nervous system's control of the breathing function:

> Neurophysiologically speaking, breathing has an ambiguous function: it is most of the time unconsciously performed, because it is controlled by the muscles attached to the autonomic nerves, and yet it can also be consciously controlled. Taking advantage of the latter fact, breathing exercise in meditational self-cultivation consciously works on the autonomic nerves so as to correct or eliminate the emotional distortion in the unconscious.[325]

The Fire Path

1.8   The Ten Sefirot of Nothingness
> *Bridle your mouth from speaking*
> *and your heart from thinking*
And if your heart runs
> *return to the place.*
> *It is therefore written,*
> *"The Chayot running and returning" (Ezekiel 1:14).*
> *Regarding this a covenant was made.*

1.12   Four: Fire from Water
With it He engraved and carved
> *The Throne of Glory*
> *Serafim, Ophanim, and holy Chayot*
> *And Ministering angels*
From these three he founded His dwelling
> *As it is written:*
> *"He makes His angels of breaths,*
> *His ministers of flaming fire" (Psalms 104:4).*

The Chayot are the "living angels" witnessed in Ezekiel's vision of heaven – the rising and falling vibrations of the "living God" (see Stanza

---

325 Yuasa Yasuo, *The Body, Self-cultivation and Ki-energy* (Albany: State University of New York Press, 1993), xviii, 58.

1.8 above). The Zohar states, "*It is said of the Hayyoth that 'they run to and fro' (Ezekiel 1:14), and so no eye can follow them. The Hayyoth which disclose themselves are those in the midst of which there is an Ofan (wheel)...*" We also know from Ezekiel 1:20 that "*the spirit of the creatures was in the wheels.*"[326]

In other words, Abraham's tone circles are the Ophanim (wheels) that contain the Chayot (tones) which are used in all of Abraham's acoustical constructions. Isaiah speaks of the Serafim[327] as "fiery, burning" angels, each with four wings and four faces, who are the caretakers of God's throne, singing *Kadosh, Kadosh, Kadosh: "Holy, Holy, Holy is the Lord of Hosts, the whole earth is full of His Glory."* [328] Their sound shook the Temple and filled it with smoke. In II Enoch they "incessantly sing" God's praises. In Christian medieval theology they are considered the angelic choir. Thus, God "*founded His dwelling,*" His "*Throne of Glory,*" "*from these three,*" "*Serafim, Ophanim, and holy Chayot.*" For Abraham "*these three*" are not just attendant angels, they comprise the fiery "Throne of Glory" itself – a throne of tone circles, tones, and a "voice" to sound those tones (see book cover for a depiction of Ezekiel's chariot-throne).

One can speculate that the mind's interactions with the autonomic nervous system defines the "Throne of Glory" as it exists within the body, i.e., the temple within. The autonomic system includes two branches: the sympathetic (usually illicting excitatory responses) and parasympathetic (usually illicting inhibitory responses), as well as the endocrine system, and the immune system. These controlling systems effect localized responses to central nervous system commands,[329] suggesting that the primordial element of fire anchors the soul's vibrations within the electrophysiology of man's nervous system. One likely path for the mind's fire would begin in the brain where the pineal gland and hypothalamus are located, and work its way down through the pituitary to the other endocrine glands, to exert a level of control over the endocrine system and emotions. Abraham's practice also appears to illicit autonomic control in the manner of a Hindu yogi's ability to slow his heart rate. This would give man the ability to effect physiological change within his inner organs and glands, and thus exert the measure of control necessary to balance the body's primordial elements.

326 Ezekiel 1:20
327 Isaiah 6:1-7; 6:2-4.
328 Isaiah 6:3.
329 Schneck and Berger, 77.

Within the context of the Book of Creation, and thus within the context of its Taoist offshoot, the primordial element of fire harnesses the energies of heaven. Man can access the fire element through non-conceptual thought around the small circle, which produces a tiny electromagnetic current that can be directed or focused at will by the meditator. The fire of thought empowers man to "engrave" like God. Wherever the fires of thought go, the chi (life force) follows with it.

In the Fire Path, one's "Yi" (mind) leads the chi down the conception Vessel, inhaling to "fan the flames," and exhaling to lead chi around the circle back up the governing channel. If the body is deficient of yang energy, or has an overabundance of yin energy, due to an excess of the water element, then one uses the Fire Path to balance one's energies. Only when these energies are balanced can the chi begin to enter the central Thrusting channel.

The Water Path

1.11 Three: Water from Breath
        With it He engraved and carved
     [22 letters from]
chaos and void
 mire and clay
He engraved them like a sort of garden
He carved them like a sort of wall
He covered them like a sort of ceiling.
     [And He poured snow over them
          and it became dust
          as it is written
     "For to snow He said, 'Become earth'" (Job 37:6).]

To quench the fires of excessive yang energy within the body's nervous system or insufficient yin energy within the body's irrigation systems, the technique called "*Water from Breath*" adjusts the various waters (Chinese: Kan) within the body to cool down its inner fire (Chinese: Lii). The element of water manifests within the semen, blood, and other liquids of the body, and the musical path taken to exercise control over water is called the Water Path. According to the principles of Chinese alchemy, semen is considered an important component of the body's water element. If not wasted through ejaculation, semen can effectively modify the Kan:Lii balance by converting it into *chi* during the small circle meditation, enhancing one's spiritual development. By altering one's breathing technique, and reversing the non-conceptual flow of mind (*Yi*) around the small circle, the Fire Path can be transformed into its reciprocal Water Path.

Within Taoism, the term alchemy refers to the creation of chi when the breath (air or wind) fans the flames (fire) of thought, and turns the semen (water) into a kind of "steam" (chi) during the small circle meditations within the "caldron" of the triple burner. The triple burner uses this steam to "cook" or metabolize food into nutrients (earth) which enrich the body. The harmonized blend of fire, water, and air then circulates around the small circle as chi, filling the 12 organ meridians and combining with nutrients to "feed" and purify the body. Chinese alchemy, as an offshoot of Abraham's teaching, can be understood as mastering the three primordial elements as tools in the meditation process: the harmonization of mind control (fire), sexual control (water), and breath control (air).

In the Water Path, the mind and breathing first lead one's chi across the nerve plexus that control the water of the kidneys and bladder (lower *dan tien*), and then continues upward to "cool" the solar plexus (middle dan tien) that control the "fires" of metabolism. The Water Path helps to quench an overabundant fire element and brings the fire-water balance back into harmony.

In Figure 87, we can see that when the six pairs of fire-water opposites are harmonized and balanced, life-force can be directed through the Wind Path within the central channel. Depending on the location within the body, various types of fire (non-conceptual thought and metabolism) are balanced by various types of water (semen, kidneys, or urinary bladder).

The highest center of mind (fire) has its opposite in the lowest center corresponding to the sexual organs (water). The six pairs of fire-water opposites become the 12 aspects of the body, positioned around the circumference of the "small circle" as key acupuncture points, which serve as the physical gates to the 12 organ meridians. The seven aspects of the soul can be found along the harmonized, central channel.

The Seven Heavens

The mind can lead chi through the "small circle" that is formed by connecting the conception vessel semicircle and the governing vessel semicircle. The third psychic vessel is the central channel, which bisects the circle and is known as the thrusting vessel, leading from the perineum and sexual organs to the top of one's head. The meditator's breath fans the flames of non-conceptual thought, but instead of leading these mental "flames" through the outer conception or governing channels, one holds one's breath slightly, with focus lingering in the "caldron" of the dan tien. If the energies are sufficiently balanced, this technique should begin to direct energy up the central thrusting channel rather than through the conception or governing channel. There are effectively three different paths possible from this configuration of channels, as depicted in figure 85: the Fire Path, Water Path and Wind Path.

Our meditation creates vibrations at various locations that would resonate with God's original *engraving* of man's body, mind and soul. Since every object in nature has its own resonance frequency, Abraham may be correct to assume that each of the 12 gates to the 12 organ meridians have their own operating frequency, perhaps related to the resonance frequency of its associated organs. Each vibration of meditative consciousness sounds a different note that might be analogous to tuning into different radio stations. Abraham would describe each tone as spinning *like a whirlwind* to find its proper location within the body's three tone circles:

> *And His word in them is "running and returning"*
> *They rush to His saying like a whirlwind*
> *And before His throne they prostrate themselves.*

Each of the 7 tones situated along the center path and each of the 12 tones situated around the circle belong to a musical scale that can be "sung" in two directions. One's daily prayers occur as a chromatic scale in either a clockwise or counter-clockwise direction, running and returning around the octave tone circle. The Sabbath prayer has considerably more intensity than our daily prayers because the Sabbath's 7 x 7 circuits results in a higher numerosity and deeper level of introspection. This enables us to better identify and atone for our sins so that we might ultimately balance the forces within and transcend the duality of good and evil, and its tugging at our soul, which keeps it earthbound.

The acoustics of the ascending and descending scales are referenced in Stanza 1.8: *"If your heart runs, then return to the place."* In other words, if the meditator has scattered or distracted thoughts when stepping through the small circle, it becomes important that one stop all such distracted behavior in order for the heart to *return to the place.* If one's concentration is not distracted, then it becomes possible to step through the ascending Fire Path from 360:720, or, as necessary, step through the descending frequencies of the reciprocal Water Path meditation from 720:360.[330]

Abraham's daily practice and intensified Sabbath practice will purify the body and balance the fire and water elements within by utilizing the reciprocal 11-note scales that exist for that purpose. Once these opposing energies are balanced we are in a position to begin directing this energy directly up and down the central channel using the Wind Path. In Figure 88, we can see that the central channel consists of the seven pure tones of the Phrygian mode, which defines the soul, and which, one might speculate, is related to the resonance frequencies of the endocrine system's seven ductless glands. To transition from the 11-tone chromatic scale to the 7-tone Phrygian mode, our meditation must somehow surpress the 6 tones that comprise "Knowledge of Good and Evil.

Figure 89 – The Tree Knowledge of Good and Evil

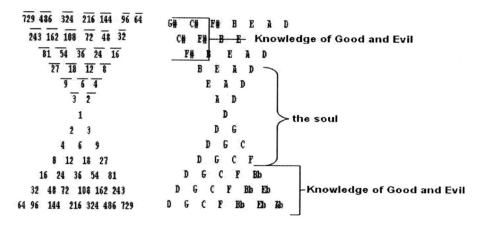

---

330 Zalman, 449. "Michael is the prince of water, and Gabriel is the prince of fire.

To accomplish this Abraham instructs us to "bridle... thinking" about the world with its inherent duality in order to transfigure our soul: *Bridle your mouth from speaking and your heart from thinking.* To enter Paradise we must not only refrain from all evil, but we must transcend all conceptual dualities of thought, such as good and evil, in order to return us to that state of innocence before original sin ensued.

Once all seven "trumpet" tones of the soul are sounded within the central Wind Path during meditation, it becomes possible to liberate the soul from the body — as long as it is not "weighed down" by knowledge of the world, or the taint of sin. Bridling one's dualistic conceptual thought implies the need to rise above one's loves and hates, attachments and aversions. Otherwise, one's life-force remains within the outer circle that resonates to those dualities.

The Gift of Prophecy

It is apparent from the text that Abraham achieved this level of development in his own meditation practice. The following passage is taken from Kaplan's Short Version translation:

6.7   *And when Abraham our father, may he rest peace,*
      looked, saw, understood, probed,
          engraved and carved,
      He was successful in creation ...
      And He bound the 22 letters to his tongue
          and He revealed to him His mystery
      He drew them in water,
          He flamed them with fire,
          He agitated them with Breath,
          He burned them with the seven [planets]
          He directed them with the twelve constellations.

Once again, we recall Aryeh Kaplan's statement that the Book of Creation appears in the form of an instruction manual, because "Hebrew is written without vowels, and therefore, the third person and the imperative are written exactly the same... '[Yah] engraved it' can also be read in the imperative, 'Engrave it.'"[331] Stanza 6.7 states that it is not only God that is

331 Kaplan, *Sefer Yetzirah*, 90.

able to "engrave" and "create" matter, but that Abraham was able to have
mastered these techniques as well. As a result, God revealed to Abraham
His mystery, binding the 22 letters to Abraham's tongue. Thus, Abraham's
Shechinah became a "wellspring of prophecy," like the Shechinah that
hovered over the Ark of the Covenant within the Holy of Holies, directly
between the "22 spans" separating the wings of the two Cherubim that
adorned the Ark. "There I will meet with you, and I will impart to you
– from above the cover, from between the two cherubim...."[332]

Running and *returning* around the tone circle manifests within
Metatron as seven clockwise ascending circuits and seven counterclockwise
descending circuits of twin serpents crisscrossing in a double helix. Each
complete circuit either ascends or descends around the "axis point where
the world and the transcendent meet."[333] The goal of one's meditative
paths around the circle is ultimately to balance the energy, enabling it to
move up and down the central channel. This will awaken the soul's seven
aspects, including the third eye's prophetic vision. "The climactic stage
of this spiritual education is the power of prophecy."[334]

Mankind must learn that prayer means learning how to pronounce
His Great Name. Once man follows Abraham's teachings and learns to
"pronounce" God's Great Name, then "all who are linked to My name"
will be brought back to Israel "from the end of the earth;"[335] "'*For the
earth shall be full of the knowledge of the Lord,*' and '*the glory of the
world will be revealed.*'"[336] "*In that day there shall be one Lord with
one name.*"[337] The prophet Isaiah tells us "*He will destroy death for ever.
My Lord God will wipe the tears away from all faces.*"[338] The Book of
Revelation prophesizes that, in the "End of Days," the seven trumpet tones
will herald the descent of the sacred cube of the "New Jerusalem" from
heaven, when all men will know the meaning of "seven circuits around
the sacred cube." Revelation echoes the prophecy of Isaiah:

> *And God will wipe away every tear from their eyes; and
> death shall be no more, neither shall there be mourning,*

332 Exodus 25:22.
333 Sells, 14.
334 Revelation 21:4.
335 Isaiah, 43:6-7, 11:12.
336 Zalman, 453.
337 Zechariah, 14:9.
338 Isaiah, 25:8; Zohar, 29a.

nor crying, nor pain any more, for the former things have passed away. [339]

If Abraham's theology were properly understood, it would have enormous implications for the three faiths. It would imply that all men who follow Abraham's teaching could acquire the gift of prophecy that accompanies the liberation of the soul. It would be the beginnings of a new egalitarian world order, in which it was not only possible for man to become an "anointed one," but it would recognized as a moral imperative; and it will soon be based on an empirical understanding of God and the soul.

A Comparative Study of Advanced Techniques

Perhaps Tibetans, more than any other modern culture, look to meditation as a way of life. It may be wise to look to them for possible insights about its subtleties, and the more advanced states of meditation. Tibetan Buddhist monks and lamas have written extensively and lucidly about the many nuances and stages of meditation. In the most advanced meditative practice of Dzogchen,[340] one is able to spiritually advance according to one's ability to live life in complete identification with one's essence energy (channel-wheels are the Buddhist equivalents of the tone-circles that Abraham calls Sefirot). A monk's entire life is viewed as meditation.

Tibetan legends portray great practitioners achieving a "rainbow body" as they maintain themselves "in the clear light" through meditation while death approaches. Legends speak about men who have locked themselves away during their final days, meditating on the "clear light" while the physical body shrinks in size, until it has been completely absorbed by its own vibrational essence into a "rainbow body," complete with several days of rainbows appearing over the Lama's enclosed tent. Achieving the rainbow body in this manner is the great goal of Dzogchen, and this phenomenon has some relatively modern witnesses. What is left

---

339 Revelation 21:4.
340 HH Dali Lama, *Dzogchen* (Ithaca, NY: Snow Lion, 2000), 125-126; Prior to Buddhism, Tibet's native religion was called Bonpo, which is said to have originated the practice of Dzogchen. Subsequently Dzogchen was incorporated into Buddhism with methods that are said to be the "pinnacle" of Buddhist practice, surpassing even those of Highest Yoga Tantra. The various Buddhist methods are appropriate to various types of people. One attempts to engage in a practice using methods most appropriate to the individual.

of the physical body is only hair and nails, which become the cherished relics of faithful followers. There are also many miraculous stories and legends of the 84 great Mahasiddhas of India, who continue to inspire men toward maintaining a serious meditation practice.

Within Tibetan Buddhism, in addition to Dzogchen, there are also the methods of Highest Yoga Tantra.[341] There are several Highest Yoga Tantras, and one of the most well-known is called the "The Six Yogas of Naropa."[342] These six yogas could be considered representative of Tibetan Highest Yoga Tantra in general. The most important is called "inner fire" yoga or *Tummo*, the basis of the other five yogas. During deep meditation a monk is said to experience four visions and then four blisses, culminating in the liberation of the soul. In other words, a controlled simulation of death causes the soul to rise up out of the physical body into what Tibetans call their illusory body. If all goes well, the illusory body will return to the physical body, and the practitioner will awaken. Tibetan Buddhist monks practice dying their whole life long using this method of deep meditation. It is the heart of the Tibetan practice just as it is the heart of Abraham's practice.

When the big moment finally comes for Tibetans, they have already perfected "running and returning" and perhaps will be "awake" and lucid enough to choose their parents for their next incarnation as they journey through the "bardo" (heaven). Perhaps they can remain in the "clear light" of the final bliss until they have attained Buddhahood, making the "return" trip of an additional incarnation unnecessary.

Monotheistic faiths and polytheistic faiths speak of those who can journey through the heavens. There is an analogous explanation for Jacob's Ladder; for Ezekiel's vision; for Mohammed's "night journey"; and for the Transfiguration of Christ. Within the Jewish tradition, the initial "etheric form" that rises out of the body is called a golem, which matures into a Shechinah. Tibetan Buddhists call this the impure illusory body, which then matures into a pure illusory body. The New Testament refers to this as Jesus' "heavenly body." Chinese Taoists, using Abraham's meditation techniques, have come to envision an actual gestation period before an "immortal fetus" rises out of the top of one's head.

---

341 Cozort, 117.
342 Glen Mullin, *Tsongkhapa's Six Yoga's of Naropa* (Ithaca, NY: Snow Lion, 1996), 62-90.

When the Talmud relates that "Rava created a man," the "golem" that Rava created was not quite so corporeal a body as Jewish tradition would have us believe, but instead was akin to the Buddhist notion of an illusory body. The heart of Abraham's message is that mankind is capable of, and responsible for, a direct relationship with God that will ultimately lead to unification with God. Once a man purifies his sacred cube along the 22 paths of Wisdom, his soul is able to ascend and descend through the seven heavens of God's Ten Sefirot

The divine light of our souls is anchored within the nervous system of our body, which we know is electrically based; our thoughts appear more like radio waves, which are also electromagnetically based. Within this context, mastering our inner divine light implies mastering our thoughts and gaining control of our nervous system. The "divine influx" of the crown that meditation binds to all the aspects of one's being is experienced as an electromagnetic pull accompanied by the flashes of light and "turbulent" visions that seem to engage both the optical and auditory nerves. In the course of one's evolving meditation practice, the meditator will typically feel the magnetic pull of the electromagnetic divine influx grow more and more pronounced over the years of one's "practice."

For Tibetans, the liberation of the soul is a simulation of death, in which the four inner elements – earth, water, fire and air – sequentially "dissolve" into one another as the experience progresses. The meditator typically closes his eyes and gazes at the blank screen of one's "third eye." As the third eye begins to open, the four initial visions describe a "mirage of water seen in the desert heat," corresponding to the earth element dissolving into the water element; this is followed by "rising plumes of smoke," corresponding to water dissolving into fire; then the flickerings of fireflies, which corresponds to fire dissolving into air; and finally, the billowing of butterlamps, which corresponds to air dissolving into "mind."

Physiologically, as the body systems quiesce during meditation, there seems to be a gradual coordination of subtle nerve impulses which are visibly perceptible as a shimmering or "mirage." This energy gradually coalesces into the slowly rising delineated waves of "smoke." As energy is led up the spine, the optic nerves perceive a "flickering" and then cloudlike "puffs" of light.

Years of following Abraham's deep meditation practice result in an audible and persistent "dripping" or "clicking." Within the Rig Veda, this is Indra's precious "soma juice." The divine "ambrosia" or "dripping" that begins to flow after years of deep meditation is a common physiological phenomenon that has been identified within the New Testament as a "true baptism of the spirit" and what it truly means to be an "anointed one."[343] This "anointing" is described in Abraham's meditation instruction in Stanza 1.11, *"For to snow He said, 'Become earth'" (Job 37:6),* which tells us to maintain a non-conceptual focus of our energies on the lowest energy centers (*Malkhut*: the element earth and *Yesod*: associated with the sexual organs and the kidneys, i.e., the water element). This initiates an electromagnetic pull downward on its magnetic opposite at the top of the head, in the most upper Sefirot, resulting in the "snow" that "anoints" a successful meditator. Within the Book of Creation this is described by *"an appearance of lightening... And He poured snow over them..."* The Tanya states that:

> A man must know that the Light which shines above his head needs oil...And King Solomon cried saying, "Let there be no lack of oil above thy head."[344]

Like the "fire path" found in both the Book of Creation and in Taoist practice, the Buddhist "inner fire" meditation, called *"Tummo,"* melts a person's "Bohdi substance" at the top of the head, which then "drips" downward in the central channel. David Corzot describes how a Tibetan Buddhist monk's meditation balances the opposing energies of white and red drops flowing in the outer channels to create a harmonized flow of drops in the central channel:

> Yogic techniques to ignite heat are indispensable to tantric practices because they cause the white and red drops – subtle substances that coat the inside of the channels – to melt and flow to various spots, bringing about intense feelings of bliss...The bliss engendered by causing the white and red drops to flow in the central channel is said to be a hundred times greater than the pleasure of ordinary orgasm.

343 Scholem, *Kabbalah*, 180-181.
344 Zalman, *Tanya*, 157; Ecclesiastes 9:8.

In the Tanya we read:

> In the terminology of the Kabbalists (this attribute) is called *tiferet* [truth], because it is made up of the two colours white and red, which allude to *chesed* [kindness] and *gevurah* [strength].[345]

Similarly, Lu K'uan Yu's *Taoist Yoga* describes the immortal seed as the union of two lights – the white light of vitality descends to unite with the ascending reddish-yellow light of the generative force.

After Buddhism's four initial visions that accompany the dissolution of the four elements into "mind," the meditator experiences the four emptinesses as four distinct states. As the Bodhi substance melts and begins to drip from the top of the head down the central channel to the heart, it is called the "mind of appearance" consisting of white drops accompanied by a flash of white light and a feeling of deep bliss or "emptiness." With the "mind of red increase," red drops move from the lower nerve plexus to the heart, accompanied by a flash of red light and a second feeling of deep bliss. The "mind of black near-attainment" occurs as the white and red drops meet in the "heart drop" accompanied by the vision of black light, while a swooning results in a brief loss of consciousness. When the two drops stabilize in the heart one experiences the final bliss, and the "mind of clear light," accompanied by a pale light. Once stabalized in the pale light, the soul will naturally begin to rise up out of the body. A Tibetan monk learns to remain in this clear light for a prolonged period of time.[346]

Tibetan Buddhists call the subtle energies of the four elemental dissolutions "winds" or "airs." In the New Testament's Book of Revelation, which is based on Abraham's teaching, "four angels standing at the four corners of the earth, holding fast the four winds of the earth, that no wind should blow over the earth, or over the sea, or over any tree."[347] The angels were poised to ride on a white horse, a red horse, a black horse, and finally the pale-green horse of death (see cover).[348]

In the Hebrew Scriptures, the prophet Zechariah describes the four winds of heaven "coming out from between two mountains" as four

345 Zalman, Tanya, 451.
346 Mullin, 76-77.
347 Revelation, 7:1-2.
348 Revelation, 6:1-8.

chariots drawn by white horses, red horses, black horses and bay horses. The two mountains are nothing less than our key acoustical constructions depicted in Genesis but without their reciprocals, changing their appearance from two trees in the Garden of Eden to two mountains.

The Shared Vision of the Prophets

The Hebrew prophets share a vision of the Celestial Chariot. Zechariah saw four chariots come out from between two mountains, drawn by white, red, black and pale horses; Revelation's four horsemen of the Apocalypse have the same coloring; Elijah was swept away in a whirlwind by a fiery chariot; Ezekiel also has vision of a fiery chariot drawn by four "creatures." This shared vision is perhaps best elaborated by Ezekiel. His vision of the "Divine Presence" offers vivid and accurate verbal description of Abraham's mathematical constructions. The *"heavens opened and I saw visions of God..."* Ezekiel's vision of the "cloud of the Divine Presence" begins with the familiar storm of primordial elements that characterizes meditation.

Figure 90 – From Between Two Mountains

"Between the Mountains" is embodied by the
transition between Abram <==> Abraham

Subset of Tree of Knowledge
Embodied by Abram

Subset of Tree of Life
Embodied by Abraham

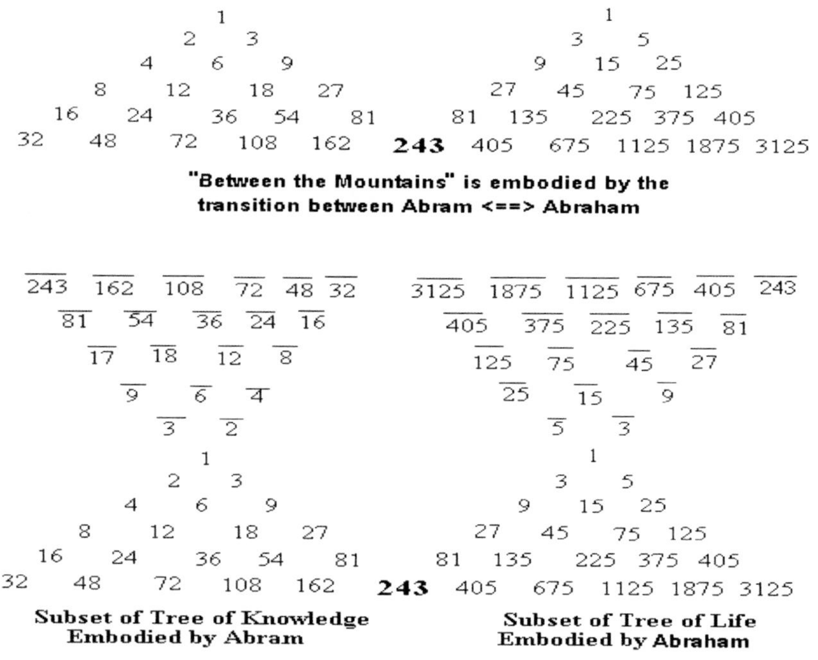

The following excerpt from the Book of Ezekiel has been depicted in the artwork on the cover of this book, in a way that is consistent with both the Hebrew Scriptures and Abraham's Book of Creation:

I looked and lo, a stormy wind came sweeping out of the north – a huge cloud and flashing fire, surrounded by a radiance; and in the center of the fire, a gleam of amber. In the center of it were also the figures of four creatures. And this was their appearance: They also had the figures of human beings. However, each had four faces, and each had four wings; the legs of each were fused into a single rigid leg, and the feet of each were like a single calf's hoof ... Each of them had a human face at the front; each of the four had the face of a lion on the right; each of the four had the face of an ox on the left; and each of the four had the face of an eagle at the back ... Dashing to and fro among the creatures was something that looked like flares. As I gazed on the creatures I saw one wheel on the ground next to each of the four faced creatures. As for the appearance and structure of the wheels, they gleamed like beryl. All four had the same form; the appearance and structure of each was as of two wheels cutting through each other. Wherever the spirit impelled them to go, they went – wherever the spirit impeled them – and the wheels were borne alongside them; for the spirit of the creatures was in the wheels. When those moved, these moved; and when those stood still, these stood still; and when those were borne above the earth, the wheels were borne alongside them – for the spirit of the creatures was in the wheels ... When they moved, I could hear the sound of their wings like the sound of mighty waters ... Above the expanse over their heads was the semblance of a throne, in appearance like sapphire; and on top, upon this semblance of a throne, there was a semblance of a human form ... There was a radiance all about him. Like the appearance of the bow which shines in the clouds on a day of rain ...[349] the House [of Israel, i.e., the Temple] was filled with the cloud, and the court was filled with the radiance of the Presence of the LORD ...[350]

349 Ezekiel 1:1-28.
350 Ezekiel 10:4.

Figure 91 – Elijah Swept Away from Elisha in a Chariot of Fire
(Gustave Dorè)

Ezekiel's vision summarizes all the acoustical constructions of the Torah already familiar to us from Part III. It is a wonderfully graphic depiction of the Divine Presence upon the Throne of Glory, "above the expanse," over the heads of four, four-faced creatures, riding in a highly mobile, noisy, fiery chariot, which Ezekiel describes as the "cloud" of the "Presence of the LORD." Ezekiel's vision no doubt depicts the same "fiery chariot" that swept Elijah away in a "whirlwind." We may recall from Part 1 that this "Cloud of the Presence of the LORD" was the "wellspring of prophecy" that hovered over the Ark of the Covenant between the two Cherubim that adorned the cover of the Ark, and hovered over Moses' tent in the desert. Ezekiel's "Cloud" contains considerably more detail than the cloud hovering over the Ark or the cloud hovering over Moses' tent.

We have already stated in Part 3, the section entitled "The Wheels of Ezekiel," that his four-faced creatures depict the "spirit" characterized by the four prime-number tone circles (2, 3, 5 and 7). The wheel of the duple progression, powers of 2, describes Ezekiel's ox, which plows the fertile earth to plant the seed of Creation. The duple progression is the octave tone circle, or female aspect that "contains" and "gives birth to" all the other tones. The wheel of the triple progression, powers of 3, is characterized by the face of man. On the Fourth Day of Creation seven tones were created from the element air, by the triple progression, to form the image of God that was breathed into Adam's nostrils on Day 6. The wheel of the quintuple progression, powers of 5, is characterized by the face of an eagle, because it represents the "eagle hovering over the nest" or the "wings of Metatron," God's highest ranking angel. The wings of Metatron can lift a sacred cube, created from the quintuple progression, through the seven heavens up to God. The wheel of the septuple progression, powers of 7, is characterized by the lion, the "King of creatures," who reigns over his subjects, just as the Shechinah is the King that reigns over Israel. In other words, man must conquer the "great beast" within for the King to reign.

The four faces of each beast correspond to four distinct tone wheels, which then harmonize and merge together into one complex tone-wheel. The spirit of the ox, man, the eagle, and the lion are "in the wheels," and integrate into the soul of the passenger in the chariot. Abraham's triangular acoustical constructions would be best described graphically as "two wheels cutting through each other." Each tone wheel corresponds to a different musical interval. The ox corresponds to the musical interval of an octave, and is usually associated with woman, because the octave "gives birth" to all the other intervals and scales. Man is represented by a tone circle of musical fifths, dividing the octave up into balanced segments. The eagle is associated with major and minor thirds, dividing the interval of a fifth up into balanced segments. The lion's tone circle is a cycle of musical sevenths. The tone circles "cut through" one another, until all four harmonize in the rainbow of sound that we call the harmonic series.

Figure 92a – Man's Soul Liberates by Harmonizing the Four Tone Wheels:
Ox = 2, Cherub = 3, Eagle = 5, and Lion = 7

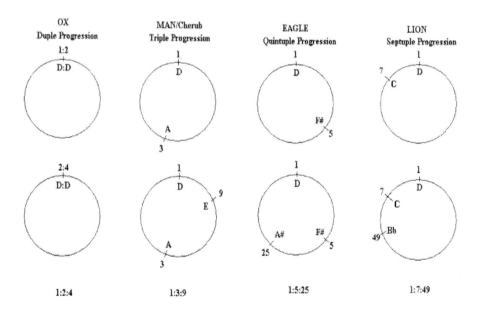

Figure 92b - Ezekiel's Wheels "Cutting Through" One Another

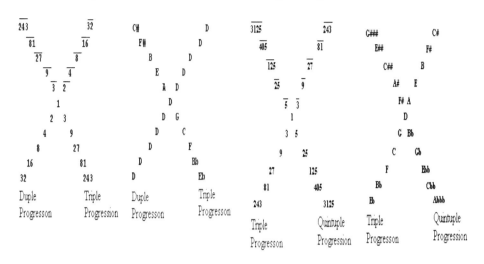

Figure 92c - Ezekiel's Wheels "with means inserted"

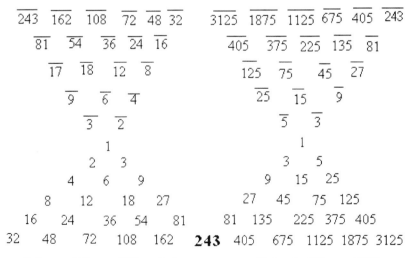

Subset of Tree of Knowledge Embodied by Abram

Subset of Tree of Life Embodied by Abraham

Figure 93 – Ezekiel's Wheelworks

Figure 94 – Ezekiel's Wheelworks

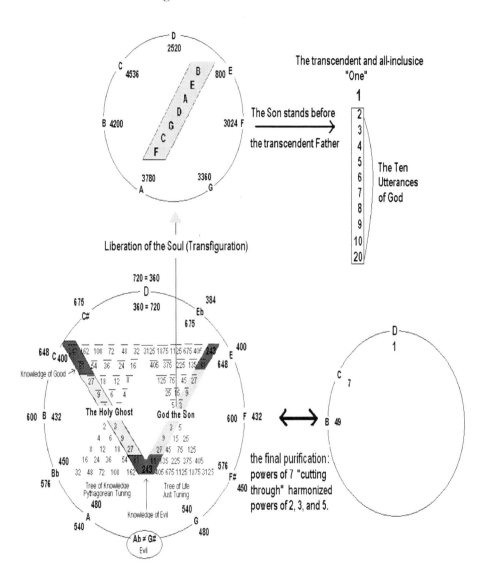

Kabbalistic tradition has defined an animal soul within us that drives man toward evil in order to fulfill its appetites. That evil resonates with the vibrational essence of Hell's octave double 1260:2520. Ezekiel's lion enables man to overcome the appetites of the animal soul and to raise his consciousness beyond the lower octave Fire Path, and through the upper octave's Fire Path, defined by the octave double 2520:5040. The "fires of heaven" enable us to atone for all sin.

The three paths to God were built from the musical "genetics" of Ezekiel's tone wheels. It is the coalescing "rainbow principle" that harmonizes the four tone-wheels, with each wheel distinguished by the face and character of the ox, man, the eagle and the lion. Enoch, Ezekiel, and Elijah, are examples of this harmonized type of being. In other words, man must integrate the wheels of Ezekiel in order to be carried to heaven in this chariot. Enoch was able to overcome sin and conquer death by liberating and perfecting his soul to "walk with God." Elijah joined this "eternal priesthood" when he was swept to heaven in a whirlwind.

Man's spiritual evolution is determined and measured by the wheels of Ezekiel. The tone-wheel of the ox, the duple progression, "cuts through" the wheel of man's triple progression to create man's soul (Figure 32a). This occurs within what kabbalistic tradition calls the world of Beriah on the Fourth Day of Creation within Pythagorean tuning. This new composite wheel of the soul ($2 \times 3 = 6$) then "cuts through" the wheel of the eagle (quintuple progression) to contain the divine light within the pure sacred cube of the body (see Figure 63c). The integrated composite tone-wheel of powers of 2, 3 and 5, within octave double 360:720 (Figure 73b), now corresponds to the vibrational essence of a harmonized mind, body and soul. In the final step (depicted in Figure 94), this composite wheel is shown "cutting through" the septuple progression tone wheel of the lion that will completely purge the taint of sin — purifying the golem into a Shechinah.

The Bahir defines the "Sphere" as the "Womb" of Creation.[351] It then tells us that the Tree of Life exists within the 12 diagonals, and the 12 diagonals exist "Inside the Sphere."[352] Inside the $2 \times 3 \times 5$ sphere (the tone wheel of Figure 94) we have therefore depicted the two trees in the garden. The gematria of Abram => Abraham marks the transition point, or lynch pin, between the two trees: Pythagorean tuning and Just tuning.

351 Kaplan, *Bahir*, 40 section 106.
352 Kaplan, *Bahir*, 34 section 95.

Once initiated into this sacred practice, the harmonization of these two trees (powers of 2, 3 and 5) integrates them into the large circle of the Divine Presence that encompasses them. This is the process of binding our mind, soul, and body to God. Abraham's sacred practice enables us to walk these paths of wisdom toward God, integrating Ezekiel's wheels into our state of being, until we are swept up in the whirlwinds of Ezekiel's fiery chariot. Once we have atoned for all our sins in the crucible of the intensified Sabbath and Jubilee prayers (integration with the final wheel in Figure 94), we will be able to conquer death, as a member of the eternal priesthood, in the manner of Enoch, Elijah and Jesus.

Figure 95 - The Astrological Origins of the Cherubim

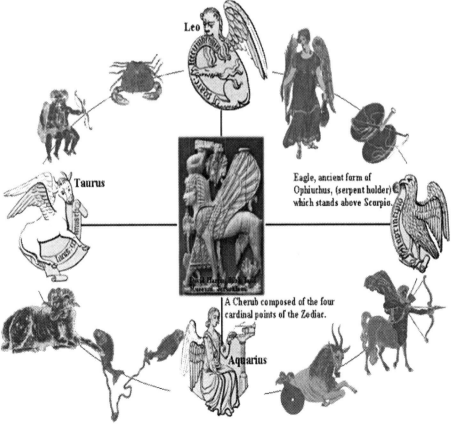

Eagle, ancient form of Ophiuchus, (serpent holder) which stands above Scorpio.

A Cherub composed of the four cardinal points of the Zodiac.

The Sum Total of Kabbalah

Man's soul is held earthbound by sin and dualistic thought. The only way to free the soul from its prison within the body is either to die or to partake of the Tree of Life, which implies seven circuits around the sacred cube. Following Abraham's practice of seven circuits will enable man to balance the three primordial elements that make up the mind, etheric body and soul – fire, water, and air, respectively. Mastering these will ultimately enable man's soul to transcend the dense earth element that makes up the outermost garment of his physical body.

The "Three Mothers" represent the three primordial elements that must be mastered during the meditation process: the fire of thought and the water of procreation, balanced by the air of breath. The mind can access these elements through the 32 paths of Wisdom,[353] which include:

1. The 11 tones of daily prayer using the Fire Path in a clockwise direction around the 12 aspects of the body's 360:720 octave double.
2. The 11 tones of daily prayer using the Water Path in a counterclockwise direction around the 12 aspects of the body's 720:360 octave double.
3. The 11 tones of Sabbath prayer using the Fire Path in a clockwise direction around the 12 aspects of Heaven's 2520:5040 octave double.
4. The 11 tones of Sabbath prayer using the Water Path in a counterclockwise direction around the 12 aspects of Heaven's 5040:2520 octave double.
5. The 7 tones of the Wind Path is the final path, ascending and descending to/from God.

A man's daily prayers, as well his Sabbath prayers, travel along the same ancient road traveled by all the great prophets — the 22 paths of Wisdom. It will balance the practitioner's opposing energies of fire and water, until a third type of meditation, the Wind Path, can liberate the seven aspects of the soul. The soul will then ascend the seven heavens toward

353 It is interesting to note that Hindustani music uses 22 Srutis, which derive from string theory within the Book of Creation's Eastern counterpart, the RG Veda..

the reordered Ten Sefirot of Nothingness that defines Supernal Man in the world of Beriah.

Since the Ten Sefirot of Nothingness in Beriah is a direct offshoot of the Ten Utterances in Atzilut, it derives from God's ten "source tones," and therefore serves as the model of resonance for all of Creation. When man's soul fully ascends it resonates with this prototype model of Supernal Man in Beriah before descending back into the body. The 3 aspects of the mind, 7 aspects of the soul, and the 12 aspects of the body, all get radiated by the divine influx during the meditation process. The divine influx (*Heh*) is fully factored into the 22 Paths of Wisdom.

Taken together the 22 Paths of Wisdom, plus the 10 Sefirot of Nothingness, constitute the 32 paths of Wisdom that is the "sum total of Kabbalah." The 11-note Fire Path and its reciprocal 11-note Water Path provide divine light to man's 12 inner organ meridians, i.e. the 12 "Directors of man's soul." The practitioner must be aware that evil inclinations derive from the twelfth spoke and must be "circumcised" or not acted upon, which is why there are 11-note paths of Wisdom and not 12-note paths. The waters of procreation must be absorbed by the 11-note Water Path and not wasted through ejaculation. The 32 paths of Wisdom include daily and Sabbath prayers, cleansing the body, atoning for sin, and liberating the soul.

The linchpin of spiritual progress is contained in the allegory of the name Abram (243) and his "crowning" transformation to Abraham (248). It may be a remarkable coincidence that the name of the patriarch of the three faiths, author of the Book of Creation, happens to have the exact numerical name (243+5=248) that serves as the spiritual patriarch of all numbers. Whether or not Abraham was a real historical figure is less important than realizing that whatever the author's actual name, it is the name, Abraham that provides the acoustical lynchpin between sin and morality. If the Name, *Yahweh*, provides the theological foundation of the three faiths, it is the name, Abraham, that provides man's moral compass. Together, these two words enable us to grasp the transcendental meaning of Scripture. Perhaps this is why the Zohar asks and answers the question: *"When did that key open the gates and make the world fruitful? It was when Abraham appeared...as soon as the name Abraham was completed the Sacred Name was completed along with it."*[354]

---

354 Zohar, 3b-4a.

PART V. SUPERSTRING THEORY: THE FOURTH FAITH

Figure 96 - Linking the Microcosm and the Macrocosm
(Robert Fludd: Utriusque cosmi II)

The Modern Quadrivium

Reuniting Religion and Science

Modern scientific man has had great difficulty relating to a God that can't be touched or seen, and no convincing link between science and religion has ever been discovered. The irony is that Abraham's monotheism was originally conceived in terms of ancient string theory, thus science and religion were born as a single entity. Needless to say, the scientific foundation of religion has been lost for thousands of years. Almost 1500 years after Abraham was believed to have lived, Plato described identical acoustical constructions long believed to have originated with Pythagoras. These constructions defined a "Music of the Spheres" that linked vibrations within seven "spheres" of the soul to the macrocosm of the seven planets and the twelve constellations. About 3500 years after Abraham, and 2000 years after Pythagoras, some corroboration came from the scientific community, when Johannes Kepler (1571-1630) "discovered his famous laws of planetary motion, in which integer ratios held between the length of each planet's year and its distance from the sun."[355]

There has been more recent corroboration as well. Since the 1950's it has been shown that "the hadrons, strongly interacting particles, are also quantum manifestations of this Pythagorean [or rather Abrahamic] ideal."[356] Within the past 22 years, unit multiples deriving harmonic waves has emerged within the scientific community as the "deep structure" of nature's framework and the organizing design principle of Creation. Since Abraham understood that harmonics provided the organizing principle of Creation almost 4000 years ago, the current whirlwind of debate about intelligent design can be completely redefined.

To explain God's light in scientific terms, it is best to begin with the nature of light itself. In 1666 Newton refracted sunlight through a triangular

---

355 F. David Peat, *Superstrings and the Search for the Theory of Everything* (Chicago: Contemporary Books, 1988), 53.
356 Peat, 53.

glass prism onto a white screen and he did not get the single spot of light that he had expected. Instead, the light was spread out in a band of colors: red, orange, yellow, green, blue and violet. It is interesting that this hidden band of inner components received the name "spectrum," which derives from the Latin term for "ghost." Newton's discovery provides an interesting perspective to the biblical story that a rainbow is God's signature to his covenant with Noah. At the time of Newton's discovery, the discovery of what we might call a "rainbow of sound," the harmonic series, was less than 50 years away.

In the twentieth century, the physics of the very large (relativity) and the physics of the very small (quantum mechanics) could never be reconciled. In the last 30 years of his life, Einstein set out to define a "unified field theory" that would describe a comprehensive mathematics tying together all four forces of nature: gravity, electromagnetism, and the strong and weak forces of the atom. He intuitively believed in a set of natural global laws that were capable of reconciling these bookends of twentieth century physics, but after 30 years, he was unsuccessful in his efforts.

Ancient science may have been primitive, but Abraham believed that the most global of all mathematical and physical laws was structured like sound. Within Abraham's cosmology and cosmogony, God's Utterances were reorganized into musical scales that defined the vibratory essence of the ancient elements: air, water, fire and earth. These four elements were then combined to form the objects and beings of Creation. The more etheric elements were closer to God, while earth, the most dense of the elements, would be the furthest away from God. Earth obscured divine light and weighed down the spirit with ignorance and dullness. Fire rises up toward God like prayer, forming the heavens; while water flowed downward and forward, like time and God's blessings. Air is the Breath of God that arbitrates between the opposites of fire and water, harmonizing the body and mind until the soul can be liberated for its return trip to Paradise.

In 1984, John Schwarz, from the California Institute of Technology, and Michael Green from Queen Mary College at the University of London finally figured out the mathematics that "ties it all together." The result of their efforts, called superstring theory, has emerged over the last 22 years as the most viable candidate for a "theory of everything" (TOE).

As it turns out, the key to Green and Schwarz's mathematics is the same theory of vibrating strings recognized by Abraham as the hand of God.

We will attempt to explain Creation within the mathematical framework of modern superstring theory, and we will see that, Abraham, the patriarch of the three faiths, is also the patriarch of ancient string theory. Abraham used the very same mathematical approach to explain Creation almost 4000 years before Green and Schwarz lived and worked. We will attempt to demonstrate that Abraham was not only the patriarch of monotheism, but also the great patriarch of science. In today's world, science and religion appear to be irreconcilable, appearing at opposite ends of the spectrum of reason and revelation. We will hopefully come to understand that, for Abraham, the terms science and theology would carry little or no distinction.

Particles & Fields

A new concept appears in physics, the most important invention since Newton's time: the field. It needed great scientific imagination to realize that it is not the charges or the particles but the field in space between the charges and the particles which is essential for the description of physical phenomena. - Einstein[357]

Newton's concept of light as particles, which he called "corpuscles," did not account for why the bands of light within the spectrum didn't collide, or why each color refracted differently. A few years later, a Dutch physicist named Christian Huygens was able to explain the refraction phenomenon by proposing that light was made of little waves rather than corpuscles, with each different-color wave having a different wavelength.[358] For hundreds of years Newton's "mechanical" view dominated physics; however, it eventually became clear that Newton's "particles" did not sufficiently explain new insights into electrical and optical phenomena, and Newton's view needed to be revised.

357 Albert Einstein and Leopold Infeld, *The Evolution of Physics* (New York: Simon & Schuster, 1938), 244.
358 Issac Asimov, *Asimov's Guide to Science*, (New York: Basic Books, 1972), 340.

This revision marked the birth of modern physics.[359] It began in the 1860s, when Michael Faraday worked out the lines of force around a magnet. James Clerk Maxwell then "evolved a set of four simple equations that, among them, described almost all phenomena involving electricity and magnetism. These equations, advanced in 1864, not only described the interrelationship of the phenomena of electricity and magnetism, but showed that the two could not be separated."[360] Magnetism was inseparably intertwined with electricity as two waveforms that continually radiated outward at 90° to one another, and that this outward radiation defined a single electromagnetic field. He also determined that visible light was an electromagnetic radiation, and that there were different types of electromagnetic radiations with either shorter or longer wavelengths. "The formulation of these equations is the most important event in physics since Newton's time...because they form a pattern for a new type of law...laws representing the structure of the field."[361]

The particle view, however, was certainly not dead. It took a major step forward in 1871, when Dmitri Mendeleyev was able to recognize different patterns within the chemical elements. This allowed him to organize the elements into different groupings and he is credited with creating the periodic table of elements. Mendeleyev didn't understand the underlying reason for these patterns, but his table proved accurate. The periodic table had gaps that were later filled by newly discovered elements toward the end of the century, underscoring the accuracy of his groupings. In is interesting to note that the periodic table's grouping into metals reflects the ancient element of earth, while its other main grouping, gases, reflect different states of the other three ancient elements: requiring the element of fire to heat water (liquid) to get air (gas); indicating that the ancient designations may have been primitive, but they were accurate reflections of the physical world.

In 1900, Max Planck may have been the first to formulate a synthesis between particle theory and field theory. He continued Maxwell's exploration of light's inner structure by describing light "particles" as electromagnetic, massless, discrete packets of energy, called photons, which are released or absorbed by electrons. Each packet of energy contained a discrete quantity of energy, and quantum theory was born.

359 Einstein and Infield, 125.
360 Asimov, 346-7.
361 Einstein and Infield, 143.

"Plank argued that radiation could be absorbed only in whole numbers of quanta."[362] Could it be that the "integer multiples" that characterize the harmonic series manifests once again as a phenomenon of nature even at the sub-atomic level? It appears so, since Planck goes on to describe light as electromagnetic waves, despite their particle-like characteristics. His theory describes wave-like properties that make particles look more like vibrations than well-defined points in space. "Planck and Einstein had related energy to the frequency of waves."[363]

The differences between particles and waves were irrevocably blurred by Einstein's famous equation: $E = mc^2$. In 1905, Einstein demonstrated the basic interchangeability between matter and energy. A very tiny amount of matter could be transformed into enormously high energies and back again. This implied that particles could be described in terms of the wave, i.e., the field, or vice versa.

"Mendeleyev's 'periodic table' (so-called because it showed the periodic recurrence of similar chemical properties)…", could not explain how increasing atomic weights resulted in recurring patterns of chemical properties because those were determined by the varying number of electrons in the element's outer orbit.[364] But this underlying reason for Mendeleyev's groupings "came some half a century later [in 1913] as the structure of atoms was untangled. Niels Bohr discovered that in going from atom to atom – starting with hydrogen, which has one electron around the central nucleus, and building up the various elements by adding electrons – a repeating pattern was formed."[365] From that pattern he developed a progressive model of atomic structure that depicted electrons orbiting its nucleus in different "shells" or orbits. Electrons appeared to move between "inner" or "outer" orbits, depending on whether specific wavelengths of radiation were absorbed or emitted.[366]

In 1923, Louis de Broglie "suggested that the wave-particle duality applied not only to light but to matter as well."[367] He predicted that an electron's wavelength would be inversely proportional to its momentum (mass * velocity). De Broglie's prediction would give electrons of

---

362 Asimov, 352.
363 Brian Greene, *The Elegant Universe* (New York: Random House, 1999), 104.
364 Asimov, 231.
365 Peat, 80.
366 Peat, 80.
367 Greene, 103.

moderate speed (i.e., frequency) a wavelength in the range of x-rays.[368] He was proven right in 1927. When de Broglie incorporated the concept of mass into the acoustical reciprocity of wavelength and frequency, he was explaining the mechanism of how God's harmonic Utterances "descended into matter."

In 1926, Erwin Schrödinger developed a mathematical description of the atom called either wave or quantum mechanics. He started by investigating the behavior of electrons as the standing waves so familiar to acousticians. He then expanded on quantum theory, by working out a mathematical system in which very small particles and forces interacted. "Schrodinger's wave equation, for example, is a differential equation, relating what is happening at one point to what happens at another point an infinitesimally short distance away."[369] The solution to Schrödinger's differential equation describing this phenomenon is called the wave function, which defines the wave at each infinitesimal point in space and instant of time. This quantified wave perspective replaced Niels Bohr's particle view of electrons orbiting like a planet around the sun. Schrodinger's electron wave was a "smeared out" orbital path around the nucleus, in which "part of it is here, and part of it is there."[370] Within this extended wave, it would prove to be impossible to take a snapshot of the electron's particle-like location.

Figure 97 – The Atom: Nucleus and Orbiting Electron Waves

"Werner Heisenberg had presented his own model of the atom. He had abandoned all attempts to picture the atom as composed either of particles or waves."[371] His method of "matrix mechanics" described the various energy levels of different electron orbits. In an effort to

---

368 Asimov, 370.
369 Peat, 21.
370 Greene, 105.
371 Asimov, 378.

pinpoint the location of electrons, he developed his uncertainty principle. Heisenberg showed that there was no way of determining both the position of a subatomic particle and its motion at the same time. He won the Nobel Prize in 1932 for his efforts.[372] Some believe that the uncertainty principle has shaken man's sure-footedness with respect to cause and effect, impacting his natural inclination to locate and touch what he believes to be an object. At first, the electron appears to us to be a point particle when viewed from a great distance (which is equivalent to viewing it at low energies), but proves to be elusive when viewed up close (at high energies), when it turns into an extended object, i.e., a wave.[373]

Our ability to peer inside the atom requires linear accelerators, cyclotrons, synchrotrons, colliders, and supercolliders, etc. These devices accelerate subatomic particles to higher and higher energies. An increase in energy translates to an increase in speed or frequency. Since we know that any increase in frequency implies a corresponding decrease in wavelength, we can expect that smaller and smaller wavelengths will require proportionally higher energies to probe smaller and smaller structures. This is because we need tiny wavelengths to explore all the nooks and crannies of a particle.[374]

When two high-energy particles are accelerated in opposite directions and then collide, a distribution of energy spectra is produced that enables us to identify the exact nature of the particles we are dealing with. Each subatomic wave-particle is analogous to a single color that gets added to the rainbow of "wave-particles" defining each particular element. In other words, each element's spectral signature is a unique combination of wave-particles that coalesce, like the colors of the rainbow, into a complex entity called the atom. The atom is therefore a prime example of God's unity from diversity, and is analogous to white light or a complex sound. The fact that each element's blend of "colors" is slightly different than the next, identifies and differentiates the elements from one another. By 1950, more than 200 subatomic particles had been discovered as short-lived resonances using these high-energy techniques.

If we can't locate an electron's position, perhaps we can approximate where it might be. In 1937, John Wheeler introduced a scattering matrix, or s-matrix, and his student Richard Feynman later refined his mentor's

---

372 Asimov, 378.
373 Peat, 63.
374 Greene, 215.

approach by introducing simple diagrams that, when taken together, add up to the total interaction between particles. This series of complex approximations is called perturbation theory.[375] It is a statistical method that has proven very accurate and practical for approximating the infinite solutions to Schrödinger's wave functions and Heisenberg's matrix. An advance in field theory came two years after Schrödinger and Heisenberg developed quantum theory:

> Quantum field theory was generally the work of P. A. M. Dirac, who in 1927,...showed how the new quantum concepts could be extended from atoms to the electromagnetic field. This field was treated as an 'orchestra of oscillators.' Where conventional quantum theory produces a wave function corresponding to each particular oscillation, the field theory creates a sort of super wave function composed out of all possible oscillator wave functions.[376]

Einstein was never able to foresee the comprehensive synthesis of superstrings over all matter and energy, but he did understand the key role of harmonics and classical string theory as it related to the inner workings of quantum mechanics, at least as early as 1938, when he teamed up with Leopold Infeld to write this passage from *The Evolution of Physics*:

> The atoms of every element are composed of elementary particles, the heavier constituting the nucleus, and the lighter the electrons. Such a system of particles behaves like a small acoustical instrument in which standing waves are produced.[377]

Global Laws of Quantization & Symmetry

Abraham's mathematics was the first to teach us that the two global laws embedded within the harmonic series are quantization and symmetry. Abraham's concept of quantization taught us to count in unit multiples of a fundamental value when describing God's Ten Utterances as Sefirot

---

375 Peat, 38-39.
376 Peat, 304.
377 Einstein and Infield, 276.

(Hebrew: counting). The second global principle that manifests within the harmonic series is symmetry. Abraham "engraves" Creation from the reciprocity of frequency and wavelength within the ancient Quadrivium. In the earlier days of quantum theory, P.A.M. Dirac "had hypothesized on purely theoretical grounds that every particle has its corresponding antiparticle, with mirror-image properties..."[378] Today, we know this to be true. "Particle and antiparticle is a fundamental symmetry of physics."[379] These two principles — quantization and symmetry — are the global laws of the harmonic series that define Creation and link the microcosm to the macrocosm.

We also know that when electrons move to higher or lower orbits within the atom, they absorb or emit discrete packets of radiation, which Max Planck first described as "particles," or "quanta" of light waves known as photons. It is these unit quanta of light that give quantum theory its name. Schrödinger's probabilistic solutions to locate the electron within higher or lower orbits occurs within the atom's grid of spherical harmonics. "The electron cannot have an arbitrary distribution in space when bound to the proton. If the distribution is to be stationary... the wave pattern must be a standing wave. This obliges the phase pattern of the electron to behave in a strictly ordered quantized fashion: the zones are separated by a whole number of meridians and parallels which form the nodes of a phase pattern...The resulting partitions of space are called spherical harmonics."[380] Quantization determines the whole-number multiples of meridians and parallels representing the possibilities of electron distribution across an atom's spherical surface.

"The spherical harmonics of an electron's orbit around its nucleus is analogous to the earth's orbit around the sun, i.e., its orbital spin.[381] There is also rotational spin around its axis, which, in the quantum world, can never be disentangled from its orbital spin.[382] Rotational spin in the quantum world, however, is not completely analogous to the earth spinning around its central axis. When a sub-atomic particle is viewed at low energies to make it appear like a point particle, there would be

378 Peat,75.
379 Peat,75.
380 Vincent Icke, *The Force of Symmetry* (Cambridge: Cambridge University Press, 1995), 151-2.
381 Greene, 170.
382 Icke, 136.

no other points next to it that could spin around a central axis.[383] That being said, "each particle is endowed with a property, called spin, which behaves like a rotation."[384]

When considering a particle's spin, there is exactly one other symmetry that many modern physicists believe exists — supersymmetry. Those particles with whole number spins are called *bosons,* corresponding to the forces of nature, such as; photons, gluons, gravitons, etc.. These spin at the integer multiples near and dear to Abraham's heart; 1, 2, 3, etc.. Although spin occurs in our space, supersymmetric spin occurs in an abstract mathematical dimension called isospin space. Here, another family of particles called fermions define all matter in the universe (electrons, protons, neutrons, mesons, etc.). Staying true to the global law of harmonics, fermions also spin at unit multiples of a quantized value, however understanding spin within abstract space is not intuitive for us. "The spin of a fermion is half an odd integer; ½, 3/2, 5/2,..."[385] Supersymmetry is counter-intuitive partly because a boson in four dimensional space must rotate 360° to complete a full rotation, however, "a fermion does not produce an exact replica of itself after rotating 360°. Instead, it requires two full turns, 720°, to make a fermion identical to what it was before the rotation."[386]

It is an interesting coincidence to note that bosons and fermions, defining the forces of nature and matter, are defined by the parameters of spin (360°) and isospin (720°), respectively. In a manner of speaking, Abraham also defined the physical world by spinning around an octave tone circle ratio of 360:720.[387] We may also recall that the "fires of heaven and hell" were created at a higher energy level by the ratios within the octave double (360*7): (720*7) = 2520:5040.

Fermions break down into quarks and leptons, while the known bosons include; gravitons (accounting for gravity), photons (electromagnetism), gluons (strong force), the Z^0, W^+, and the W^- intermediate vectors bosons (weak force). Supersymmetry states that "fermions and bosons could be

383 Greene, 170.
384 Icke, 137.
385 Icke, 145.
386 Icke, 141.

387 It should also be understood that although there are 360° in an octave tone circle of ratio 1:2 (in this case 360:720), Abraham's sub-divisions of the octave are all integer ratios of frequency and wavelengths and not a measure of degrees on a compass.

transformed one into the other [as mirror images] and all particles could be gathered into a single great family."[388]

What would we be left with if we eliminated the mean between two opposing forces? Presumably, just the two opposing forces, with no way to reconcile them. However, what nature exhibits instead, is that the duality of opposing forces could be completely eliminated if we were somehow able to raise the energy level to recreate the conditions that existed immediately before and immediately after the Big Bang.

For example, as in spin space, there is a basic two-valuedness of "up" or "down" within isospin space. The electron can be thought of as having a special spin in either one of these two directions within isospin space. "Spin up would signify a proton and spin down a neutron."[389] "Heisenberg guessed that if the electromagnetic field could be mathematically switched off [which happens at high energies], then the proton could not be distinguished from the neutron."[390] At high energies, this type of nongender particle would be called a *nucleon* (neutron + proton). It could be mathematically expressed as "rotationally symmetric," i.e., all spin directions would be equivalent.[391] Switching the electromagnetic field back on (which happens at low energies), breaks this mirror symmetry and clearly differentiates the proton from the neutron. In other words, the way to unite two harmonized, but opposing forces, is to raise its energy level. We can speculate that man similarly raises his energy level as he learns to transcend the world's dualities during the meditation process.

Electromagnetism is now seen as a gauge field between two opposing electron properties (electricity and magnetism). Could it be that what is true for electromagnetism is also true for the strong and weak nuclear force, and even for the gravitational force? Are the four forces of nature simply on-off switches for local particle symmetries? "Whenever nature exhibits some form of global symmetry,... it is probably the result of a powerful local symmetry plus a gauge field."[392] Within the parlance of string theory, a gauge field "harmonizes" wave-particle opposites.

---

388 Peat, 92-3.
389 Peat, 76-7; Of course, in isospin space "up" and "down" don't mean the same thing as in our space.
390 Peat, 76.
391 Icke, 192.
392 Peat, 85.

Einstein believed that underneath it all there was a unity to nature; that the different local symmetries could all be resolved by underlying global laws that would ultimately unify all force fields and particles. For example, without gravity tugging particles downward, who is to say which way is up? Similarly, without electromagnetism the particles become uniform; who could then tell which particle has a positive charge and which a negative? If the various gauge theories, such as gravity, the strong force, the weak force, and electromagnetism could be "turned off," then all particles would become rotationally symmetric. If it were then turned back on like a mathematical light switch, then the unity of that symmetry group would be broken and we would suddenly know up from down, a positive charge from a negative charge, etc.

If one turns one's attention from the physics of the very small to the physics of the very large, Einstein's general theory of relativity shifts the study of electromagnetic waves and quantum waves to a larger scale where large amounts of energy correspond to large masses, curving space-time itself. This curvature of space-time caused by the gravitational field around planets is analogous to the way a magnetic field can be delineated around magnets. Einstein and Infeld state, "Maxwell's equations are laws representing the structure of the field." When formulating his general theory of relativity Einstein was only generalizing Maxwell's field equations to include gravity. Einstein's gravitational field theory and Dirac's quantum field theory could both be considered logical extensions of Maxwell's original electromagnetic field theory equations.

Special relativity implies that if an event (like an orbiting, spinning planet) and the event's observer are moving at different speeds, then as their speeds approach the speed of light, strange things happen; the space coordinates can get mixed up with the time coordinates. Because of this confusion, it would be important to give space and time coordinates together, as a space-time continuum, when translating between the two different coordinate systems. Each coordinate system is relative to its viewing perspective, and all local symmetries must be translated to global terms in an effort to find the invariant underlying global laws.[393]

Einstein's famous equation, $E = mc^2$, provides an underlying framework for the different coordinate systems possible within the space-time fabric. The distortion of the space-time fabric by objects approaching the speed of

393 Peat, 105.

light is described by special relativity, while the warping of the space-time fabric by large masses is described by general relativity.

Whether one's frame of reference is at the relativistic scale of planets and gravity, the quantum scale of protons and the strong force, or the human scale of visible light and the electromagnetic force, it is the commonality of wave theory and harmonics that comprises the global law. Like the ripples caused by a pebble thrown into a lake, scientists are able to follow the universe's acoustical trail backward in time, to about 13.7 billion years ago, by analyzing the faint background harmonics of the Big Bang. Ultimately, we would converge on a point that might be called the primordial superstring of God's harmonic utterances. In the beginning, all local symmetries were melded together in an intense caldron of heat and compression — the unrealized potential of everything — the ultimate unification of symmetries that we call God. The Big Bang (coincidentally?) appears to result in a ten-dimensional universe.

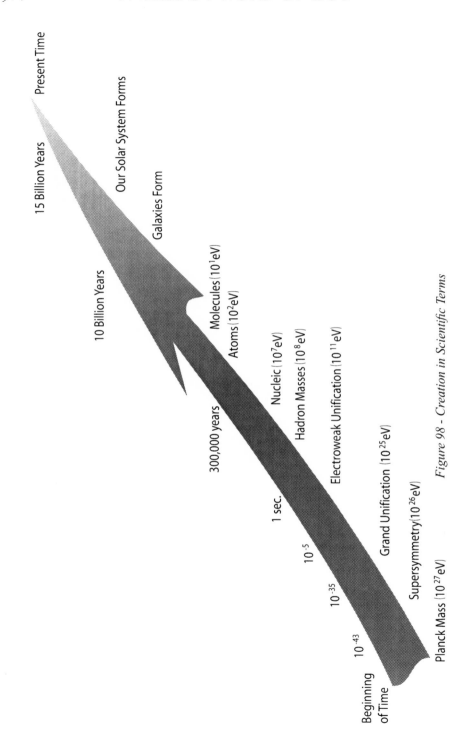

Figure 98 – Creation in Scientific Terms

The Breaking of Symmetries

Creation & the Big Bang

Abraham's account of Creation begins with his mathematical representation of God as the number 1, i.e., the undifferentiated "One" or Monad. God's extended oneness becomes the unifying "rainbow principle" of unity from diversity. His Ten Utterances of divine light would continue to fill and then overflow all sacred cubes, breaking each vessel, until expansion reached the final sacred cube, representing the hypothetical boundaries of the universe. The initial expansion of divine light that occurs on Day 1 of Creation within the Torah, parallels what modern scientists call the "Big Bang." After the high energies of Creation's big bang, expansion and cooling lowers energy levels, causing the various mathematical symmetries to break, one after another, to reveal the duality of matter at each level, until the universe unfolded to its current state.

Abraham's mathematical definition of God before Creation, is analogous to what scientists call supersymmetry, a state of undifferentiated symmetry that existed prior to the Big Bang. At this point there was no differentiation between bosons and fermions, there was only the undifferentiated energy of the Monad. Abraham describes Creation as a result of five acoustical events. The first of these events, on Day 1 of Creation, is God's Utterances, revealing the harmonic series that provides the deep structure of Creation. That event is analogous to the the vibrations of the primordial superstring exploding into ten dimensions.

In four subsequent acoustical events, God's light descends into matter to define four distinct "worlds." Kabbalistic tradition calls this the "Breaking of the Vessels." Science calls it the breaking of symmetries. Creation in terms of modern scientific cosmology describes a parallel process; the initial Big Bang expansion of a highly compactified primordial superstring within ten or eleven dimensions, followed by the breaking of four additional symmetries as a result of cooling after the initial expansion.

The mathematics of superstring theory requires ten (or perhaps eleven) dimensions; six additional hidden or compactified dimensions, plus the four revealed dimensions of space-time. Ancient string theory defines Creation in terms of ten divine utterances which then gets reordered to expand in ten directions: the six directions of space, two directions to define Time, and two directions to define the soul. Abraham's Day 2 mathematical description of the Heavenly Firmament as the womb of Creation has a modern analog in Schwarz and Green's mathematical description of the SO(32) symmetry within the language of superstring theory:[394] Peat gives us some sense of their breakthrough moment in overcoming the many scientific and mathematical hurdles:

> It became possible to create a superstring theory that had all the features physicists had been dreaming of. It was chiral, supersymmmetric, and free of ghosts, tachyons, infinities, and anomalies. It accounted for the forces of nature and the symmetry patterns of the elementary particles. The theory of everything had been born.[395]

Supersymmetry was broken by cooling and expansion immediately after the Big Bang, exposing gravitons, bosons and fermions. In other words, fermions (all matter in the universe) and bosons (the four forces of the universe), can be considered opposing modes of vibration that exist on the same ten-dimensional superstring. Supersymmetry's gauge field is the gravitational field of the graviton (a massless, spin 2 vector boson). When cooling and expansion lowered the universe's energy level, supersymmetry's light switch turned on this gauge field — supergravity — exposing fermions and bosons as the basic duality of nature. This is how Abraham's metaphysical doctrine of "opposites and the mean" manifests as global law within the physical universe. This is the modern analog of Day 3's creations within Genesis.

394 These different symmetries get their name from scientists who group elementary particles into various patterns of 3, 8, 10, etc. Each grouping of particles is characterized by mirror reflections within various types of space, such as three-dimensionsal space, space-time, isospin space, strangeness space, etc.
395 Peat, 119.

Creating Matter & Life

After SO(32) was broken by further expansion and cooling, the next symmetry occurred at grand unification energies, SU(3) * SU(2) * U(1). Before the momentous discovery of superstring theory, particle physicists had their day in the sun:

> The grand unified theory was supposed to be the great success of contemporary theoretical physics, the Holy Grail that would finally be grasped after decades of searching.[396]

Cooling and expansion of the universe lowers its energy level and "turns on" the gauge field for grand unification, SU(3) * SU(2) * U(1). This exposes the strong force that bind hadrons together SU(3) as well as the forces that characterize lepton interactions SU(2) * U(1).

The various types of hadrons (like the proton and neutron) are bound together in the nucleus by a gauge field called the strong force SU(3), which is carried by gluons. Very high energy collisions of hadrons helped us to peer into their inner structure, suggesting a sort of internal "graininess" in which tiny internal gritty pieces were considered evidence of the elemental building block of hadrons, known as the quark.[397] Physicists developed the "standard model" of all matter in the universe as a view of grand unification energies with the local symmetries of quarks and leptons linked by the gauge fields: SU(3) * SU(2) * U(1).[398] Grand unification energies are the modern analog for Day 4 of Creation — the harmonization of quarks and leptons, before the formation of atoms and molecules.

With the advent of bigger accelerators in the 1960s, additional abstract mathematical symmetries helped organize the zoo of particles that had been discovered since the 1950s. This required more mathematical symmetry mirrors to be erected in abstract space. Principles of symmetry reveal properties that describe the structure of the underlying forces within these new particles. Additional symmetries enable particle theorists to organize particles into various families. For example, a threefold pattern of quark organization became known as color. The color symmetries were named *red, green,* or

396 Peat, 97.
397 Peat, 82.
398 Peat, 89-90.

blue.[399] A six-quark symmetry was then developed called flavor: *up, down, top, bottom, strange* and *charmed.* Each of three colors of quark could come in six flavors creating the possibility of 18 different types of quark.

One second after the Big Bang, the constant exchange of gluon particles bound the different types of quark together into more complex structures called *hadrons.* Meson hadron patterns are two-quark composites, while baryon hadron patterns are three-quark composites. Protons and neutrons, for example, are three-quark composites called baryons. A proton is usually composed of two up and one down quark, but other combinations are possible. A neutron can be composed of two down and one up quark. Based on quantum numbers, the permutations of combining three quarks enable creation of eightfold and tenfold patterns of resonances called *symmetry relationships,* which are then collected together to form the SU(3) symmetry group. The eightfold pattern of hadron resonances is based on the fact that there are three types of quark with roughly the same smaller size mass, *up, down,* and *strange.*[400] The diagrams that follow are 4000 years apart, but they both correspond to a three-fold pattern of symmetry to create a tenfold pattern of resonances. Like Mendeleyev's periodic table, these patterns of resonance within the modern Quadrivium predicted missing elements.[401]

Interactions between leptons (such as the electron), and between quarks and leptons, occur as the weak SU(2) and electroweak (SU(2) * U(1) forces. The gauge field between leptons is the electromagnetic force U(1) carried by neutral, massless photons. The weak force that characterizes radioactive decay, SU(2), is carried by two gauge field vector bosons W+ and W-, as well as the neutral vector boson Z°.[402]

The exposed hadrons began to form nuclei, and about 300,000 years after the Big Bang, began to interact with leptons to form atoms and then molecules, gradually defining all matter. About 10 billion years after the Big Bang, galaxies and our own solar system were born. The most primitive forms of life began about 700,000 million years after the earth was formed, and fossilized worms were discovered about 1.1 billion years ago. Modern humans first appeared about 130,000 years ago.

---

399 Icke, 208.
400 Icke, 216.
401 Peat, 78.
402 Peat, 89.

Figure 99a,b,c,d – The Resonances of the Quadrivium[1]

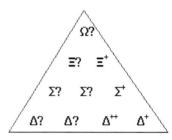

The Ancient Quadrivium - Ten member pattern of elementary resonances derived from the "Three Mothers" within a classical string.

The Modern Quadrivium - Ten member pattern of elementary resonances derived from a three-fold pattern of up, down, and strange quarks within the hadron portion of a superstring.

Tone Wheels
of Divine Light

Electron Orbits
and Photons of Light

---

1 Peat, 79.

Creating Superstrings

To incorporate both quantum mechanics and relativity, the classic Newtonian string must become a superstring by becoming both "relativistic" and "quantized." In order to get some insight into what is involved in this process, we will start with a simple formula:

$$f = \frac{1}{2L} \sqrt{\frac{T}{m}}$$

Figure 100 - Classic Newtonian String [403]

This formula relates the fundamental frequency f, the length of a string L, its mass m, and its tension T. In classical mechanics, we would write down the calculus describing the physical quantities of the oscillating string. These equations map each of the overtone waveforms in terms of their periodic trigonometric functions (sines and cosines) into the geometric coordinates of space-time. Solutions to these equations for any given instant would enable us to determine the velocity and location of any point on the string.

To get a very high level view of the mathematical rigor required to create a superstring. We would first need to transform our Newtonian string into a "relativistic string" with its highest energy wave functions moving at the speed of light. From the formula above we can see that increasing the frequency of a vibrating string to the speed of light would have an inverse effect on wavelength, reducing it to approximately "Planck's length" of 10^{-32} cm. In order to travel at the speed of light as relativity requires, it must also be massless, while the tension on the string would be enormous: 10^{39} N. Even though the highest energy wave functions of a relativistic string would be massless, lower harmonics would decrease in tension and begin to pick up mass, until the fundamental of the superstring, which would have the lowest frequency, largest wavelength, and would be the most massive wave-particle within any given element.

The next major step in creating a superstring would be to "quantize" this "relativistic string." Heisenberg's uncertainty principle requires that the terms representing the various wave functions be converted to quantum

403 Peat, 53.

mechanical operators. These quantum operators become statistical and probabilistic determinants of what was previously a definitive process. The final step in creating a superstring requires us to ensure that the string's vibrations are supersymmetric and adhere to the correct particle symmetry groups, as previously discussed, to enable the mathematics to work out appropriately.[404]

After pointing out the similarities between the classical and quantum equations, Einstein and Infeld comment:

> Analogously, in the case of an electron, a certain function is determined for any point in space, and for any moment. We shall call this function the *probability wave*... It does not tell us the position and velocity of the electron at any moment because such a question has no sense in quantum physics. But it will tell us the probability of meeting the electron at a particular spot, or where we have the greatest chance of meeting an electron. The result does not refer to one, but many repeated measurements.[405]

The discrete "packets" of energy, or "quantum numbers" that define each of these different quantum states, give us the various wave resonances. The different masses that we created from the wave functions of a relativistic string now take on the different characteristic energies, quantum numbers, and symmetries associated with each of the subatomic wave-particles. A superstring creates a rainbow of diverse wave-particles framed by the bookends of relativity and quantum field theory, that coalesce into each atom's complex unity.

---

404 Peat, 109-110.
405 Einstein and Infeld, 288-289.

*Figure 101 - Seven Angels Heralding the New Jerusalem's Descent from Heaven
(Illustration by Charles Bentz)*

The Path to Peace

Toward an Empirical God

Galileo, often called the "father of modern physics," wrote that "the language of God is mathematics." He was forced to recant his scientific findings to avoid being burned at the stake and spent the remaining eight years of his life under house arrest. After his heresy trial, science and religion went their separate ways. In 1992, Pope John Paul II finally acknowledged in a speech that the Roman Catholic Church had erred in condemning him. Even in today's modern world, Christianity is still struggling to come to terms with Darwin and the theory of evolution.

Today, many people of faith believe that God can be found in the common thread running throughout all of Creation, bringing order and an "intelligent design" to nature. Abraham, the great patriarch of Judaism, Christianity, and Islam, would not disagree. But, he would tell us that this "common thread" is more like a vibrating string – the same vibrating string that is at the heart of superstring theory, the "Holy Grail" of modern theoretical physics and today's leading candidate for a "theory of everything."

It was Galileo who formulated a modern scientific conception of vibrating strings, but Pythagoras (5th century BCE) is generally considered the "father of mathematics and music," and was historically credited with being the first in the ancient world to explore the mathematics of vibrating strings to create a cosmology that scholars in the Middle Ages called the "Music of the Spheres." I am, of course, convinced that it was Abraham who should rightfully be considered the father of ancient string theory. Abraham, or whoever was responsible for the Book of Creation's content, lived somewhere between 500 and 1500 years before Pythagoras. It was Abraham who first explored the unseen hand of monotheism's God and the organizing "rainbow principle" of Creation called the harmonic series.

Since the 1950's physicists have once again been thinking about vibrating strings. In 1984, two physicists named Michael Green and John Schwarz, finally succeeded in working out the mathematics that had confounded Einstein for the last 30 years of his life. Superstring theory provides a comprehensive framework to reconcile the great book-ends of 20th century physics: relativity and quantum mechanics.

Professor Ed Witten put it best, "That silly little formula describing vibrating strings organizes all matter and forces in the universe.[406] It was Yoichiro Nambu's pioneering work in the 1970s that helped set the stage for success,[407] so that by 1984, Green and Schwarz could directly apply the theory of relativity and quantum mechanics to the classically vibrating string — and superstring theory was born.

It replaces the standard model of particle physics which accounts for only three out of four forces of nature: the strong force, the weak force, and the electromagnetic force, but did not include gravity until the abstract dimensions necessary for supergravity were borrowed from superstring theory. Superstring theory accounts for all four forces of nature.

For the mathematics of superstring theory to work out correctly there must be either ten or eleven dimensions, rather than the usual four dimensions of length, width, depth, and time. The extra dimensions within abstract mathematical space continue to be explored. Superstring theory has often been called the best hope for a "theory of everything" because it reconciles two of the greatest physics revolutions of the twentieth-century, quantum mechanics and general relativity: "That has been the problem of problems in physics...For some years, it's been clear that string theory does, in fact, give a logically consistent framework, encompassing both gravity and quantum mechanics."[408]

Princeton professor Ed Witten was touted as the new Einstein in a 1987 *New York Times Magazine* article, and he believes that science will find a way to prove string theory correct within the next 100 years.[409] His description underscores the importance of the harmonic series to Creation from a scientific perspective:

406 Cole.
407 Peat, 51.
408 P.C.W. Davies and J. Brown, eds., *Superstrings: A Theory of Everything* (Cambridge: Cambridge University Press, 1988), interview with John Ellis, 165; 97.
409 K.C. Cole, "A Theory of Everything," *New York Times Magazine*, October 18, 1987.

In the case of a violin string, the different harmonics correspond to different sounds. In the case of a superstring, the different harmonics correspond to different elementary particles. The electron, graviton, the photon, the neutrino and all the others, are different harmonics of a fundamental string just as the different overtones of a violin string are different harmonics of one string.[410]

Referring to string theory's "long forgotten" roots, Witten states:

String theory is a long forgotten theory that turns our current picture of the physical universe on its head...the most revolutionary idea in physics in more than half a century - as revolutionary as relativity; as revolutionary as quantum theory.[411]

The Book of Creation mathematically embeds the harmonic series in the holiest name of God, the Holy Tetragrammaton, which by now can be understood from a scientific perspective as the organizing principle of Creation. Today's empirically minded naysayers are scientists who appear frustrated by the inherent difficulties in devising appropriate experiments to prove superstring theory. Their problem seems to be that they can't touch and feel the stone that was metaphorically cast into the lake. If we can accept the apparent fact that the stone may have to stay at the bottom of the lake, and all we may ever be able to see are the ripples that travel away from its point of entry into the lake. Science may never be able to view the tiny vibrating string at the core of every atom, because it exists at the unviewable size and impenetrable energies of Planck's length and mass (10^{-32}cm and 10^{27} GeV). If scientists can understand the ripples in the lake well enough to prove superstring theory correct, then there may be no need to find the stone. Until then, the naysayers will ramble on, calling it philosophy rather than science. What can be said is that string theory is the science of the great philosophers and religions, however, even before it is proven empirically, perhaps we can learn to appreciate the value of mathematics and music as the universal language of God.

---

410 Davies and Brown, 93.
411 Cole.

Redefining Intelligent Design

The raging debate about Intelligent Design pits evolutionists against creationists; science versus theology; rationalism versus revelation. One of the modern standard-bearers for atheism and Darwin's natural selection is the evolutionary biologist Richard Dawkins. To a creationist, the miracle of functionality, beauty and complexity of a human organism is a masterwork of intelligent design that only God could have executed. Dawkins compares creationism to a forbiddingly steep cliff, and compares natural selection to the other side of the mountain – an easily scalable, gradual slope of evolution.[412]

In his new book "The God Delusion," Dawkins paraphrases Darwin's own admission that "The creationists are right that, if genuinely irreducible complexity could be properly demonstrated, it would wreck Darwin's theory."[413] In other words, the scientific community maintains that everything is reducible to a gradual, step-by-step process. There are mountains of scientific evidence to support the step-by-step evolution of man over time. Darwin's influence spread well beyond biology. Even atoms can be shown to have evolved from quarks and leptons soon after the Big Bang. We also understand how molecules evolve from atoms, and how planets, solar systems and earth's geological formations evolve. So we must ask ourselves, "Where is the recognizable hand of God (or should I say fingerprint?), that is a complex phenomenon, but is not ultimately reducible to some link in the evolutionary chain?" It appears that both creationists and scientists are at a loss to find what Darwin called a genuinely irreducible complexity, whether at the point of origin or later in the evolutionary chain. Where is that truly unscaleable cliff? Where is the irreducibly complex blueprint of creation that we can call God?

As we have seen, the scientific proof of God's existence, comes to us from monotheism's most authoritative source: the *Sefer Yetzirah* (the Book of Creation). The irriducible complexity that defines God is the harmonic series, as exemplified by the rainbow and complex sound. Abraham saw the hand of God in the harmonic series, and since 1984, modern theoretical science has been trying to empirically prove that he was right.

---

412 Richard Dawkins, *The God Delusion* (New York: Houghton Mifflin, 2006), 121-123.
413 Dawkins, 125.

A rainbow manifests the diversity of Intelligent Design while God manifests its unification. We can study this blueprint of Creation as it applies to the complexity of white light, which breaks up into constituent colors when directed through a prism. The complexity of a sound is similarly comprised of a rainbow of sound when directed through a harmonic analyzer. Similarly, every atom on the periodic table is a holistic merging of a rainbow of wave-particles. Each atom has its own spectral signature that uniquely identifies it on the periodic table of elements when directed through a super-collider. Just as there are nuances of loudness (amplitude) within the mathematical structure of sound that determine how a violin differs in sound quality (timbre) from a clarinet, there are mathematically analogous differences within the rainbow of sub-atomic wave-particles that define how the spectral signature of oxygen differs from that of Helium. The mathematics of the harmonic series translates across all mediums within the continuum of energy and matter, including: gravity, light, radio waves, electricity, sound, and the strong and weak forces of the atom, are all made of vibrating wave-particles.

America's founding fathers got it right. The theory of everything that defines God can be described by our national motto: E Pluribus Unum. The irreducible complexity of the rainbow principle describes the essence of creation's diversity coalescing into unity of the "white light of God." If the Book of Creation is the cradle of both religion and science, as I believe it to be, then evolutionists and creationists must learn to coexist. God's intelligent design, the harmonic series, unites the essence of nature's diversity into what Abraham called the Living God.

Revelation of the Word

It is possible that the Bible was created as a way to bring Abraham's complex theological treatise to the masses. If that is the case, as this author believes it to be, it certainly succeeded in its bid to reach a wide audience. Biblical parables and allegories should not be interpreted literally because they encrypt the most profound and significant aspects of Abraham's writings. It is not enough to recite the words of Scripture without understanding its intended meaning. Abraham teaches us that the inner meaning of Scripture is a profound but very learnable body of knowledge.

Abraham's gnosticism could not logically be considered heresy, since it provides the foundation of Scripture.

Abraham's text is the cradle of both religion and science and constitutes nothing less than the "objective truth about God." What Princeton professor Ed Witten calls the "silly little formula" describing vibrating strings – the harmonic series – turns out to be the basis of both religion and science. It is revolutionizing modern physics, and my profound hope for mankind is that it will revolutionize religion before religion annihilates us all.

Abraham's tiny treatise uses God's "rainbow principle" to demonstrate "unity from diversity," establishing monotheism as the global law of Creation. Abraham's words can bring peace to the troubled spirit of his progeny. Although the Jewish people hold this book in the highest esteem, they are only its caretakers; it rightfully belongs to all three faiths, and should be shared with the world.

With a proper understanding of the Book of Creation, rabbis, imams, priests, and even atheists who believe only in modern science, may find themselves on common spiritual ground for the first time. The true birthright of Abraham's children, Isaac and Ishmael, was never really about inheriting the physical land of Israel. Abraham's true legacy is in defining a spiritual "high ground," where lasting peace is attainable by everyone. Within the Book of Revelation, Christians call this high ground the "New Jerusalem." A proper reading of the Book of Creation brings us a renewed hope that the spiritual evolution of man will enable us to live in the peace and harmony of a New Jerusalem.

The "high ground" of a New Jerusalem will begin to manifest as we learn to master Abraham's practice of "seven circuits around the sacred cube." We will be praying from the same book that, in some way, has instructed all the ancient prophets, including: Moses, Jesus, and Mohammed. Practicing this teaching religiously will cause our worldly wanderings to gradually slow and eventually cease, until we come to a place of contentment within ourselves. As we continue this practice, contentment gradually transforms into joy and compassion for those who aren't experiencing it with us. That is the point we must all reach one person at a time. A true and lasting peace requires the patience and compassion born of spirituality, wisdom, understanding and knowledge, that can only come from mastering Abraham's practice.

I have no doubt that string theory is the language of God, and it will prove to be the "theory of everything" for both religion and science. Abraham's seven "tone circles" around the sacred cube were used by Joshua and his generals armed with trumpets to conquer Jericho. On the seventh circuit his generals would sound their trumpets to tear down the "walls of Jericho." The walls are symbolic of the walls between men, and between man and God. In other words, the "veil of pomegranites" that separated the High Priest from the Holy of Holies was the veil between life and death that only the High Priest knew how to negotiate, by "pronouncing" the Word of God. The true High Priests of old were members of the "order of Melchizedek" — the eternal priesthood — who guarded this knowledge with their life. They were the "anointed ones" who were able to liberate or transfigure their soul and go behind the veil of life and death.

The Messianic message has been hidden in the *Sefer Yetzirah* for 4000 years. Revelation of the transcendental meaning and pronunciation of the Word of God will enable Abraham's descendants to reclaim their lost legacy. We must all become "anointed ones" by practicing seven circuits around the sacred cube. Only Abraham's practice will enable the three faiths to tear down the walls that separate them from each other and from God.

The revelation of Abraham's ancient teaching to his descendants is allegorized by the Book of Revelation's descent of the New Jerusalem from heaven. And so, we open a "little scroll," and sound the seven trumpets to herald the New Jerusalem's descent from heaven. Once Abraham's descendents learn to pronounce the Word of God *there shall be no more death, neither sorrow, nor crying, neither shall there be any more pain; for the former things are passed away.*

WHEELS WITHIN WHEELS: *A Prayer for Peace*
by Jonathan Clark

Wheels within wheels, the galaxies revolve,
Amidst great gaseous clouds, and purpling
Of star stuff, and the brilliant furnaces of Creation.
Who can see the endless majesty
Of the Universe, and remain unmoved?
The Sacred Chord that sounded eons ago,
From which emerged all we know, and all
We shall ever know, brings its sonic glory
To every vibration of the Cosmos.
Here on Earth, every winnowing wind,
Every ripple on the water, every peal of thunder
Above the mountains and the valleys,
Asserts that kinetic energy which had its source
In the sound that was the Word that made the world.
Shall we exalt the Holy One, blessed be He,
Or pretend to an omniscience we do not possess,
Secretly hoping He indulges us
Like the errant children we are?
Wheels within wheels, the galaxies revolve,
Like lenses of awe, concentrating
Our prayers and meditations into a beam
That merges with the white Light of God.
Avinu Malkenu, our Father, our King,
Permeating all You have created,
Let the Universe ring once more
With Your creating Word, creating within us
More perfect hearts, and souls with the divine tropism,
To bend toward You and Your commandments.
Perfection that You are, as we in our limited way
Understand it, You made us in Your image,
For the Universal Mind that uttered the Sacred Chord,
Governs all life and process in the Universe alike.
May the time not be distant, O Lord, which finds us
Ready for transformation, and peace shall reign
On Earth, and the heart's honey cell shall overflow
With such sweetness at such a realization.
Wheels within wheels, galaxies revolve,
O dizzying tilt to my longing for salvation!

Appendix - The Ancient Quadrivium

The Arithmetic of the Quadrivium

Given two numbers, ancient mathematicians devised different types of "means" or average values for them. Three of them have particular interest for us: the arithmetic mean, geometric mean and harmonic mean. The simplest of the three is the arithmetic mean. It is what most of us think of as the "average" value of two numbers. The arithmetic mean of two numbers, a and b, is $(a + b)/2$. The arithmetic mean preserves the distances between numbers. The arithmetic mean of 10 and 20 is 15, and the distance between 10 and 15 on a number line is the same as the distance between 15 and 20. An arithmetic progression of more than two numbers will always have equal increments, e.g., 2, 4, 6, 8, 10 ...

A second type of mean is called the geometric mean. Rather than preserving distances, it preserves ratios. The geometric mean of two numbers, a and b, is the square root of their product. The geometric mean of 5 and 20, for example, is the square root of $5*20 = \sqrt{100} = 10$. Look at the sequence of numbers 5, 10, 20. Notice that the ratios, 5/10 and 10/20, are equal. This will always be the case with the geometric mean. A geometric progression of more than two numbers will always have equal ratios, e.g., 1, 2, 4, 8, 16 ...

The harmonic mean is probably the least familiar of the three. The harmonic mean of two numbers, a and b, is twice the product divided by the sum, or $2ab/(a + b)$. This is equivalent to taking the product of the two numbers and dividing by their arithmetic mean. For example, the harmonic mean of 6 and 12 is $(2*6*12)/(6 + 12) = 144/18 = 8$. We'd get the same result by taking the product, $6*12 = 72$, and dividing by the arithmetic mean of 6 and 12, which is 9.

We've said that the arithmetic mean preserves distances and the geometric means preserves ratios. The harmonic mean combines the two and preserves the ratios of distances. For example, the harmonic mean of

6 and 12 is 8. If we take the sequence of numbers 6, 8, and 12, and look at the two ratios, (8 - 6)/6 and (12 - 8)/12, we'll get the same number, 1/3, in both cases. This will always be the case for harmonic means. The ratios of distances from the mean to the endpoints are always equal.

The reciprocity of frequency and wavelength is reflected in the reciprocity of arithmetic and harmonic proportions. For example, a harmonic proportion with relative frequency ratios of 6, 8, and 12 when inverted gives its wavelength in an arithmetic progression: $1/6 = 4/24$, $1/8 = 3/24$, $1/12 = 2/24$. This implies that the formulas for arithmetic and harmonic means are in a reciprocal relationship. We can show this to be true if we substitute the reciprocals of a, b and x into the formula for the arithmetic mean $(a + b)/2 = x$, to get $1/x = 1/2(1/a + 1/b)$. When we solve for x, we find that x is equal to the harmonic mean, $2ab/(a + b)$.

The Music of the Quadrivium

A small primer to elucidate the science of sound is important. Modern scientists call most sounds we hear in the everyday world, *complex sounds.* Each complex tone is made up of an infinite number of pure tones in the way that white light is made up of all the colors of the spectrum. The harmonic series provides the internal structure of sound, and the structure of sound is determined by stacking pure tones, called sine waves, one on top of the other. But, before we begin stacking tones to create our own "rainbow of sound," it is important that we understand the difference between absolute and relative pitch.

Today, musical notes are named by their juxtaposition to concert A, which has been fixed as a world standard to 440 cycles per second. In Abraham's day, tones were not fixed to specific frequencies. The starting point for a musical scale slid around within the continuum of frequency. And, since Abraham had no concept of cycles per second, he had to use integer divisions of a string as his standard of measurement. What was fixed in Abraham's day were therefore the integer ratios that determined the relationship of one tone to another from some arbitrary starting point. For this reason, Figure 15b, our diagram for each day of Creation, would always begin from "God's Holy Palace," on the note D, even if its beginning integer were the numeral 3, 60, 360, or 1260, etc..

By today's absolute standard, the row beginning with a numeral 3 would differ from our D starting point by the musical interval of a perfect fifth. Instead, each Day of Creation brought an entirely new musical context that was tied to the Heavenly Firmament's integer ratios.

Today, an orchestra would do its best to tune up to concert A, at 440 cycles per second. The concert master would play what he believes to be a standard concert A. But, a machine, or someone with "absolute pitch" — the rare ability to identify specific frequencies — could be sure to find that standard 440 cps concert A. The rest of the orchestra would still need to tune their instruments relative to the concertmaster's best efforts.

To get a better feel for the structure of the harmonic series we will simulate a harmonic series by building it from scratch. If the concertmaster were able to play a concert A as if it were a pure sine wave,[414] it would vibrate at 440 cycles per second. On top of this, we would stack another pure tone vibrating twice as fast (another A, eight notes away from the first, vibrating at 880 cps). Then stack another sine wave vibrating three times as fast (an E vibrating at 1320 cps); another four times as fast; five times as fast, etc. (the human ear can perceive about 16 of these harmonics). If all these tones were played at the same time, we would produce the rainbow of sound that we call a complex tone. Building a complex tone from pure sine waves is called additive synthesis, while filtering sine waves from a complex tone is called subtractive synthesis.

A modern device known as a harmonic analyzer can accurately deconstruct a complex tone into its constituent sine waves; a mathematically analogous process to the way a prism breaks down white light into its constituent colors. The defining mathematical principle of the harmonic series can be simply stated as "sine waves occurring at integer multiples of a fundamental frequency." The lowest frequency sine wave of a complex tone is called its *fundamental*, while the higher frequency harmonics can also be called *overtones* because they are "over," or higher in frequency than, the fundamental tone. The term "overtone series" is often used interchangeably with the term harmonic series.

The story goes that as Pythagoras was walking by a blacksmith's shop he noticed different tones coming from the various sized anvils as

---

414 It would have to be an imaginary violin since no real instrument can create a pure sine wave when played; it's always a complex tone that is produced.

the anvils were struck by the blacksmith's hammer.[415] After measuring the weight of the various anvils in question he concluded that he could predict the frequency (the highness or lowness of pitch) based on the size and weight of the anvil. A more familiar example would be to observe how the different sizes of church organ pipes were related to one another by the ratio of integers, i.e., pipes that were twice the volume, three times the volume... The ratio 1:2 represents the fundamental tone compared to a tone with twice the frequency. The ratio 1:3 represents the fundamental versus a tone with three times the frequency. Thus the harmonic series within any complex tone can be defined by integer multiples of a fundamental frequency: 1:2:3:4:5:6:7:8:9:10...

Multiples and divisions of a vibrating string have defined the act of counting for civilization. Only by sticking to exact integer ratios will all the tones of the sonic rainbow be heard. The real difference between the ancient and modern view of the harmonic series was the 18th century discovery that each sound is really a complex sound, containing an infinite number of harmonics, all sounding at the same time. If a complex vocal sound is put through a harmonic analyzer it can be viewed. It is not unlike a fingerprint, in that there is infinite variation between the sounds of people's voices. The most significant reason that each person's voice sounds noticeably different is the subtleties of relative loudness (amplitude) for each of the overtones. Variation in sound quality is known as "timbre."

Because the harmonic series explains the "deep structure" of sound, it is not surprising to learn that the evolution of Western musical practice from ancient times until modern times sequentially incorporates the tones produced by the harmonic series, one by one, into the musical vocabulary of the time, accounting for an orderly evolution of music and music theory over the centuries.[416]

---

415 Leonard Mlodinow, *Euclid's Window* (New York: Simon & Schuster, 2001), 17.
416 Howard Schatz, "The Chord of Nature and the Evolution of Music Theory," in *Music in Human Adaptation*, eds. Daniel Schneck and Judith K. Schneck (Blacksburg: Virginia Tech, 1997), 423-436.

The Geometry of the Quadrivium

In his book *Introductio Arithmetica*, the ancient Greek arithmetician Nichomachus of Gerasa (ca.100 CE) tells us that the first triangle is potentially formed by the number 1 but actually created by the number 3, the next triangle is created by the number 6 … Numbers that can be arranged in triangular arrays are called *triangular numbers*, while those that can be arranged equilaterally in squares became the *squared numbers* (n^2): $1*1 = 1$; $2*2 = 4$; $3*3 = 9$; $4*4 = 16$ … As one studies these patterns of equilaterally arrayed pebbles, it shouldn't take long to discern some repeating patterns. For example, every sequential form, whether triangles, squares, pentagons, hexagons, etc., has sides that increase by 1 pebble with each successive increase in size. We observe that the first triangular number creates a triangle with a side 1 unit in length, the second triangle has a side 2 units in length, the third triangle has a side 3 units in length, and the fourth has a side 4 units in length, etc. The same thing can be said of the length of each side for the other two-dimensional forms – squares, pentagons, hexagons, etc. A second important pattern also becomes evident: if one takes the difference between adjacent sets of triangular numbers 1, 3, 6, 10, 15 ..., we get a difference of 2 between the first two triangular numbers: 1 and 3, and a difference of 3 between the next two triangular numbers, 3 and 6, a difference of 4 between the next two triangular numbers, etc.

Figure 102 – Calculating Geometric Numbers

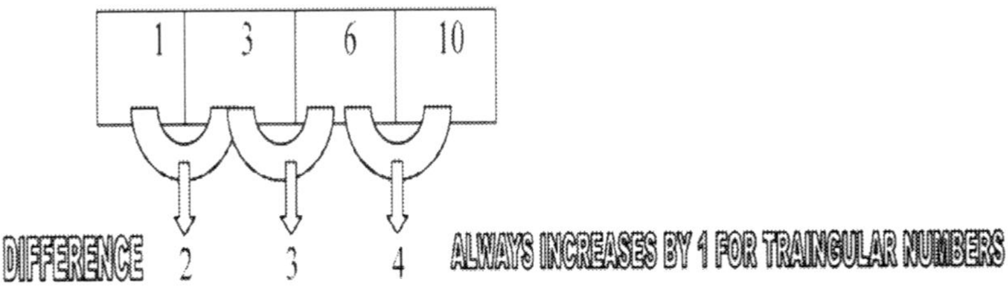

Similarly, when we take the difference for adjacent square numbers 1, 4, 9, 16, 25..., we begin with a difference of 3, and then get a difference of 5, a difference of 7, etc., always increasing the difference by 2. When we consider pentagonal numbers 1, 5, 12, 22, 35..., differences will always increase by 3, while differences between hexagons will always differ by 4, etc. From this pattern of differences, we can follow Nichomachus' example and create the table that follows, identifying the various geometric forms by their corresponding number.[417]

Table 17 – Table of Geometric

Triangles	1	3	6	10	15	21	28	36	45	55
Squares	1	4	9	16	25	36	49	64	81	100
Pentagonals	1	5	12	22	35	51	70	92	117	145
Hexagonals	1	6	15	28	45	66	91	120	153	190

Using this method of construction, Table 15 can be extended to as many rows and columns as desired. Nichomachus also points out that every square can be diagonally divided into two triangles, and if we refer to the table we can see that every square number also resolves into two successive triangular numbers: $4 = 1 + 3$; $9 = 3 + 6$; $16 = 6 + 10$, etc. Just as a square is made of two triangles, a pentagon can be made from joining square to a triangle. This also holds true with respect to the numeric table above: $5 = 4 + 1$; $12 = 9 + 3$; $22 = 16 + 6$, etc. Similarly, any hexagon is comprised of the pentagon appearing immediately above it in the table, added to the previous column's triangle, $6 = 5 + 1$; $15 = 12 + 3$; $28 = 22 + 6$, etc., for every geometric form. We consider the triangle as the most elemental two-dimensional geometric shape because every other shape can be broken down into triangles. On Day 4 God extends the two-dimensional triangular array of "opposites and the mean" into a three-dimensional tetrahedron, by simply juxtaposing a fourth pebble over a 3- pebble equilateral triangular base.

---

417 Nicomachus, Introduction to Arithmetic II, Chapter XII.

Figure 103 - Day 4's Extension into Matter

Day Four generated the 4th tonal "pebble"

Triangular base (Days One, Two & Three)

If we view the Creation allegory from Abraham's perspective, then a planer triangular base came into existence as a result of Days 1, 2 and 3 of Creation. Day 4 generated the fourth tonal "pebble," extending our structure into three dimensions. This 4-pebble tetrahedral structure can be further "extended into matter" by juxtaposing it over the next successive triangular base of 6, to get a 10-pebble tetrahedron. We can extend it still further into matter by juxtaposing the 10-pebble tetrahedron over the next triangular base of 10 to get a 20-pebble tetrahedron; a 20-pebble tetrahedron over a 15 triangular base is 35, etc. Our three-dimensional tetrahedron series is therefore 4, 10, 20, 35, etc., which we may notice is a progressive accumulation of the series of triangular numbers: 1, 3, 6, 10, 15, 21… From the Hebrew musical perspective, God extends the geometry of the tetrahedron's triple progression by echoing the geometric proportion of wavelength ratio 3/2 into the lowest realms of matter and evil.

Figure 104 – Extending the Triple Progression

$$F \leftarrow C \leftarrow G \leftarrow D \longrightarrow A \longrightarrow E \longrightarrow B$$
$$2/3^3 \quad 2/3^2 \quad 2/3 \quad 1 \quad 3/2 \quad (3/2)^2 \quad (3/2)^3$$

Triple progression + Extension into matter

Within the holistic context of the ancient Quadrivium, it is easy to forget that geometry should be understood as having a musical aspect. However, with little appreciation for its cosmological context, or accurate knowledge of its derivation, Western music theorists generally believe that Pythagoras invented the diatonic scale (ca. 550 BCE) based on this triple progression. The tones of the diatonic scale are obtained as a series of five successive upper fifths and one lower fifth. [418]

The successive echoes of musical fifths, called a *circle of fifths* (shown above), can be transposed to the same octave by doubling the frequency of the low F (2/3 x 2 = 4/3) and then dividing the extension notes by the appropriate power of 2.

Figure 105 – The Rising Tetrachord

$$T \quad T \quad S \quad T \quad T \quad T \quad S$$
$$C \rightarrow D \rightarrow E \rightarrow F \rightarrow G \rightarrow A \rightarrow B \rightarrow C$$
$$1 \quad 9/8 \quad 81/64 \quad 4/3 \quad 3/2 \quad 27/16 \quad 243/128 \quad 2$$

The derived notes are sequenced above as a rising diatonic scale, transposed to the key of C, because that key is easily recognizable as the white notes on a piano. Two cumulative intervals of 9/8 (indicated as T for tone), are followed by one semitone interval of 256/243 (indicated as S) to create the pattern T T S T T T S. The Pythagorean semitone ratio 256/243 was called either a *leimma* ("leftover" interval) or *diesis* (difference) because it was obtained by subtracting two whole tones from the perfect fourth. This pattern of tones and semitones can be maintained when transposing to another diatonic key (bringing black notes of the keyboard into play). With each different key, the scale would still be called diatonic rather than chromatic as long as the pattern of tones and semitones is maintained. It is important to remember that God's extension into matter first took place within musical and geometric terms, until Day 5, when God added motion to geometry and created Astronomy.

---

418 Willi Apel, *Harvard Dictionary of Music* (Cambridge, MA: Harvard University Press, 1972), 709-710. Apel's diagram must be understood as ratios of frequency rather than wavelength.

The Astronomy of the Quadrivium

In Abraham's day, the precision of time intervals determined by the rotation of the heavenly bodies was limited by the use of integers in calculations. The day is the rotational period of the Earth and is reflected in the Book of Creation as 24 hours; the 7-day week has no foundation in astronomy and appears to be solely determined by the Book of Creation, which then appears in the Creation allegory of the Bible; the month is linked to the period of the Moon and is reflected in the Book of Creation as 30 days; and the year is linked to the Earth's orbit around the Sun and is reflected as 360 days plus 5 festival days.

The discovery of inaccuracies in the calendar year is often attributed to a student of Plato and Archytas named Eudoxus.[419] Eudoxus provided the first geometric model of the cosmos and proposed the calendar adopted by Julius Caesar 300 years later in 46 CE. The Julian calendar was used in the West until 1582. Each year contained 12 months and there was an average of 365.25 days in a solar year. It introduced a year of length 365 days with a leap year every 4 years of 366 days. The discrepancy between the actual length of the year, 365.24219 days, and the Julian year of 365.25 days, may not seem like much, but it adds up over centuries. Therefore the change from the Julian calendar to Pope Gregory XIII's present-day Gregorian calendar required a change only to the rule for leap-years. In the Gregorian calendar century years would only be leap-years if they were divisible by 400.

Today, we realize that a lunar year has approximately 354 days, which averages to 29.5 days per month, while there about 365¼ days in a solar year. So, even the Gregorian calendar has problems when an approximately 29.5-day lunar cycle is being measured against a yearly solar cycle of approximately 365.25 days. The Jewish calendar has a "leap month" to compensate for these "inaccuracies." In order to help the Jewish lunar calendar coincide with the Gregorian solar calendar, an extra month is added on leap years. In the Jewish system, every 19 years includes seven leap years (the third, sixth, eighth, eleventh, fourteenth, seventeenth and nineteenth years). In a leap year, a thirteenth month, called Adar Sheni (the second Adar), is added. The Muslim calendar is also a lunar

---

419 Clawson, 42-43.

one, although it does not use a leap month and therefore experiences the constant shifting of holidays against the Gregorian calendar.

For Abraham, within the perfect world of God's essence, the length of the lunar year should match the length of the solar year, but there is a considerable shortfall of lunar days within the solar calendar. Abraham's acoustical constructions were based on the assumption that integer relationships which defined the inner world of God's perfection used 30 days to define a lunar month and 12 lunar months to define a 360-day solar year.

Within Just tuning, that shortfall has its musical analog in a musical diesis, defined by the musical interval separating two tones that should be equivalent, but aren't: Ab = G#, or 3500:3584. When this ratio is reduced to its smallest terms we get 125:128, or $5^3 : 2^7$. In other words, when three major thirds, created by the quintuple progression, are taken in relation to the octave's duple progression, the tones don't match. When comparing Just tuning within Day 5 to Just tuning within Day 6, the size of the "flawed" interval within a 30-day lunar cycle is roughly comparable to the size of the flawed interval within the 360-day solar cycle.

So, where does the truth in measurement lie? Abraham believed that God could not create a vibratory puzzle with pieces that don't fit together, it must therefore be man's "Fall from Grace," as manifest in the "outer light" of the quintuple progression, and in the primordial element of earth, When the physical world was brought into existence and it became difficult to perceive and measure the inner, unseen world of God. We still need time to empirically prove that superstrings are the harmonic essence of everything, but many of today's physicists are confident that it will happen in this century. Man's objective view of God and the essence of everything, has been, and will always be, tied to the harmonic series. Man must establish his meditative focus on the harmonic series that comprises the essence of his soul in order to evolve spiritually, and to maintain his mental, emotional, and physical equilibrium amidst the world's imperfection and turmoil.

Bibliography

Apel, Willi, *Harvard Dictionary of Music*, Cambridge, Massachusetts: Harvard University Press, 1972.

Armstrong, Karen, *Islam: A Short History*, New York: Random House, 2000.

Armstrong, Karen, *A History of God*, New York: Random House, 1993.

Austin, William W., *Music in the Twentieth Century*, New York: W.W. Norton, 1966.

Asimov, Isaac, *Asimov's Guide to Science*, New York: Basic Books, 1972.

Barbour, J. Murray, *Tuning and Temperament: A Historical Survey*, East Lansing, Michigan: State College Press, 1953.

Barrett, Helen M., *Boethius*, New York: Russel & Russel, 1965.

Bloom, *Jesus and Yahweh: The Names Divine,* New York: Riverhead Books, 2005.

Boethius, *The Consolation of Philosophy*, trans. Richard Green, Indianapolis: Bobbs-Merrill, 1962.

Brinton, Craine and Christopher, John B., and Wolff, Robert Lee, *A History of Civilization*, Vol. I. Englewood Cliffs, New Jersey: Prentice Hall, 1960.

Campbell, Joseph, *The Masks of God*, New York: Viking Press, 1964.

Chumash: Artscroll Series, eds. Nosson Scherman and Meir Zlotowitz, Brooklyn, New York: Mesorah Publications, 1998.

Clawson, Calvin, *Mathematical Sorcery*, Cambridge: Perseus, 1999.

Cole, K.C., "Theory of Everything," *New York Times Magazine*, October18, 1987, 20-26.

Coogan, Michael D., ed., *The Oxford History of the Biblical World*, New York: Oxford University Press, 1998.

Cozort, Daniel, *Highest Yoga Tantra*, Ithaca, New York: Snow Lion, 1986.

Dali Lama, *Dzogchen*, trans. G.T. Jinpa and R. Barron, Ithaca, New York: Snow Lion, 2000.

Davies, P.C.W. and Brown, J., eds., *Superstrings: A Theory of Everything*, Cambridge, UK: Cambridge University Press, 1988.

Dawkins, Richard, *The God Delusion*, New York: Houghton Mifflin, 2006.

Dawood, N.J., trans., *The Koran*, New York-London: Penguin Books, 1956.

DeMar, Gary, "Denying Sola Scriptura: The Attempt to Neutralize the Bible," *Biblical Worldview*, December 1993.

Einstein, Albert and Infield, Leopold, *The Evolution of Physics*, New York: Simon & Schuster, 1938.

Fairbanks, Arthus, *The First Philosphers of Greece*, London: Kegan Paul, Trench, and Trauber, 1898.

Farmer, Henry George, "The Music of Ancient Egypt," *The New Oxford History of Music,* London: Oxford University Press, 1957, Vol.1, 275.

Gaon, Saadia, *The Book of Beliefs and Opinions,* trans. Samuel Rosenblatt, New Haven, Connecticut: Yale University Press, 1948.

Grout, Donald Jay, *A History of Western Music*, New York: W.W. Norton, 1960, 1973.

Greene, Brian, *The Elegant Universe*, New York: Random House, 1999. Halevi, Z'ev ben Shimon, *Kabbalah and Exodus,* Boulder Colorado: Shambhala, 1980.

Harkavy, Alexander, ed., *The Holy Scriptures*, New York: Hebrew Publications, 1936.

Helmholtz, Hermann, *On the Sensations of Tone*, translated by Alexander Ellis, New York: Dover Publishing, Inc., 1954.

Heninger, S.K. Jr., *Touches of Sweet Harmony: Pythagorean Cosmology and Renaissance Poetics*, San Marino, California: Huntington Library, 1974.

Hindemith, Paul, *Craft of Musical Composition*, Book I, trans. Arthur Mendell, New York: Associated Music Publishing, 1942.

Icke, Vincent, *The Force of Symmetry*, Cambridge: Cambridge University Press, 1995.

Idel, Moshe, *Studies in Ecstatic Kabbalah*, Albany: State University of New York Press, 1988.

Kaplan, Aryeh, *Bahir*, York Beach, Maine: Samuel Weiser,1979.

Kaplan, Aryeh, *Meditation and Kabbalah*, York Beach, Maine: Samuel Weiser, 1982.

Kaplan, Aryeh, *Meditation and the Bible*, York Beach, Maine: Samuel Weiser, 1978.

Kaplan, Aryeh, *Sefer Yetzirah*, York Beach, Maine: Samuel Weiser, 1990.

Kayser, Hans, *Lehrbuch der Harmonik*, Zürich: Occident Verlag, 1950.

Laurence, Richard, trans., *The Book of Enoch*, London: Kegan Paul, Trench, and Trauber, 1883.

Levarie, Siegmund and Ernst Levy, *Tone: A Study in Musical Acoustics*, Kent, Ohio: Kent State University Press, 1968.

Levy, Ernst, *A Theory of Harmony*, unpublished, 1951.

Lewis, Bernard, *The Arabs in History*, New York: Oxford University Press, 2002.

Lippman, Edward A., *Musical Thought in Ancient Greece*, New York: Columbia University Press, 1964.

Macoy, Robert, *General History, Cyclopedia and Dictionary of Freemasonry*, New York: Masonic Publishing Company, 1869.

Mann, Felix, *Acupuncture*, New York: Vantage Books, 1962, 1971.

McClain, Ernest G., *The Myth of Invariance: The Origin of the Gods, Mathematics and Music from the RG Veda to Plato*, New York: Nicolas-Hays, 1976.

McClain, Ernest G., *The Pythagorean Plato*, New York: Nicolas-Hays, 1978.

McClain, Ernest G., "A New Look at Plato's Timaeus," *Music and Man*, 1, no. 4, 1975.

Mlodinow, Leonard, *Euclid's Window*, New York: Simon & Schuster, 2001.

Mullin, Glen, *Tsongkhapa's Six Yoga's of Naropa*, Ithaca, New York: Snow Lion, 1996.

New Testament, New York: Catholic Book Publishing, 1952.

Ni, Maoshing, trans., *The Yellow Emperor's Classic of Medicine*, Boston: Shambhala Publications, 1995.

Odeberg, Hugo, ed., *Hebrew Book of Enoch*, New York, KTAV, 1973.

Patch, Howard Rollin, *The Tradition of Boethius*, New York: Oxford University Press, 1935.

Peat, F. David, *Superstrings and the Search for the Theory of Everything*, Chicago: Contemporary Books, 1988.

Plato, *The Republic*, trans. G.M.A. Grube, Indianapolis: Hackett Publishing Company, 1974.

Plato, "Laws," in *The Collected Dialogues of Plato*, ed. by Edith Hamilton and Huntington Cairns, trans. A.E. Taylor, Princeton, NJ: Princeton University Press, 1961.

Plato, "Timaeus," in *The Collected Dialogues of Plato*, ed. by Edith Hamilton and Huntington Cairns, trans. Benjamin Gowett, Princeton, NJ: Princeton University Press, 1961.

Porter, J.R., *The Lost Bible*, Chicago: University of Chicago Press, 2001.

Rameau, Jean-Philippe, *Treatise on Harmony*, trans. Philip Gosset., New York: Dover Publications, 1971.

Rameau, Jean Philippe, *Harmonic Generation*, trans. Deborah Hays, doctoral dissertation, Stanford University, 1968.

Rand, Edward Kennard, *Founders of the Middle Ages*, Cambridge, Massachusetts: Harvard University Press, 1928.

Reese, Gustave, *Music in the Renaissance*, rev.ed., New York: W.W. Norton,1959.

Renard, John, *Understanding the Islamic Experience*, New York/Mahwah: Paulist Press, 1992.

Riemann, Hugo, *History of Music Theory*, trans. R.H. Haggh, Lincoln, Nebraska: University of Nebraska,1962.

Rinpoche, Sogyal, *The Tibetan Book of Living and Dying*, ed. P.G. Gaffney and A. Harvey, San Francisco: Harper Collins, 1994.

Sachs, Curt, *Our Musical Heritage*, New York: Prentice Hall, Inc., 1948.

Schatz, Howard, ed.by Schneck, Dr. Daniel J. & Judith K., "The Chord of Nature and the Evolution of Music Theory," *Music in Human Adaptation*, Blacksburg, Virginia: Virginia Tech, 1997.

Scherman, Rabbi Nosson, ed. *The Chumash*, Brooklyn, New York: Mesorah Publications, 1998.

Schneck, Daniel J. and Dorita S. Berger, T*he Music Effect: Music Physiology and Clinical Applications*, London: Jessica Kinglsey Publishers, 2006.

Scholem, Gershom, *Kabbalah*, New York- Jerusalem: Keter Publishing House, 1974.

Scholem, Gershom, *Origins of the Kabbalah*, ed. R.J. Zwi Werblowsky, trans. Allan Arkush, Princeton, New Jersey: Princeton University Press, 1962, 1987.

Sells, Michael A., trans. and ed., *Early Islamic Mysticism*, New York-Mahwah: Paulist Press, 1996.

Sperling, Harry and Simon, Maurice, trans. *Zohar*, London: Soncino Press, 1984.

Tanakh: The Holy Scriptures, Jerusalem: Jewish Publication Society, 1985.

Thimus, Albert von, *Die harmonikale Symbolik des Altherthums*, Köln: M. DuMont-Schauberg, 1868 and 1876.

Waite, Arthur Edward, *A New Encyclopedia of Freemasonry*, New York: Random House, 1970.

Wilhelm, Richard and Baynes, Cary F., trans., *The I Ching*, Princeton, New Jersey: Princeton University Press, 1950, 1977.

Yasser, Joseph, *A Theory of Evolving Tonality*, New York: American Library of Musicology, 1932.

Yu, Lu K'uan, *Taoist Yoga: Alchemy & Immortality*, York Beach, Maine: Weiser, 1973.

Yasuo, Yuasa, *The Body, Self-cultivation and Ki-energy*, Albany: State University of New York Press, 1993.

Index

F

Faraday, Michael 304
fauxbordon 168
fermion 310
Feynman, Richard 307
filioque 75
Fire Path 137, 139, 141, 145–146, 209, 212, 230, 235, 244, 251, 269–270, 273, 275–278, 294, 296
First Ecumenical Council 71–73
Five Books of Moses 9, 64
five pillars of Islam, 2
five Platonic solids 152
fixed tones 174
four-horned altar 83, 179, 222, 198, 199
four horsemen of the Apocalypse 286
Franklin, Benjamin 187
Freemasons 2, 11, 13, 76, 173, 188, 189
frequency 28
Fuller, Buckminster 151

G

galgul 123
Galileo 28
Gamaliel 82–84
Gaon, Saadia 4, 5, 162
gauge field 311–312, 316–318
Gemara 10
gematria 22, 23, 31, 211, 294
geodesic dome 151
geometric mean 157, 331
geometric progression 34, 160, 162, 331
Gevurah 159, 237, 240
ghazu 96
gifts that traveled East 105, 266
Gikatilla, Joseph 1
gluons 310–311, 317
Gnosticism 71–73
God's Covenant with Abraham 9, 86, 223, 233, 236
golem 65–67, 237, 282
governing channel 275
governing vessel 276
grand unification 317
gravitons 310–311, 316
great abyss 249, 251

I

Iamblichus , 34
illusory body 67, 282–283
immortal fetus 282
Incarnation 13, 71
Indra 57, 178, 283
inner light 152, 176–177, 181, 194, 200–201, 212, 230
inner struggle 13, 53, 77, 92, 251
intelligent design xiii, 27, 301
Isaac 9, 46, 48, 50–53, 81, 83, 103, 181, 184, 236, 327
Ishmael 48, 49, 50–52, 103, 105, 327
isospin 310–311, 316
Israel 4, 9, 21, 46, 48, 51–52, 55, 58–61, 64, 69, 84, 98, 103, 121, 181, 184–185, 199,
    225, 232, 236, 262, 264, 280, 287, 327

J

Jacob 9, 46, 48–49, 81, 159, 179, 230, 236, 239, 282
Jacob's ladder 179, 230, 239
Jefferson, Thomas 187
Jehovah 1, 46, 187
Jesus 5, 13, 49, 66, 68–69, 72–74, 76, 78–79, 81, 83–89, 89, 91, 105–107, 109, 163,
    181, 182, 282, 295, 327
jihad 13, 53, 91–92, 97–100, 108, 251
John the Baptist 81
Josephus, Flavius 16, 45
jubilee 244
Julian calendar 339
Julius Caesar 339
Just Tuning 117, 141, 169, 174, 181–182, 185, 200, 211, 215, 221–222, 233, 235–236,
    242, 294, 340

K

Ka'bah 2–3, 13, 44, 49, 51–53, 57, 61, 93, 95–98, 59, 100–103, 165, 240, 251
kav 26–28, 31, 32, 33, 122, 137, 153–154, 160, 163–164, 199, 201, 208
kavanah 64–65, 67, 239, 89
Keats, John 16
kelim 184
Kepler, Johannes 301
Kituvim 9
Koran 1, 40, 51–52, 61, 68, 91, 95, 96, 99–100, 102, 107, 227
Kundalini 248

L

lambda 34, 158, 160, 163
lambdoma 34
language of God xii, 325–326
leap year 247, 339
leimma 338
lepton 317
lesser jihad 92, 97–99
Leviathan 250
Lincoln, Abraham 65
Logos 73, 74, 75–76, 84–85, 116
Lost Word 2–4, 11, 13, 23, 31, 50–51, 61, 77, 81–82, 83, 187, 188, 240, 253, 297
Lubavitch 159
lunar month 340
Luria, Rabbi Isaac 184–186

M

magic 2, 14, 48, 65, 84
mahasiddhas 106
Maimonides 4–5
Majlis 93–94
Malkhut 284
mandala 123, 227, 242, 253
Manetho 16
mantra 185
mark of the beast 175, 248, 249
Mary 87, 106
matrix mechanics 306
Maxwell, James Clerk 304
Mecca 2, 13, 51–53, 61, 92–93, 95–98, 100–101, 165, 240
Medina 52, 94, 96–97
Melchizedek 45–46, 68, 71, 77, 80–81, 259, 328
Mendeleyev, Dmitri 304–305, 318
Mesopotamia 19, 105, 165, 179, 232
Metatron 84, 85, 193–196, 237, 253, 280, 289, 198
Midot 159
milah 238
Mishnah 10
Mispar 24
Mohammed 5, 52, 91–94, 96–99, 102, 107
Moses 5, 9, 12, 55, 67–68, 79, 106–107, 171
Mount Horeb 55, 178, 182
Mount Meru 57, 178
Mount Sinai 9–11, 55, 57, 62–64, 178–179, 249

Printed in the United States
79688LV00004B/40-57